THEY PASSED THIS WAY

THEY PASSED THIS WAY

The United States of America,
The States of Australia and World War II

BARRY RALPH

Kangaroo Press

First published in Australia in 2000 by Kangaroo Press
an imprint of Simon & Schuster (Australia) Pty Limited
20 Barcoo Street, East Roseville NSW 2069

A Viacom Company
Sydney New York London Toronto Tokyo Singapore

National Library of Australia
Cataloguing-in-Publication data

Ralph, Barry.

They passed this way: the United States of America, the states of Australia
and World War II.

Bibliography.
Includes index.

ISBN 0 86417 951 0.

1. World War, 1939-1945 - Social aspects - Australia. 2. Australia -
History - 1939-1945. 3. United States - Armed Forces - Australia.
I. Title

940.540973

Set in Sabon 11/15
Printed in Australia by Griffin Press

10 9 8 7 6 5 4 3 2 1

CONTENTS

To my mother and father

PREFACE

For a major part of World War II Australia was under the threat of invasion. However, when the invasion came it was not the enemy that passed this way, but the American serviceman.

Between December 1941 and August 1945, an estimated one million Americans were stationed in Australia to counter the Japanese threat. Soldiers, sailors, airmen, nurses and entertainers were posted down-under, either permanently or temporarily. They came from all over America, from a mixture of classes and races, and each of them has a story to tell, an experience to share.

This book is an account of the trials and tribulations of many of these men and women who served in a strange, isolated country far from home. Some of them, like Douglas MacArthur, have become historical figures. But there were many others who enjoyed a less public profile but whose experiences were equally compelling. It is my intention to rescue many of these people from the mists of history and give them once again a voice, a presence.

Of course the Australians who greeted the Americans, and those who fought with them, are no less worthy of recognition. The Yanks created a stir wherever they went in Australia. Most reactions were positive, but not all, and for many the prosecution of the war was not entirely confined to the battlefields of the South Pacific. For that reason I have paid particular attention to the cultural, social and domestic impact of the American presence in Australia during the war. We are still feeling its legacy.

No single book on this subject can be definitive, however, and this work is merely an account of a unique military alliance and cultural coalition bonded by war.

In researching this book I was fortunate in being able to interview many veterans of World War II, both military and civilian, and to be given access to several unpublished memoirs. For anyone writing an account of this period it is virtually obligatory to call on Major Bill Bentson. Although he retired from the army over 30 years ago, he has never really left the service; he simply no longer wears a uniform. His lucid memory and extensive archives are a bonanza for any historian and I was not the first to have benefited from his enthusiastic cooperation and his ability to answer virtually any question about the Australian–American alliance. I also appreciate his generosity in reading some of my manuscript and the challenges he faced in keeping my errors to a minimum.

For the hours in which I incessantly tested their patience and invaded their inner thoughts, my thanks to Professor John Lillback and to Leslie and Yvonne Cottman, and to Joy Foord for being so honest.

There are many others who I would like to thank, first amongst them Neville Meyers, who helped organise the trip but never took the journey. His wife, Lynn, who is a librarian offered invaluable advice and archival knowledge. Sid Bromley is the Bill Bentson of Australian jazz and entertainment. While his recollections of his military service were valuable, his encyclopaedic knowledge of anything musical was truly a major inspiration, as has been his friendship of the past two decades. Beryl Lynagh was a prime source of information on life on the home front. Her late husband, Ted, rarely spoke about the effect the war had on his generation, but when he chose to he offered many invaluable insights.

American musicians Zeke Zarchy and John Best were candid in recalling what it was like to serve your country as a musician during the war. Larry Adler and Barbara James also recalled their experiences as entertainers during the war — as did Michael Pate, who is probably unaware of the impact of our fleeting conversation. There is little new that can be said about Artie Shaw. His ability as a musician is obvious, but I am grateful that I have also experienced many of his non-musical virtues — not the least his talent as a creative writer and the encouragement he gave me.

There are many people who did not pass this way but who have an intimate knowledge of those who did. Writers, collectors and historians Mike Sutcliffe, Rupert Goodman, Bob Piper, Bob Alford, Roger Marks, David Vincent and Col Benson offered sympathetic and constructive support.

A special thank you is reserved for Allan Campbell, who turned up late in the project but just in time to provide some rare photographs and valuable insights. Allan served in the Intelligence Section, Northern Command, Brisbane, and had much to do with MacArthur and LeGrande Diller, amongst others. They are a durable breed, these veterans. Allan is 96 years old and still operates his advertising and public relations company in Brisbane. He allowed me much of his valuable time.

My thanks also to the late Cec Parsons, who never knew about this project but was instrumental in stimulating my enthusiasm for this unique era. Thanks to Cec Shaw, George Lester, Loyde Adams, Cliff Leeman and Arch Broadbent, wherever you are, and to Ben Jansen, Elaine Hamilton and particularly Duncan Richardson for helping with the manuscript. I would also like to thank my brother Brian for his support and encouragement.

The national and state archives were, of course, invaluable and there are still many revelations and historic jewels awaiting researchers with the time to peruse their holdings. The staff of the Queensland State Archives found many rare, formerly classified documents, including the correspondence from John Curtin relating to the Battle of Brisbane riots and contemporary accounts of the events that led to the apocryphal story of the Battle of the Trains.

The State Library of Queensland offered valuable secondary reference sources and microfiche copies of all the nation's newspapers during this period. While the press coverage of the war was heavily censored and is of uncertain value to the historian, most newspapers gave excellent coverage of social and domestic issues and convey a genuine insight to the mood of the people.

The search for photographs was an adventure in itself. In addition to the kind donation of many personal photographs, which I gratefully acknowledge, the cooperation of the John Oxley Library and the Brisbane *Courier-Mail* in letting me examine their vast photographic archives is very much appreciated.

Particular thanks are due to the forbearance of my family, who for so long had to contend with me being more concerned with matters past than matters present. The state of the grounds is a sad reflection on my recent priorities.

Finally, I would like to express my admiration for everyone who either served in, or lived through, that momentous period when the world was at war. Most are now gone, but their efforts in creating a new order resulted in my generation not having to contend with another global conflict. The least we can do by way of thanks is acknowledge those who passed this way and those who went in other directions on the roads that finally led to peace.

CHAPTER 1

OVER HERE

It is my melancholy duty to inform you officially that, in consequence of the persistence by Germany in her invasion of Poland, Great Britain has declared war upon her and that as a result Australia is also at war.[1]

At 9.15 pm on 3 September 1939, the illusion of peace was finally shattered when Prime Minister Robert Menzies made this announcement to the people of Australia. The country was once again drawn into another war against an enemy which posed no direct threat and in battlefields half a world away. A generation earlier Australia had sent 330 000 volunteers to aid the Mother Country in the Great War. The First AIF (Australian Imperial Force) suffered 68 per cent casualties, including nearly 60 000 killed.[2] Few would have understood the motives or tactics of that cruel conflict, where nineteenth-century methods of warfare confronted twentieth-century technology.

During the years between the wars the average Australian was more concerned with dealing with the Great Depression than the growing tension in Europe or the emerging Japanese threat in the Pacific.

A census taken early in 1939 had numbered the predominantly Anglo-Celtic population at just over seven million.[3] The great majority of its citizens were city dwellers living on the east coast, with the bulk of the remainder in scattered townships and outback areas of six states and two territories.

The lifestyle of the white, overwhelmingly British, Christian and democratic Australian was basic in many ways. However, there was much to admire about the people of the young nation. There was a social code, respect for women and comparatively little violence. In the year the war started, there were 64 249 marriages and 3137 divorces.[4] Inflation was low and stable. A pocket watch advertised for ten shillings in 1930 would still cost ten shillings in 1939. A wage of £6 for a 44-hour week was good money. A couple could buy a new home for around £500, furnish it for £200 and mortgage the property at an interest rate of 3.5 per cent.[5]

Australia had always been influenced by British customs and attitudes, but the country's window to the outside world was the cinema. American cinematic heroes became Australia's as well — men wore singlets like Gable, and women their hair like Harlow. A Saturday evening visit to one of the many picture theatres was the preferred entertainment.

In 1939 Australia possessed an insulated culture, the product of an isolated continent. Few Australians travelled overseas and very few tourists visited Australia. Robert Bruce Menzies, a former barrister, led the United Australia Party (UAP) to success at the polls in April 1939. The threat of war prompted his government to introduce a national register of manpower, resulting in the registration of all males aged between 18 and 64. 'The objects sought in this bill,' explained Geoffrey Street, Minister for Defence, 'are, first, a general survey of manpower and, secondly, the establishment and organisation of a national register for use in preparing for a national emergency.'[6]

Soon, men across the country were filling out registration cards — nominating their occupations, qualifications and other skills. The perceived need to compile the register was yet another indicator that war clouds were gathering. The government and the people of Australia awaited events that they could not influence. Rather, the events would influence them.

Just three days after war was declared, the government announced that censorship would be imposed on news, on the radio and in the press. Other forms of communication, such as telegraph, telephone and postal services, were also subject to censorship and telephone services to Great Britain were suspended indefinitely.[7] On 15 September, Menzies announced that after discussions with Britain as to what form of military assistance could be offered, there would be an immediate formation of a division which would be called the 6th Division of the Second AIF. It would comprise 20 000 volunteers, whose enlistment was to be for the duration of the war.[8]

On 20 October, Menzies announced that compulsory military training for home defence was to be introduced to ensure that numbers in the militia were at an acceptable level. All single men who turned 21 in the year ending 1 July 1940 were called up for three months training. The existing militia force of 80 000 part-time volunteer soldiers, affectionately known as 'Chockos', were also called to arms. The formation of the 6th Division was the priority, with preference given to single men who were not employed in essential civilian jobs.[9]

The rush to enlist was not as enthusiastic as it had been a quarter of a century before, but the men of the 6th Division were soon in training. For the eager young men rushing to the recruit reception depots throughout the country expecting to be attired in dashing uniforms, there would be a major disappointment. Initially, there was not enough clothing on hand to cater for the massive influx of army personnel. The men soon found that, like the peppercorn wage, the uniform was essentially of Great War vintage. It was, in fact, very eye-catching but for all the wrong reasons! Americans, later in the war, kidded that Aussies wore uniforms made from old army blankets.[10] Although the standard of uniforms subsequently improved, they would never dispel the impression that, even if the Australian soldier was amongst the most formidable of fighting men, he was also amongst the worst-dressed.

The ill-wind of war had at least blown some good fortune on the Australian economy. Six months after the start of the war, unemployment had decreased by more than 300 000. Attendance was booming at sporting events and motorists created a record for petrol sales the day before rationing was introduced.[11]

The role of women in Australia in the early war years was perceived as being wholly domestic. Except for the nurses attached to the new AIF divisions, there were no women in uniform aiding the war effort and women in war-related industries were very much in the minority. There was a distinct reluctance by the War Cabinet to consider women for the armed forces. The Air Force eventually took the initiative when it formed the Women's Auxiliary Australian Air Force (WAAAF) in February 1941, 'for the employment of women in musterings where trained men are not available or are not suitable for the work required'.[12]

The unpopular Menzies was soon having major problems with his United Australia Party and the Australian people. With the war situation already grave, and seeming to become worse in the first two years of the war, Menzies resigned from his position as prime minister in August 1941 and was replaced, briefly, by Arthur Fadden. The Labor Party, headed by John Curtin, came to office on 7 October 1941.

Meanwhile, more divisions within the Second AIF had been formed. The 6th Division, under the command of Lieutenant-General Thomas Blamey, was despatched to the Middle East on 10 January 1940 and the 7th Division soon followed. The 8th and 9th Divisions were being formed with the intention of serving overseas. The Empire Air Training Scheme, begun in late 1939, resulted in many Australian aircrews seeing action in the skies over Europe very early in the war. Australian ships soon joined the British Mediterranean fleet and served with distinction. HMAS *Sydney* thrilled the nation with the heroic feat of attacking an Italian cruiser squadron, sinking the *Bartolomeo Colleoni* and seriously damaging the *Giovanni delle Bande Nere*.[13]

The 6th Division performed well in the Libyan campaign in early 1941 and the 7th and 9th Divisions were also despatched to the Middle East. The 6th was committed to the futile Greek and Crete campaigns and suffered heavy losses: 6734 killed, wounded or captured. The 9th Division gained immortality during the siege of Tobruk, denying Rommel's Afrika Korps the valuable port for seven months. At the same time that the 7th Division was fighting the pro-German Vichy French forces in Lebanon and Syria, the 8th Division, under the command of Major General Gordon Bennett, was on its way to Singapore to become yet another garrison division for the British bastion in what was still known as the Far East.[14]

It was while escorting units of this Division that HMAS *Sydney* would meet her fate. Late in the afternoon of 19 November, the Sydney engaged the German raider, *Kormoran*. After a brief and savage battle both ships were sunk. Survivors from the German ship were rescued or captured on the Western Australian coast. The *Sydney* was lost with the entire ship's company of 645 men. Initially listed as overdue, the reality soon became apparent and on 30 November Prime Minister Curtin announced to the nation the extent of the disaster.[15] The Australian people had heard bad news before, but the loss of the *Sydney* broke the heart of the nation. Eight days after the loss the *Sydney*, HMAS *Parramatta* was torpedoed off the Libyan coast with the loss of 140 men.[16]

The seeds of further disaster were being sown as Australians grew more anxious about the ever-increasing Japanese menace. The island continent and its widely scattered population seemed to be in a perilous and vulnerable position.

It was December 1941. A factory in Port Kembla had started constructing the first of 45 457 of the locally designed Owen sub-machine-guns.[17] James Joyce's novel, *Ulysses*, was once again banned.[18] Newsprint was rationed to 55 per cent of the pre-war level[19] and the petrol ration was reduced even further. Walter Lindrum scored 100 billiard points in 46 seconds.[20] Bob Dyer, an expatriate American hillbilly performer, was first heard on the wireless.[21] *Sun Valley Serenade* was first seen at the Regent Theatre[22] — and the Japanese bombed Pearl Harbor.

To Prime Minister Curtin fell the responsibility of undertaking another of those melancholy duties, to inform the public of yet another war and yet another enemy:

We shall hold this country and keep it as a citadel for the British-speaking race and as a place where civilisation will persist.[23]

The Prime Minister and the nation may have had the resolve, but there was very little else left to contribute to the war effort or to national defence. Australia had become the orphan of the South Pacific. Never in the history of the nation had there been such impending peril.

On 22 December 1941, as Japanese forces stormed seemingly inexorably through Malaya and the Philippines, a convoy of American ships sailed unexpectedly into the port of Brisbane.

CHAPTER TWO

OVER THERE

The role of the United States of America during World War II was similar to that which it played in the first global conflict — a reluctant protagonist, drawn and provoked into combat, but whose participation was as authoritative as it was decisive.

Although belated, America's entry into the Great War ensured a relatively swift victory for the Allies. The great majority of the American people believed that the nation should never again become involved in the European predilection for warfare and destruction.

The country's focus during the decade before World War II was not on European or Far Eastern affairs but on the Great Depression. When elected in 1932, President Franklin Delano Roosevelt was faced with 14 million unemployed, one in three families without any income, shanty towns, soup kitchens, breadlines, destitute farmers, banks foreclosing mortgages and closing banks. Roosevelt instigated emergency legislation and the parameters of the New Deal were formulated. But while America had demonstrated that it was capable of dealing with any domestic crisis, it had remained aloof from and indifferent to international tensions.

In 1939 the great bastion of democracy was enjoying a joyful and dynamic isolationism. America was a country so vital and progressive that seldom a day went by without a major innovation or achievement.

In San Francisco, the Golden Gate Bridge had opened.[1] The dynamic Howard Hughes flew around the world in less than four days. *Gone With The Wind* was playing to capacity houses throughout the nation. Two young men, Jerry Siegel and Joe

Shuster, developed a new hero for Action Comics with a good American name — Superman. The 'man of steel' almost created as much furore as the stockings made from nylon, which went on sale in October.[2] The stock market continued to recover. The Fair Labor Standards Act set the minimum wage at 40 cents an hour for a maximum 40 hour working week. It was great to be an American. The 130 million populace could enjoy an average life expectancy of 63 years. The boundless optimism and dynamics of the nation were demonstrated when the New York World's Fair, The World of Tomorrow, opened to universal acclaim on 30 April 1939.[3]

Some citizens may have been a little concerned about newspaper reports relating to the belligerence of some overseas countries. Japan was still the aggressor in China and there were now signs that she had aspirations even further afield. Hitler and Mussolini had thriving fascist dictatorships. However: 'America does not want war,' Roosevelt declared on one of his radio chats, 'We shall remain neutral'. The President knew public opinion well. Only 8 per cent of Americans were interventionists; the remainder wanted nothing to do with a foreign war.

On 3 September 1939, Great Britain and the Commonwealth, together with France, declared war on Germany two days after Poland had been invaded. Roosevelt was on the air that night, still emphasising neutrality, but many Americans could see the signs that the country would slowly be drawn into the conflict. On 3 January 1940, Roosevelt submitted a $1.8 billion national defence budget to Congress.[4] Three weeks later, the United States refused to renew the United States–Japan Trade Treaty which had been in force for 30 years.

The American public did not know how committed the government was to supporting England and her allies. However, when Roosevelt was returned to the presidency for an unprecedented third term in 1940, aid to Britain was escalated, as was the national defence budget to almost $11 billion.[5] Shortly before Roosevelt embarked on his third term, Congress passed the Selective Training and Service Act. This was the first peacetime draft in the history of the nation. The conscription initiative would involve all American males aged between 21 and 35.[6] Each of the 48 states of the Union would also mobilise their National Guard militia divisions.[7] Two of these, the 32nd Division from Wisconsin and Michigan and the 41st from north-western states, were soon to enjoy an adventure in Australia, and a nightmare in New Guinea.

All the while, the Japanese imperialistic thrust was incessant and threatening. The Rising Sun was flying over Manchuria and much of the rest of eastern China and, in 1940, French Indochina.

In March 1941, Congress authorised a new program to enable aid to be sent to Great Britain and her allies while America remained theoretically neutral. At a press conference Roosevelt explained the new Lend-Lease Act in simplistic terms: 'Suppose my neighbour's home catches fire. If he can take my garden hose and connect it up with his hydrant, I may help him to put out the fire.' The Lend-Lease Act was a major public relations triumph. It authorised the President to give military aid to whoever he desired. However, FDR knew from the start that he would never get his hose back.[8]

By late 1941, the Allies knew that war with Japan was likely. The Americans, English and Dutch had ceased exporting any oil to Japan in response to its armed aggression in the Far East.[9] Roosevelt had even frozen all Japanese assets in America. If Japan was to continue with its policies, then it would need access to the necessary raw materials. The oil-rich Netherlands East Indies and Malaya became major Japanese objectives.

The greatest deterrents to Japanese occupation of the East Indies were the American Pacific Fleet based at Pearl Harbor and, to a lesser extent, the British naval base at Singapore. But where would the Japanese strike? And when? The Philippines was considered a potential Japanese objective. In mid-1941, Douglas MacArthur, former US Chief of Staff, was there in the employ of Filipino President Quezon, developing defence strategies and training the

Filipino army. Roosevelt returned the aging warrior to the active list and commenced reinforcement of the islands. The possibility of a raid on the Pearl Harbor naval base in Hawaii was also contemplated, but it was heavily defended and isolated. It was felt that the Japanese would attack at great risk and would surely be detected before they could strike.

In the first week of December 1941, the war in Europe was at a crucial stage and the Axis powers at their zenith. Hitler had at last ordered an offensive against Moscow; units of the Australian 9th Division were still resisting the onslaughts of Rommel and the Afrika Korps in the Libyan port of Tobruk; Malta had just endured its one thousandth air raid and the British capital ships, *Prince of Wales* and *Repulse*, known as Force Z, had arrived in Singapore.

On the morning of 7 December, 1941, aircraft of the Empire of Japan attacked the American Pacific Fleet and installations at Pearl Harbor. The Japanese knew that Sunday morning was a good time to strike. They fully expected some resistance but caught the American forces totally by surprise. The Japanese sank four battleships and seriously damaged four more.[10] Many other vessels were sunk or damaged. All but five of the 166 aircraft destroyed were caught on the ground. There were 2403 Americans killed in the attack.[11] Yet it was not a decisive victory. The American aircraft carriers were at sea and, on shore, the large oil and petrol tanks and other essential facilities were mostly undamaged. In fact the attack was a gamble. Japan believed that Germany would defeat Russia and, therefore, Russia would no longer threaten Japan's aggressive expansion into China. However, its most disastrous miscalculation was in gauging America's response and the depth of her resolve. Within hours of the attack President Roosevelt announced to 90 million people, through 56 million radio receivers, that America was at war. The nation was at last unified and galvanised. After 23 years of peace Uncle Sam was once again intervening in another world war. Isolationism had suddenly lost its appeal and the word was removed from the American lexicon.

It seemed that everyone wanted to wear a uniform. Roosevelt had barely completed his epoch-making speech when 16 million men swamped the country's 6175 draft boards[12] — truck drivers, factory hands, taxi drivers, accountants, farmers, musicians, movie stars and more. It was a poor man who did not look good in a uniform. The girls obviously thought so, with a thousand couples being married every day.

Within 72 hours of the attack on Pearl Harbor, Germany declared war on the United States. Roosevelt cabled Churchill, 'all of us are in the same boat with you'.[13] Churchill's reaction to the entry of America into both theatres of war was perceptive, even at this early and precarious stage: 'So we have won after all'.[14]

Despite the national call to arms, America was ill-equipped and unprepared for the conflict. The Chairman of the Joint Chiefs of Staff, General George Marshall, told Roosevelt at the beginning of the war that, militarily, America was a third-rate power.[15] The priority that was given to Depression-related domestic building programs, coupled with an aloofness from foreign affairs and a desire for neutrality, had resulted in insignificant financial endowments for defence. At the start of hostilities in Europe in 1939, the American armed services were undermanned and with meagre equipment, most of which was antiquated and obsolete. The turning point came with the initiatives that the Roosevelt administration had implemented, including the mobilisation of all National Guard units and the Selective Services Act. This generated manpower to the extent that, by late 1941, there were a million men in training camps across the land. Still, it took six months before the nation's great production capacity started to bear an influence on the war. Officers in the War Plans Division of the General Staff called this period 'D plus 180'.[16] Until then, difficult decisions would need to be made and military deployment of resources would become crucial.

On 21 November 1941, a convoy of ships containing munitions

and troops and escorted by the USS *Pensacola* had departed San Francisco for Manila. After the attack on Pearl Harbor, the convoy was ordered to change course and await orders. General MacArthur was desperate for the convoy to reach its intended destination, but Roosevelt's advisers told him that the convoy would doubtless be lost before it reached the Philippines. Despite the protests of MacArthur, it was decided that the convoy would be diverted to another port until such time as it would be prudent to continue the voyage.

On 12 December, the War Department ordered the *Pensacola* convoy to set course for the east coast of Australia and to arrive in the port of Brisbane no later than 22 December.[17]

CHAPTER THREE

OVERTURE

During World War II, an estimated one million Americans occupied Australia for operations against Japanese forces. However significant this period was for both countries, it was not the first time American servicemen had visited the strange land down-under.

Over 100 years before, in November 1839, two American warships, under the command of Lieutenant Charles Wilkes sailed unexpectedly into a quiet Sydney Harbour. The locals who gazed upon Sydney Cove the next morning were startled to see the USS *Vincennes* and USS *Peacock* at anchor.[1] The Americans were given an enthusiastic welcome and 40 of them deserted, preferring Australia to their next destination, Antarctica.[2]

The next time the Americans sailed into Australian ports, in 1908, it was by invitation. Prime Minister Alfred Deakin sent an invitation to President Theodore Roosevelt inviting the Great White Fleet of America to visit the country during its world cruise. Deakin's telegram stated: 'I doubt whether any two peoples could be found who are likely to benefit more by any thing that tends to knit their relations more closely'. In closing, there was a guarantee that seemed to remain in force for the next 50 years: 'Australian ports and portals would be wide open to your ships and men'.[3]

From the time the American Fleet docked in Auckland Harbour, the Australian public began gleefully anticipating its arrival in their own country. A correspondent from New Zealand told the *Daily Telegraph* in Sydney that the fleet had sailed from Honolulu on a war footing. The *Wisconsin* had lost a man overboard. A furious gale was weathered by all ships with little damage and the best feature of the long voyage was that the coal requirements were less than anticipated. This was fortunate, in that most of the colliers were lagging behind, due to the speed of the fleet.[4]

On 20 August, it was a sight to behold — sixteen warships in stunning white, anchored between Kirribilli Point and Bradleys Head. The fleet stayed a week in Sydney and in Melbourne. For the general public, most of whom had never seen an American in the flesh before, it was a curious experience. Most Yanks 'looked different' — they were lanky, some were scraggy, some were swarthy and all of them talked funny. Public holidays were announced, parties and other social events continued around the clock, the 14 000 American sailors enjoyed their first taste of Australian hospitality. The Great White Fleet left Australian waters at the end of August, having publicly cemented the two countries' relationship.

In July 1925 the Americans were back, yet again under the guise of a training cruise. Fifty-six ships with 25 000 officers and men under the commands of Admiral S.S. Robison and Admiral R. Coontz arrived in July — one group in Sydney, the other in Melbourne.[5]

Other foreign vessels often visited Sydney, dropping anchor in the magnificent harbour. One of the last German fighting ships to visit Australia prior to World War II was the light cruiser *Koln* in 1933, under the command of Fregattenkapitan Otto Schniewind. The ship had started its Australian tour with a visit to Fremantle. Anxieties regarding the 'new' Germany had yet to be felt and Schniewind, who had an audience with Prime Minister Joseph Lyons, assured the media that, 'Although the *Koln* was built for war, it was hoped that she would be a messenger for peace'. He also suggested that, 'Adolf Hitler would prove of great benefit to Germany, having accomplished a bloodless revolution'.[6] The *Koln* left Sydney on 16 May 1933. The watch officer on the cruiser was 31-year-old Theodor Anton Detmers. On 19 November 1941, as Fregattenkapitan Detmers, he was in command of the German surface raider *Kormoran* when she sank the HMAS *Sydney* off the Western Australian coast.[7]

The American Navy made another visit in February 1938, during which 14 000 sailors were to enjoy another taste of Aussie hospitality. The official reason for the visit was the 150th anniversary of white settlement in Australia. However, the British Foreign Secretary, Anthony Eden, had suggested that a display of naval power in the Pacific may be 'useful' in response to Japanese aggressions and intentions. Vessels from England, New Zealand, Italy, France, Holland and the United States joined Australian ships for the celebration. The Japanese were apparently unmoved and even suggested that they would have sent a cruiser — had they been invited.[8]

The American representation was the largest and most powerful. The cruisers *Milwaukee, Memphis, Trenton* and *Louisville* arrived and anchored in Sydney Harbour. Regardless of the objective or the motive for the event, however, it was not the arrival of the ships that proved memorable, but an incident that occurred during their departure.

At 2.00 pm on the afternoon of Sunday, 13 February 1938, the *Louisville* weighed anchor and left her berth at Woolloomooloo. Hundreds of people were on the wharf and there were shouts and cheers as the ships started for the Heads. The *Louisville* looked magnificent. Its crew of 900 had kept her in top shape and 600 of them were lined up on the decks and superstructure, shoulder to shoulder, resplendent in their white uniforms. Numerous spectator craft bobbed in and out of the ship's wake with sirens and horns sounding almost as loud as the cheers.[9] The *Rodney*, a small, double-deck harbour ferry, was one of many pleasure craft in service. The master was Mr C. Rosman. On that day there were no spare seats and little standing room as passengers pushed their way onto the ferry. Even as the gangplanks were removed, they jumped from the wharf. Many almost fell into the water as they desperately climbed aboard.

As the *Rodney* approached the *Louisville*, Rosman announced that he would cross over to the cruiser's far side. This resulted in the ferry passing under the larger ship's stern. The ferry master's action surprised the crew of the *Louisville*. There were many vessels of all sizes — but this one was closer than most. Indeed it was so close that some of the *Louisville*'s crew could even recognise a number of the girls who had by now made their way to the upper deck of the ferry.[10] The recommended capacity on the top deck was 60 people.[11] As the wake of the cruiser lashed against the side of the ferry, over 100 passengers rushed over to the left railing, waving, cheering and crying. The last moment of exuberance was recorded by a photographer on the *Louisville*. The shutter had barely closed when the *Rodney* turned over. Other craft were in the area, but it was only when a large harbour ferry sounded four blasts of its siren that most of them realised something was wrong. The crew of the *Louisville* did not need any signal of distress. The upturned hull of the *Rodney* was only a few feet from their ship. Six crewmen dived into the water so quickly that they had not removed their caps. A hundred more would have followed had not Captain Mathewson ordered them to stand fast.[12] The *Louisville* stopped and launched four whalers and two motor launches to assist in the rescue. One hundred and fifty lifejackets were thrown overboard. Survivors and the dead were taken aboard the cruiser where the ship's doctors, orderlies and crew members struggled with a situation they could never have imagined. Nineteen was the final death toll; fifteen of the victims were under the age of 25.[13]

The *Louisville* continued its voyage to Melbourne and later, after a ceremony on board, the cruiser's aircraft dropped a wreath at sea. Some crew members also received permission to fly to Sydney to attend funeral services for the *Rodney* victims.[14] Prior to the final departure of the *Louisville*, Prime Minister Lyons sent a telegram to Captain Mathewson:

The loss of life, while indeed tragic, would have been much more but for the heroic work of the personnel of your vessel.

The Government is most appreciative of your prompt action in rendering assistance. I should be glad if you would convey to all concerned our warmest thanks.[15]

While many thousands of American sailors had visited Australia, resident Americans were comparatively rare in the prewar years. Some had moved to Australia for domestic or professional reasons. The 1921 census listed 6604 US-born citizens living permanently in Australia. Twelve years later, there were only 6066.[16]

The average Australian knew little about Americans. All that they knew — and liked — were the appealing, glamorous, righteous and courageous characters that were portrayed on the silver screen. There was no other medium to challenge these stereotypes. Due to a publishing agreement, Australia only imported books from Britain. Magazines were too few and outdated to have any impact. American history had no part in the education system. There was no tourism, little air travel and very few visitors arrived not wearing a uniform. As a consequence, to the average Australian the typical American *was* the character in the pictures, the performer on a record, or someone they heard on the wireless.

In March 1941, when President Roosevelt finally got his contentious Lend-Lease Act through Congress, it was a cause for celebration amongst those who desperately needed the help of Uncle Sam. Roosevelt wanted a show of unity and strength, he wanted ships 'to pop up everywhere', alerting friend and foe alike of American intentions and resolve. By no coincidence, there were naval squadrons of American ships en route to Australia and New Zealand when the announcement came that the Lend-Lease Bill had been passed law. Roosevelt asked if they could visit. As bureaucrats made hasty arrangements and politicians organised last-minute receptions, the public waited to greet what was to be the last American fleet to visit under a flag of peace. The nation's gravest hour had not yet arrived, but there was relief that an ally was about to visit and fascination that 'big brother' was American.

On 19 March it was announced in the Brisbane *Courier-Mail*:

Seven American warships from the United States Pacific Fleet, comprising two cruisers and a flotilla of five destroyers, will enter Sydney Harbour early on Thursday morning on a goodwill visit, which will last until late on Saturday.

The squadron will consist of the cruisers *Chicago* and *Portland*, the flotilla leader *Clark* and the destroyers *Cassin*, *Conyngham*, *Downes* and *Reid*.

The squadron will be under the command of Rear-Admiral Newton, whose flag is on the *Chicago* and it will have a complement of 2166 men. Although the ships are described as being on a training cruise, their visit to Australia, coinciding with the visit of a similar squadron to New Zealand and following dramatically and immediately on President Roosevelt's pledges of help and goodwill to the Empire, has caused profound satisfaction in the highest official quarters in Australia.[17]

For the great majority of the crews, this would be the first visit to Australia. They knew little about the country to which they were about to convey goodwill, but they had been told to expect an enthusiastic welcome and to be on their best behaviour.

Parliament started the loyal hysteria by demonstrating that the squadron's visit was big news — even bigger than running the country. Acting Prime Minister Arthur Fadden proposed an adjournment of parliament so that members could welcome the ships in Sydney. Opposition Leader John Curtin and the Minister for the Navy, Billy Hughes, promptly agreed. Mr Curtin also issued a statement:

I know it is the wish of the Australian people that we should welcome this visit as a compliment to our nation — a compliment which we will seek to acknowledge by the warmth of our welcome to these men and their ships. I hope that every officer and every man of the American squadron will in future years recall pleasant memories of this visit.[18]

Mr Hughes picked up the refrain:

The Australian people cherish happy memories of other visits by the American Navy. But the coming of this squadron, following upon the epoch-making speech by President Roosevelt, will stir them to their depths, because they will hail it as a sign of the goodwill and friendly encouragement of the people of the great Republic to the people of Australia in the fateful struggle in which we are involved.[19]

Australia was ready and the reception started before the ships were even in sight of land. Shortly after dawn, on Thursday, 20 March, the few aircraft that the RAAF had were circling the squadron and pointing the way to Sydney Heads. Although it was raining when the ships docked at Woolloomooloo, it was fine when the sailors started to march. The *Sydney Morning Herald* described the event: 'Sydney never before showed itself so ecstatic, so eager to demonstrate its feelings as it did to-day in welcoming the United States naval squadron'.[20]

A 600-strong contingent from the ships marched through the city streets. The crowd was estimated at 750 000. They blotted out every foot of pavement, every window, every awning, balcony and rooftop. One thousand policemen were on duty. When American flags had sold out, vendors sold Union Jacks instead. The New South Wales Police Band was in the front as the procession headed towards Martin Place from Macquarie Street. Thundershowers of confetti and streamers from buildings submerged the marchers and crowd and when stocks were exhausted balloons, flowers and then office waste were thrown. The crowd cheered wildly and hoarsely. The visitors waved their hands and doffed their hats. Some women broke the lines and embraced the sailors. Others asked for autographs. The *Herald* also reported that: 'There were many women who were anxious to offer private hospitality'.

The mayor was waiting at Town Hall. The Americans called it a Broadway welcome and nothing like it had ever been seen in the history of the city. You knew your place on the political and social pecking order if you received one of the 800 invitations to be a guest at the government-organised official reception at the Town Hall. Fadden offered a toast to Admiral Newton, who replied:

We have been here one short day, and already we feel as much at home as if we were among Americans. From the reactions I have heard, the passage of the Lend and Lease bill and President Roosevelt's speech have acted on the democracies like a transfusion.

There were similar transfusions of enthusiasm as sailors took to the city for their own less formal receptions. 'Attaboy' was the caption on Ian Gill's cartoon in the Brisbane *Courier-Mail* on Tuesday, 25 March. Pictured was a kangaroo, with the Stars and Stripes in one hand and the Union Jack in the other. In the kangaroo's pouch was a large key with a tag that read 'Freedom of Brisbane'.[21]

A Sydney newspaper stated that, 'The fleet was on its way to an unknown northern destination.' This was taking censorship a bit too far. Everyone knew the ships were on their way to Brisbane. The front page of the *Courier-Mail* carried a photograph of an attractive young lady with a sailor's cap and a multitude of American flags and this caption:

Symbolic of the cordial welcome which awaits the United States Squadron on its arrival in Brisbane this morning. There will be no lack of Stars and Stripes to display in honour of the visitors and no shortage of willing arms to wave them.[22]

Admiral Newton had sent a telegram to the media saying that his men anticipated great pleasure in the forthcoming visit and how fortunate he and his men were.

Brisbane had never seen an American naval squadron before. The goodwill visits in the past had not ventured north to anchor in the relatively shallow and narrow Brisbane River. 'Yankmania' gripped the locals. The McDonnell & East department store took full-page advertisements in the newspapers offering Yank caps. You could buy a navy blue felt for 9s 11d or a white linen gob for 3s 11d. There were also suggested fashions to wear for the visit of 'our American cousins'.[23]

The ships gathered at Cape Moreton for their berthing at Hamilton and Newstead. What awaited them was, proportionately, the greatest public display of enthusiasm and emotion in the history of the country, even breaking the previous record set in Sydney only two days before. The multitude was there long before dawn, lined up on both sides of the river, waiting.

The *Cassin* was first ship to be seen, at 5.10 am, then the *Conyngham*, the *Reid*, the *Downes* and the *Clark*. The big ships appeared shortly after. Pleasure craft converged and tugs sounded whistles. Four hundred military signallers waved welcome. Seemingly out of nowhere, a group of Lockheed Hudsons flew over, followed by eight Wirraways. The *Courier-Mail* aircraft dipped its wings as the photographer took aim. The ships had their crews on deck. The khaki-clad marines contrasted with the whiter-than-white apparel of the sailors. They were cheering too, but were easily drowned out by the crowd. Faces appeared from every porthole. Crew members on the stern were waving frantically, while the marines remained rigid and formal. There were laughs and cheers as the crowd finally spotted a rating blowing kisses from high in the crow's nest of the *Chicago*. A signal lamp sent a message, not to the crowd, but to the *Portland*, warning her to be careful of the pleasure craft, some of which were bouncing off the sides of the *Chicago*. An official launch containing cabinet ministers, aldermen and other bureaucrats was frantically trying to convey the official welcome. It was unprecedented; it was madness — it was only 7.00 am.

The march from Fortitude Valley to the city hall was even more spectacular than in Sydney. Mounted police led the parade, the band from the *Chicago* followed, then came the marines and the sailors, while a few Australians brought up the rear. The band, which comprised 25 musicians led by a baton-twirling drum-major, played 'Roll out the Barrel'. Somebody threw a bottle of beer into the ranks of marchers. A Yank caught it cleanly, much to the delight of the crowd.[24]

The Brisbane Lord Mayor, Alderman Chandler, presented the Americans with the freedom of the city. The authorities had expected 160 000 people to welcome the ships but 280 000 was the estimated figure. This was nearly 85 per cent of the population of Brisbane. It was the biggest public demonstration in the history of the city.

As the sailors wandered around the streets, people ran up to pat them on the back or shake their hands. Girls gave them written messages and phone numbers and cars pulled up and offered lifts. A tram conductor, observing a large party of Yanks walking towards town, stopped and ordered his passengers to vacate his vehicle. This they quickly did and the Yanks jumped aboard. One tram, immersed in streamers, paper and flags, caught fire. Seven people were injured in various road accidents.

Streamers were thrown to the ships and sailors threw nickels and chocolate bars, which children rushed to retrieve. When tobacco was thrown, adults became children. Signing autographs was the main duty for the sailors that day. There was a sea of girls all clamouring for attention. 'Sign here. Sign here, please,' was their chorus. 'Girls! Girls! Stop now! I've got to weigh anchor. I've got to get back to the ship!' exclaimed one of the besieged visitors. Uncle Sam could have put this scene on recruitment posters. Sailors returned to their ships with dozens of names, addresses and phone numbers. The ships' laundries also had the task of removing hundreds of names from the white uniforms, while many caps had been given away or stolen. The men were chased and mobbed as the city virtually came to a stop. Dan Hayes, from the *Portland*, had been signing autographs for an hour before calling it quits with a plaintive, 'Girls, I gotta go. Honest girls, I gotta headache in my hand!'.[25]

No American was alone for long that day, but not all enjoyed the adulation. Some sat in bars, talking to Diggers; others took photographs. Some even went to see Kit Carson at the Regent or Melody Ranch at the Tivoli. Some took girls, others went alone. Many enjoyed meals in homes throughout the city, meeting family members, neighbours — and usually everybody in the street.

The big event ashore that night was a dance for enlisted men that the state government had organised at the City Hall. The officers would enjoy a separate, more formal function. To limit the girls to 800, invitations had been carefully distributed. Representatives from the Women's National Emergency Legion, Women's Auxiliary Transport Service, Red Cross Link and the Air Force Club were some of the recipients. Others obtained them somehow, through fair means or foul. It was the social event of the decade if you could get an invitation and during the evening police formed a human chain around the venue to keep back the crush of uninvited girls, many weeping in their formal gowns.

Inside, Seaman Ralph Woolridge from the *Chicago* jitterbugged with Miss Irene Stack. Miss Rene Asmar was dressed in a Stars and Stripes gown that her mother had made. She was photographed with George Faulk, also from the *Chicago*.[26]

The departure of the fleet was almost as inspirational as its arrival.

Not everyone wanted to say farewell, however, and two ratings from the *Chicago* watched the squadron depart without them. Soon the daily newspapers reported: 'Queensland police have now been posted with the descriptions of the two American sailors reported missing from the vessel, *Chicago*, flagship of the squadron which visited Brisbane last week'.[27]

Evidently, Seaman Albert F. Hudson, 18 years of age and Yeoman Joseph E. Olsen, 21, thought it preferable to discharge themselves from the United States Navy and enjoy life down-under. Although the two young men were in breach of several major regulations, the escapade created much goodwill. The two surfaced eleven days later, in Toowoomba, 130 kilometres west of Brisbane. They walked in to the local police station and alerted Chief Constable Stephenson to their identity.

'Sure we left the Navy because we didn't like it,' Olsen told a newspaper reporter. 'We left our uniforms in a clothing store in

Brisbane and bought us some new outfits. We thought giving ourselves up easiest and I guess it would lift a lot of worry off our folks who are getting old.' Hudson, when asked how he liked Australia, said, 'Boy, this is a grand country and the people are swell folks. I sure hope that we can come back here one day. The Australian people are the nicest I've met'.

The two Americans were in the Toowoomba lockup, with unlocked doors. Locals bought them refreshments, cakes, biscuits and knitted clothes. When not in their cells, they were at the rear of the police station playing tennis with the constables. They were taken on a drive into the country to try and see some kangaroos, which was always an item high on the list of requests from the Yanks. At the station, they received long lines of visitors. The sailors were also allowed to walk around the city, usually with Constable Stephenson's young son Edward.

An Australian sailor called Walsh, who had met the two Americans when their ship was in Sydney, drove up from Brisbane to visit them. 'G'day Bert. G'day Joe,' said Walsh. 'Jesus, what are you blokes doing here?

'We just got ourselves into a little trouble,' said Hudson.

'Don't worry about it, mate. You'll be all right. Do you need any smokes?'

'Brother, we've got everything,' Olsen replied.

'These are two bonza blokes,' said Walsh to a policeman as he left the station.

Constable Stephenson became the most hated man in Toowoomba when he notified the CIB in Brisbane that he had the men in custody. It was an emotional scene when Detective Constable Cook arrived in town to take the men to the train station for the trip to Sydney, where they would be handed over to the American Consul for transfer back to the States. There were tears all round as the crowd farewelled the sailors. 'What part of America are you from?' a newspaper reporter asked Olsen, but it was young Edward Stephenson who replied, 'Joe is from Ohio, where the tall corn grows.' Olsen ruffled the boy's hair as he corrected him, 'Not Ohio, kid, it's Oia. Now c'mon buddy, don't cry, don't cry. If I had a basket big enough I'd smuggle you onto the train.' Cook gestured for the men to move towards the train. 'What's going to happen to them?' asked a child, who, like dozens of others, had been given the day off school. 'They're going back to their school to get the cane', replied the mother.

It was a sombre experience as the train pulled out of the station. Olsen and Hudson had left an indelible impression on the people of Queensland. They also left with enough tobacco to last for months, enough cakes, biscuits and scones to feed the train and, seemingly, the names and addresses of half the population of Toowoomba.[28]

Five weeks after the squadron left, the two sailors were waiting on a Sydney pier for their voyage home. They had captured the hearts of the people — and the headlines of the press. Uncle Sam might not have approved of the methods, but the desertion had become a public relations bonanza. It was Albert Hudson who, through the medium of the press, had the final word to the people of Australia. The sincere, but somewhat indiscreet, former sailor of the USS *Chicago* told reporters:

Australia is a great country and the people are more like Americans than any others. The police are wonderful as well; in Toowoomba they put us in a lockup, but let us walk around and play tennis and visit with folks.[29]

In August 1941, two heavy cruisers, the USS *Salt Lake City* and the USS *Northampton*, paid a surprise visit to Brisbane. This time there were no large crowds to greet them. Ostensibly, they had docked for fuel and supplies but they were a welcome presence for a nervous population increasingly concerned about reverses in the war. The American Consulate also had more to contend with, as on this visit seven men jumped ship.

Soon the fleet visits, the marches, the receptions and the autographs were superseded by the intensity of war. For the men and ships that visited Australia before and during the war, the future would provide few training exercises and even less goodwill. Most of the ships and many of the men would not survive the conflict. The *Cassin* and the *Downes* were destroyed, side by side, at Pearl Harbor; such was the fury of the blast that the ships were welded together in a mass of metal.[30]

The *Chicago*, however, was luckier. Stationed at Pearl Harbor, Admiral Newton had taken her, with two other cruisers and the aircraft carrier *Lexington*, to reinforce Midway Island the day before the Japanese attacked. Later, she was anchored off Garden Island in Sydney Harbour when the Japanese midget submarines attacked in May 1942. Captain Bode and several of his officers were being entertained ashore when the alarm sounded at 11.00 pm.[31] The *Chicago* opened fire at periscope sightings with her small-calibre auxiliary armament. After a confusing action, the ship retrieved her officers and pulled anchor, making for the open sea and narrowly avoiding two torpedos in the process.

Ten weeks later, the *Chicago* was one of several warships protecting the 1st Marine Division's landings on Guadalcanal and Tulagi.

Early on the morning of 9 August the *Chicago*, with HMAS *Canberra* and two destroyers were stationed south-east of Savo Island. The northern force of three heavy cruisers were adjacent to Savo Island. Both groups were a protecting screen for transports which were unloading men and equipment ashore. A Japanese cruiser squadron from Rabaul, under the command of Admiral Mikawa, sailed into the area undetected and destroyed the *Canberra* before she had time to sound action stations. The *Chicago* lost its bow to a Japanese torpedo and turned away from the battle.

The failure of the *Chicago* to warn the northern group of the attack was a major factor in the loss of the cruisers *Quincy*, *Vincennes* and *Astoria*. As a result, the American Navy suffered its worst defeat at sea and over 1000 sailors died.[32] After an inquiry into the disaster, Captain Bode took his own life.[33] The *Chicago* did not long survive him. On 29 January 1943 she was torpedoed in the Battle of Rennell Island and the next morning the damaged cruiser was taken in tow by the *Louisville*. Some hours later, 24 Japanese aircraft finally despatched the *Chicago* to her final resting place, two miles beneath the surface.[34]

The *Portland* was involved in the Coral Sea and Midway encounters before being a part of the American force for the naval battle of Guadalcanal in November 1942. The ship performed well in a close-quarter battle of unprecedented ferocity with the Japanese. Two American admirals, Callaghan and Scott, were killed that night and several ships were lost. Badly damaged, the *Portland* was towed to Tulagi where it was engaged again, this time by friendly forces. Captain Du Bose had no sooner concluded an altercation with the captain of a tug when the cruiser was attacked by American PT boats. 'I have fired both my torpedos at a large unidentified ship entering the anchorage,' exulted the voice of a PT skipper on the ship's radio.[35] Fortunately, they missed. It was the last straw for Captain Du Bose who had been on the bridge for the past 48 hours. He now knew why American ships were reluctant to enter the sound patrolled by the Tulagi PT 'cowboys'.[36] Some skippers feared them as much as the Japanese.

These small, fast craft had achieved a high profile and much glamour when John D. Bulkeley's boat, PT 41, rescued General MacArthur and his entourage from the Philippines. Few knew when, in June 1943, a group of them sank Admiral Turner's flagship, the USS *McCawley*.[37] Two months later a Tulagi boat, PT 109, under the command of Lieutenant John F. Kennedy, ran across the bows of the Japanese destroyer *Amagiri* and was cut in two.[38]

The USS *Northampton* was sunk by Japanese destroyers in the Battle of Tassafaronga on 1 December 1942.[39] The USS *Pensacola* was severely damaged in the same action. Her sister ship, USS *Salt Lake City*, had been damaged in the Battle of Cape Esperance six weeks earlier. Both ships suffered heavy casualties and were out of action for a year. The USS *Reid* was destroyed by Japanese surface ships in the Leyte Gulf in December 1944 with the loss of 150 men.[40] The *Conyngham* performed gallantly all through the war, only to suffer the ignominy of being sunk as a target ship in 1948.[41]

The visits to Australian waters for these ships in the years before the United States entered the war served as an introduction to the population of the military might and cultural disposition of United States forces. During the war years, the visits had decidedly different motives.

CHAPTER FOUR.

ANOTHER OP'NIN', ANOTHER SHOW

When a convoy of American transports docked in Brisbane on 22 December 1941, there was no media attention or fanfare. The majority of the local population were astonished to see the Americans arrive in such force and so soon after Pearl Harbor.

The odyssey had begun a month earlier when the transports *Republic* and *Holbrook* left San Francisco for the Philippines with 2700 men and their equipment. The Japanese threat had resulted in the American forces being reinforced and the ageing commander Douglas MacArthur, previously retired, being returned to active duty. The two ships rendezvoused in Honolulu with other heavily laden transports *Bloemfontein, Chaumont, Meigs, Coast Farmer, Admiral Halstead* and the fleet tender USS *Niagara*. The convoy was under the protection of the heavy cruiser USS *Pensacola*.[1]

Observing security and blackout conditions, the ships sailed at a determined ten knots on a south-westerly course for the Philippines. On the morning of 7 December the *Republic* received an alarming report. The American base at Pearl Harbor was under attack by Japanese forces. Many thought that it was just another military exercise, but later came the definitive: 'Japan has started hostilities — govern yourself accordingly'.

While the *Pensacola*'s aircraft mounted search patrols, the ships of the convoy covered their markings with battle grey and defensive measures were taken. Artillery pieces were set up on deck and shells stacked nearby. The *Republic* mounted machine-guns on deck and riflemen on station. Whatever the practical value of these measures, it was good for morale. Corporal Willard A. Heath, a member of B Battery, 148th Field Artillery, was on the Holbrook:

Our escort ships let out tow targets. Marksmanship wasn't good at first, but after a couple of rounds it got better. The Idaho National Guardsmen with their old model 75 mm guns were the most accurate cannoneers in the convoy. Jack Allured's gun crew of B Battery blew the target out of the water. The guys cheered. It took our minds off things.[2]

The convoy continued sailing around in circles awaiting orders. The uncertainty of the situation was not helped by the latest war news being piped over the PA. The Japanese had landed in Malaya and Hong Kong. There was also a report that the marine garrison on Wake Island was being attacked. There was more bad news. The Philippines had been attacked and two British warships had been sunk by Japanese aircraft in the South China Sea.[3]

Rumours about the destination were rampant. The most alarming was that the convoy would still proceed to Manila. More comforting was the rumour that the ships were going back to the States.

Meanwhile, the convoy was still in the middle of the Pacific and still sailing in circles. Finally, on 12 December, orders were received. As the ships navigators scanned charts, the ship's PA system announced: 'Attention all hands, this is the captain speaking. We have been ordered to proceed to Brisbayne, Os-tral-yah'.

The ships' companies were stunned. 'Where did he say?' 'Brisbayne, where's that?' 'Are they on our side?'[4]

After a refuelling stop in Suva, the ships set course for Australia. The task force was under the command of Brigadier General Julian F. Barnes.[5] He would also be appointed commander of United States troops in Australia and report directly to MacArthur, who still expected the cargoes of men and equipment to be sent to Manila.

The convoy arrived in Australian waters where the cruisers, HMAS *Canberra* and HMAS *Perth,* waited to escort the ships to their new destination. Brisbane was to be a temporary stop until supplies could be unloaded and the aircraft assembled and flown to the Philippines.

MacArthur's chagrin over his loss of the ships was justified. The convoy carried 52 Dauntless dive bombers and 34 Kittyhawk fighters. There were 7 million rounds of .50 calibre ammunition, 5000 bombs, ranging from 30 to 500 pounds, and 3000 barrels of fuel and oil.

The personnel comprised 48 pilots, 2000 technicians, mechanics, support personnel, casuals, the 2nd Battalion, 131st Field Artillery, and two National Guard regiments, the 147th and 148th. The total personnel, excluding ships' companies, was approximately 4600 men.[6]

The American military had always recognised the value of Australia as a base for communications, equipment and personnel. The United States government had even allocated funds for a project to build airfields and unloading facilities, mostly in northern Australia. Darwin in particular seemed an ideal forward base for the despatch of men and supplies to MacArthur in the Philippines. Lieutenant-General Lewis Brereton had been on MacArthur's staff in Manila before he visited Australia a few weeks before Pearl Harbor to examine potential supply routes and logistics. He had discussions with the Australian government and the military, who were clearly delighted with any American involvement and commitment.[7]

The men of the Pensacola convoy knew nothing about this. The ships crawled up the Brisbane River, the hulls of their heavily laden ships almost dragging the bottom. There was much curiosity as men wrestled for vantage points on deck. Soon a flotilla containing an official welcoming committee arrived. Senior Australian army and naval personnel and Colonel Merle-Smith of the Melbourne Consulate boarded the *Republic*, formally welcoming General Barnes and his staff to the city of Brisbane. By 5 pm Barnes and his officers had established their headquarters and accommodation at the new Lennons Hotel in Brisbane city.[8]

After the ships berthed at Brett's Wharf, the first of the 4600

American personnel stepped off the gangplanks and on to Australian soil. The men were glad to finally get off the stinking, confined holds of the transports, and on the wharf. There was a small welcoming committee including a brass band. Second-Lieutenant Mark Muller from Kentucky recalled:

The band played, 'While We Were Marching Through Georgia', a Union victory song from the Civil War. Anyone on board from the South who heard that song would not have thought it appropriate, but it didn't matter. Not after the voyage. We had been on board that long that we were down to one meal a day. There was nothing left. We were broke and dirty.[9]

Nobody knew where they were going as they formed lines on the pier. It didn't matter that they didn't have a dime, or were dirty and tired. They might have been nervous and anxious, but they were safe. Seaman 2nd Class John Leeman remembers:

The rest of us had gone to a racetrack called Doomben — the other one was called Ascot. Australian army guys were there to help us. Diggers is what you called them. They wore hats with one side turned up and they all seemed to be smoking. But they seemed okay, offering us a smoke and a drink at the pub; we gathered that it meant a saloon. Some of them asked if we wanted a few bob till we got paid. We lived in pyramidal tents on mattresses filled with straw; some of the guys slept on the ground. The cheering from the Aussies on the way from the ships made us feel good. From what we were hearing there wasn't too much cheering for the guys in the Philippines. We had been promised some fresh food and a glass of cold milk. Jesus, it was hot in the tent. We didn't know how anyone could sleep in the heat. To hell with it, we thought — this place ain't so bad.[10]

Hollis G. Allen, a Texan from the 131st Field Artillery, was initially confused but soon got to know his hosts well:

The Aussies were hard to understand, and we had to ask them two or three times what they said. They either ran their words together, slurred them, or cut each word short. However, after spending about a week there, most everyone could understand them pretty well. They had plenty of nice things to say to the Americans; they liked us, as we did them. We were broke, and they paid for our visits to town, bought us beer, cold drinks, and sandwiches.[11]

Willard Heath was looking forward to a hearty breakfast:

We lined up for what we hoped would be a long awaited, real breakfast. I held out my mess kit to the congenial cook, and plop ... a mutton chop, with the grease already beginning to congeal. To our host mutton was a treat, so they figured we'd enjoy it. We looked forward to a good cup of coffee. Nope, watered down tea with too much milk and sugar. But there was always plenty of fresh bread.[12]

The Australian soldiers were equally as curious about their visitors. Clem Sorenson remembers:

They were a friendly bunch, every one is their buddy, they say Ma'am to every woman. You couldn't understand a word they were saying. We didn't think the girls would go for them.

Bugger them, we thought, if they don't like the tents, nobody asked them to come here and what's wrong with mutton? None of them wanted to touch it. Instead of tea they wanted coffee and what about wanting ice-cream. We used to say, 'Hey Yank! Don't you know there's a war on?'[13]

Jack Newcomb was on sentry duty at the front gate of Camp Ascot: 'I had never seen so many Yanks before. They kept on coming. I thought that they would look tall and strong, but this lot looked tired and buggered. Some could hardly carry their gear.'[14]

There was no publicity about the ships but word spread as crowds gathered around the wharves and the river. They could not board the American ships, nor could they even get near the dock facilities. Thousands still watched from across the river, absorbing the might and majesty of the warships and the dull grey lines of the freighters — their decks humming with activity. There was the odd wave and whistle but soon it was nightfall. The crowds remained on the far side of the river even when it was dark and quiet.

No lights or sounds came from the ships, just the slapping of water and the glitter of the river in the moonlight. The locals knew the men were still watching from the ships — they could feel them. Someone on the river bank began singing. Laughter broke out and more singing. Soon the night air trembled as hundreds sang 'Waltzing Matilda'. At first the ships were silent, and when the singing from the shore ceased the night was still. Then from the ships came a lone American voice, and then another. Before long a male choir began singing 'You Are My Sunshine'.[15] This was Christmas 1941, on the Brisbane River. For many, this would be their most profound memory of the war. They no longer felt alone.

After a month on the ships and several days in the tents, the men received liberty and back pay. John Leeman and others walked in to the city of Brisbane.

We knew nothing about this place. It was like from another world. Houses on stumps with red roofs. Cable cars in the middle of the roads; the Aussies call them trams. The city looked sort of empty and quiet. Some girls were in town; they looked pretty, dressed well — kinda classy. They would giggle when you said something to them; they were sorta shy, but some of them called out — 'G'day Yank' and waved. There were plenty of hotels and movie theatres, but nothing was open. It was a Sunday, the day after Boxing Day, but it was so quiet. We kept running into guys from the ships. Most of the guys were sitting in the park; some were talking to Aussies.

The Aussie money was something else. Instead of dollars and cents they had pounds, shillings, pence and halfpennies; there were no quarters or dimes, but florins and shillings and things. Then they talk about quids and bobs. Nobody could figure it out. What we used to do was to buy something and then put our hand in our pocket and bring out the change and say, 'Take what ya want'.[16]

There was to be no Christmas vacation. The ships had to be reloaded and despatched to priority destinations. It was then that the United States armed forces met one of their most formidable and unexpected adversaries — the Australian waterside worker.

The Americans sensed potential problems when they were told that wharf labourers would be required to assist them in unloading their ships. Australian waterside workers had long been protected by a strong and militant union which was even more powerful under the wartime Labor government. One American historian concluded that the wharfies were 'trying, none too efficient and costly. They were also insolent, thievish and resentful of the US Army.'[17]

There was also much concern about the lack of productivity, limited working hours, overstaffing and poor skills. The wharfies resented the arrogant domination often displayed by the Americans when it came to logistics. There was also much resentment by the Australian wharfies when it became apparent that the Americans had little or no respect for existing industrial and labour regulations.

Despite the gravity of Australia's plight in the early period of the war, there were many industrial strikes for a multitude of reasons. Disputes and stoppages within the mining, munitions, transport and waterfront industries caused the government considerable concern. Although the working days lost to strike activity were less with the Labor government, Curtin felt compelled to take aggressive action against the more militant unions. He ordered naval personnel to unload a ship in Sydney and also stated: 'The men who are not in the fighting forces and who, at the same time, will not work are as much the enemies of this country as the directly enlisted legions of the enemy'. Curtin also warned that men who did not work in their protected industry would lose their exemption from military service.[18]

Although the Australian Communist Party was a minority group (5000 members in 1940) and was often challenged by the government, it was an active organisation that gained some influence in various trade unions.[19] Much is revealed about the Communist Party and the waterfront workers in one of their newsletters distributed at the height of the war in 1943.

Communist Party Member Mick Healy addressed the problem

of day gangs of wharfies unloading the cargo from a ship while the night gang reloads the same cargo later in the day:

Only the actions of the workers on the job can expose those responsible for such bungling and inefficiency. They must be severely dealt with and removed from their positions by the Curtin Government as hindering our successful war effort against the Fascist Axis. The Waterside Workers' Federation cannot overlook such an incident. Wharfies demand an immediate investigation. We stand for the utter destruction of the Fascist Axis. It is to help smash fascism that we support a maximum war effort on the waterfront, not by speed-up tactics, but by more efficient use of available man power so that the work shall be spread as evenly as possible.[20]

The United States military and the Stevedoring Industry Commission would never achieve the level of harmony or compatibility found in other relationships forged during the alliance.

For most of the men of the *Pensacola* convoy, the visit to Brisbane would be a brief one. On 27 December 1941 the *Holbrook* and *Chaumont* left with the National Guard regiments for Port Darwin. Soon the remainder of the convoy would be redeployed. The 131st Field Artillery Regiment boarded the *Bloemfontein* and were despatched to Java. Fifteen hundred men were posted to Townsville and 1100 remained in Brisbane.[21]

By January 1942 the Japanese had secured Guam, Manila, and Hong Kong and were advancing through Burma, the Netherlands East Indies and Thailand. It seemed that nothing could stop the Japanese and their southward thrust — except Singapore. In Canberra Prime Minister Curtin believed that the Pacific war should be viewed as distinct from the European theatre, but equally important. It should not be treated as a subordinate part of the global conflict.

England had always assured the dominion that, if threatened, it would forsake all and come to the rescue. However, this could not seriously be contemplated in 1942. At any rate, Singapore was the bastion of colonial power in the Far East. There were four

Commonwealth divisions garrisoned there and the defences were believed to be impregnable.[22]

Australia, at this time, was virtually helpless. The country had meagre defence resources and poor mobilisation potential. Most of the best troops were overseas and involved in campaigns that were not a direct threat to the country. As Curtin fought with Churchill for the return of the Australian Middle East divisions, substantial Americans forces began to disembark in Australian ports. The media were not permitted to acknowledge their arrival or presence. However, this fooled no-one and Curtin acknowledged the implication of United States involvement in an interview published in the Melbourne *Herald* on 27 December 1941:

Without any inhibitions of any kind, I make it quite clear that Australia looks to America, free of any pangs as to our traditional links or kinship with the United Kingdom.

We shall exert all our energies to shaping a defence plan, with the US as its keystone, which will enable us to hold out until the tide swings against the enemy.[23]

This was a dramatic departure from the traditional Australian external policy. It was not a divorce from Mother England, but the duo had become a trio. The speech was a direct response to American plans to increase the defence capability of Australia with more United States involvement.

On 28 December 1941, Lieutenant General George H. Brett arrived in Australia to take command of all United States forces. General Barnes would be Chief of Staff and General Brereton, who had arrived from the Philippines, was in command of all air forces. The headquarters moved from Brisbane to Melbourne which had superior facilities and was also the location of Australian Army Headquarters.

The Americans began to establish a series of organisations to handle the distribution of supplies and personnel throughout a large and unfamiliar country. The organisations were referred to as numbered base sections of the United States Armed Forces in Australia (USAFIA). The essential objective was to operate service commands, to receive and assemble all United States troops and supplies arriving in Australia, and to forward them to the areas designated as ordered by High Command. The following base sections were allocated on 5 January 1942. Darwin as Base Section 1; Townsville, Base Section 2; Brisbane, Base Section 3; and Melbourne, Base Section 4. On 3 March 1942, Adelaide and Perth were designated as Base Sections 5 and 6. Sydney became Base Section 7 on 19 April.[24]

Although not acknowledged by the government or the press, more American troops were arriving into Sydney and Port Melbourne. On 1 February 1942, after an uneventful two-week cruise from San Francisco, 4550 Americans disembarked from the *Mariposa* and *President Coolidge*. The convoy escort had been the heavy cruiser USS *Phoenix*. The 22 000 ton *Coolidge* had been a Pacific passenger liner before being requisitioned by the United States government for service as a troopship.[25] Both ships were to meet extraordinary fates.

The end for the *Coolidge* was ignominious. She struck an American mine while entering the US base of Espiritu Santo in the New Hebrides. There was only one fatality as the ship sank in shallow water, ultimately becoming a popular tourist attraction and diving location. The *Phoenix* survived the Pacific war, but not one in another ocean 40 years later. Sold to Argentina in 1951 and renamed the *General Belgrano*, she was torpedoed and sunk by the British Submarine HMS *Conqueror* in May 1982 — an act which escalated the Falklands War.[26]

The 52nd Signal Battalion was one of the first outfits ashore. One of the soldiers to disembark from the *Mariposa* was a 24-year-old soldier from New York called Eddie Leonski.

A fortnight later, on 15 February 1942, Lieutenant General Arthur Percival walked towards the Ford factory in Singapore. He and other senior officers were on their way to meet General Yamashita and agree to an unconditional surrender. Also surrendering, but not present, were 130 000 Commonwealth troops. It was the greatest capitulation in the history of the British Empire. Colonel Phillip Parker placed the following on public record: 'The end — an inglorious end — had come; no last desperate struggle; No Dunkirk or Crete. Just the pathetic fizzle and the splutter of a damn squib.'[27]

It had taken a numerically inferior Japanese force 70 days to capture the impregnable fortress. The Australian public was not aware of the immediate ramifications of the fall of Singapore, and nor were they aware that nearly 2000 men of the 8th Division had already been killed in the fighting and over 15 000 were being marched into Japanese captivity.[28] This was the most disastrous single event in Australian military history. In percentage terms, the equivalent effect for American forces would have been the loss of 20 divisions.

The Japanese had effectively eliminated all serious resistance to their conquest of the South Pacific. The problems confronting them in early 1942 were purely logistical. Four days after the fall of Singapore, the Japanese bombed Darwin causing major damage to the town, port and shipping. Two hundred and forty-three were killed and hundreds more wounded. Australia had reached its darkest hour.

On 21 March, with the fanfare and reception worthy of royalty, General Douglas MacArthur arrived in Melbourne. The General, his family and staff had escaped from the Philippines and after a dramatic journey through Japanese-held territory, MacArthur had been appointed Supreme Commander of all Allied Forces in the South-West Pacific Area.

By that time there were about 15 000 US personnel scattered throughout the nation.[29] Now that MacArthur had arrived, the media told the public what they already knew: The Yanks Are Here. Most readers treated the statement as a joke. The Americans had been a familiar sight on the streets in all the eastern capital cities. They had fought at Darwin, built airfields and bases, and

some local girls had even married them. However, the announcement of the American presence seemed to escalate the 'invasion'.
Soon they would be everywhere.

The main influx of American troops to Australia occurred when
two large divisions, the 32nd and 41st, arrived. These were National
Guard divisions consisting largely of conscripts from Wisconsin,
Michigan and north-western states. Departing San Francisco in
late March on the *Queen Elizabeth, President Coolidge* and
Mariposa, the 41st arrived in Sydney on 6 April. The *Queen
Elizabeth* had to wait at the Heads for the *Queen Mary* to pass
before entering the harbour. The meeting of the world's largest
ships caused a great deal of excitement for passengers and crews.[30]

The two *Queens* had been converted to troopship status at the
beginning of the war. They were large enough to carry a division
and fast enough to outrun a menacing submarine.

In October 1942, while off the coast of Ireland, the 80 000-ton
Queen Mary, at a speed of 28 knots, collided with the escorting
British cruiser *Curacoa*, slicing the 4200-ton ship in two and
drowning over 300 men.[31]

There were no incidents that day in Sydney when the majestic
liner docked with its cargo of Americans. Sergeant Bill Bentson of
the 163rd Infantry Regiment was one of the few Americans who
knew something about Australia. 'A missionary had visited our
school once and spoke about the Aborigines and showed some
artefacts,' he recalled in 1997. 'I had also seen some photographs
of animals, like kangaroos, emus and koalas and things.'

Bentson, who also had a Boy Scout penfriend in Sydney, was
one of the better informed. Most of the Americans knew virtually
nothing about Australia and its people. Bentson remembers his first
day in a strange country:

We were stuck on the ship until after 11.00 pm when we were told to get up
and get our barracks bag. We got on a barge and then a ferry to shore and
then we were on a train.

The train was noisy and uncomfortable. Nobody slept and at every small town we stopped or slowed down the kids would run alongside the train. We would throw some American money and chocolates to them. We would have meals at some of the stations. Breakfast was usually sausages and mashed potatoes, which the Aussies called bangers and mash. Some of the stations had a bar and the guys would buy all the booze they had.

We arrived in Albury late in the afternoon. We were told to get off the train, so we thought we must be at our destination, but it was a different track gauge and we had to change trains. What sort of system was that when each state has a different track gauge?[32]

The 163rd Regiment of the 41st Division finally arrived at its new base in the Victorian town of Seymour. Bentson was a specialist in communications and with 35 other men he was directed to proceed to Melbourne. It was pitch black and after midnight when the group camped at a park in some makeshift tents. Even the hay cots were welcome after the arduous day. Then the men heard noises. It was the sound of animals — lions, elephants, monkeys and other creatures. Bentson remembers the reaction from the men of the 41st Division. 'It couldn't be. We weren't told about this. Jesus Christ, what's going on? Kangaroos and koalas, that's okay — but what else is in the bush?' When the sun came up, the men saw the outline of the city of Melbourne and with a great deal of relief they realised that they were camped in Victoria Park — right beside the Melbourne Zoo.

On 9 April, Bill Bentson and twelve other ranks were told to report to the headquarters of the United States Armed Forces in the Far East. The address was the Trustees Executive building, located at 408 Collins Street, Melbourne. The building was empty but it was to be converted and equipped with all haste. It was here that General Douglas MacArthur was to commence his war and prepare for the long road back to the Philippines.

By June 1942 there were nearly 90 000 Americans stationed in Australia. This included 29 000 Army Corps personnel, many of whom were posted in northern Australian towns and remote outback airfields and strips. The remnants of the Asiatic submarine force of old S-boats and their tenders had arrived from the Philippines. They operated from facilities in Fremantle and, from 15 April 1942, in Brisbane.[33]

The Americans arrived in a nation facing the prospect of invasion. Most of the population knew little about the war, other than what was being conveyed through very tightly controlled media. However, no censorship could disguise the disastrous news about the fall of Singapore, the bombing of Darwin and the fact that the best of the Australian Army were fighting battles thousands of miles from home. In a period when brownouts were common, air-raid drills obligatory and where the most admired dwelling was one which boasted a bomb shelter in the backyard, the arrival of the Americans was not unlike the arrival of the cavalry in the movies — a fortunate deliverance portrayed in the last reel of every second Western.

The cavalry captain was MacArthur. When his arrival in March 1942 led to official revelation of the presence of the Americans, newspapers quickly exploited his undoubted charisma. 'The Great son of a Great Father; Greatest Scion of a famous family! ... That is General Douglas MacArthur, who now occupies the brightest military spotlight of the world.'

The *Truth* newspaper also stated that Australia would observe a national MacArthur day, and for the enemy there was this grim prediction: 'MacArthur is the man to whom the civilised world looks to sweep the Japs back into their slime'.[34] Copies of the sanitised MacArthur biography by Francis Miller were air-mailed from America so newspapers could serialise his exploits. Bookstores eagerly awaited bulk shipments by sea.

At the same time, the tools for MacArthur's crusade — men and munitions — were arriving in every major Australian port. MacArthur quickly sent a cable to General Marshall in Washington requesting more men and equipment. It was clear that he wanted to go on the offensive almost immediately. Marshall reminded him that the essential mission for the South-West Pacific Command was to secure Australia as a base for future operations.

It was not just the size of the American endeavour that impressed those who witnessed it, but the methodical calm and ingenuity displayed by Uncle Sam in the business of war.

Base Section 3 Headquarters were established in Somerville House, five kilometres from the Brisbane city centre. It was formerly an exclusive girls' boarding school, but the pupils had been relocated when the specialists moved in. Before long, Somerville House was a fully fledged, fully equipped Base Section facility. The beautiful coloured windows installed 50 years earlier were carefully removed and stored, while a more durable and practical replacement was installed.

There were a number of little things that frustrated the Yanks. In Brisbane there was a shortage of telephone handsets. When informed that it would take several weeks to fill the requisition, a detachment of American technicians immediately removed handsets from every public phone box in the city area. All were replaced when new stocks arrived.

There was no time for formalities. If a wharf was not big enough, it would be extended. If there was no road to the wharf, one would be built. The American Purchasing and Contracting Section requestioned everything necessary and much that was not. Automobiles, timber, steel and a thousand other items were requisitioned on a priority basis that was second to none. Seemingly, the Americans thought of everything. Immediately upon arriving in Brisbane they even leased a portion of the Lutwyche cemetery for nationals who would lose their lives, not just in battle but by accident and through sickness or misadventure. Later in the war a larger plot was required in a cemetery at Ipswich, 40 kilometres from the city.[35]

If books on MacArthur were being read by Australians, then booklets about Australians were being read by Americans. The visiting GI (universal slang for US soldier) had a formidable kit, including his weapon, utensils, two uniforms, two ties, two hats, and other essentials which were a cumbersome and ultimately useless gas mask and a small library of booklets.

The first to be issued was a pocket Bible. It carried this message from President Roosevelt. 'I take pleasure in commending the reading of the Bible to all who serve in the armed forces. It is a fountain of strength and now as always, an aid in attaining the highest aspirations of the human soul.'

There was also an *Army Song Book* containing 67 singalong ditties. However, the compiler at the Office of Armed Forces Information and Education must have been a musical square. The popular songs of 1942 were 'Elmer's Tune', 'Jeepers Creepers', 'Don't Sit Under the Apple Tree' and 'Blues in the Night'. The *Army Song Book* contained songs from another war and was treated as a joke. In 1942 there were few willing vocalists for 'K-K-K-Katy', 'It's a Long Way to Tipperary', 'By the Light of the Silvery Moon' and even 'Oh, Susanna'.

With so many troops overseas, the Special Services Division provided 'The Pocket Guide to ...' handbooks. There were pocket guides to England, Canada and to everywhere. After April 1942, the *Pocket Guide to the Philippines* became a collector's item.

The *Pocket Guide to Australia* contained information and handy hints for getting along with the mysterious and enigmatic Aussies. There was a brief explanation of the history and heritage of the country and the fact that, apart from 70 000 'Abos', the Aussies are from Anglo-Saxon stock. An Australian soldier is called a Digger and he is simple, direct and tough — especially if he comes from the outback. To him, the 'bloody thank yous' and 'pleases', are a bit sissified. The worst thing a Digger can do is let his mates down. 'Rough as bags' is a 'tough guy' and if a Digger tells you that you are as 'game as Ned Kelly', you should feel honoured because he was a courageous backwoods highwayman and an outlaw like Jesse James and Billy the Kid. There was also the invaluable vernacular translations:

Sheila = A babe
Crook = Feeling lousy
Tucker = Chow
Dinkum = Gospel truth
Pub = Saloon
Cobber = A pal
Tea = Supper

The guide was an honourable attempt at a crash course in Australian culture. But you learned much quicker if you took a Sheila for some supper, or met a dinkum cobber in a saloon.[36]

The early days of the American occupation was a love affair. The Yank was a saviour and a novelty. He was always well dressed, usually well mannered and a marvellous diversion from the ever increasing problems of the war. Betty Laing from Hendra in Brisbane may well have been the first to forge a marital alliance when she wed Laurence Ducker from the United States in early March 1942. This was even before it was officially announced that the Yanks were in Australia. 'He looked so lonely that I took him home for some tea,' said Mrs Ducker. 'It was love at first sight.'[37]

From then on, there was a procession to altars all over the country. One girl loved the Americans so much that she married two of them. Another Melbourne woman married an American sergeant and found herself in the Supreme Court on a bigamy charge: the 22-year-old mother of a 3-year-old child told her RAAF husband that she had been transferred to Sydney with her job. There was a tearful confession and nobody lived happily ever after.[38]

By April 1942, 20 Australian girls had married American servicemen. The Roman Catholic archbishop of Brisbane, the Most Reverend James Duhig, told the Melbourne *Sun News-Pictorial*: 'These men did not come to Australia to marry, they came to fight and I think the US authorities should introduce a complete marriage ban'.[39]

The federal government and the American military issued ominous and stern warnings about the perils and pitfalls of service marriages. Next month there were 30 marriages.

While some women wanted nothing whatsoever to do with the Yanks, many found them irresistible. Apart from their good looks and attractive uniforms, they were well paid. An American private earned more than £18 a month including overseas allowances. Whichever way you calculated it, the Yank earned twice as much as the Digger.[40] Things became even more unequal with the rise in rank. This remuneration was not designed to embarrass the Australian soldier; it simply reflected the buoyant American economy.

It was not only the women who loved the Yanks. The world of commerce found them to be the best thing yet in a miserable war. Taxi drivers, picture theatres, pubs, shops and virtually every amusement or service industry grew fat 'on the hog' with the American. Even more so when you could supply his essentials like hamburgers, tobacco, coffee, chocolates and ice-cream. These commodities were always hard to get and very few Yanks objected to paying a little and sometimes a lot more for them. Black market trade was soon rampant. While many establishments were fair and ethical, others saw it almost as a national duty to rip off a Yank. Walking into a Brisbane cafe in 1942, an American officer asked why there were two prices on the menu. 'It's like this, mate,' said the owner, 'the printed price is for the Aussies and the pencil price is for the Yanks.' Most Americans would not make an issue of it: however, on this occasion the matter reached the local magistrates court and the cafe proprietor received a substantial fine.[41]

Ignorance of the currency and the customs, coupled with a desire to impress, plenty of money, boredom and loneliness, were the factors that led to exploitation. Few Yanks complained and they learned quickly. The affluent visitors caused a financial boom for most commercial establishments. They had done well with the Second AIF before they were sent overseas, but this was much more lucrative.

Regardless of several unfortunate incidents, by mid-1942 the American serviceman and the Australian citizen had virtually consummated their relationship and for better or worse they were bound together by turbulent circumstances for the immediate future.

When General MacArthur moved his headquarters north to Brisbane, Staff Sergeant Bill Bentson and other specialist staff also relocated. Bentson soon became a keen observer of Australian culture:

One of the many things I noticed were the young children of fourteen and fifteen who were in the workforce. Evidently this was not a direct result of the war but a recognised custom. They were in shops, offices, selling newspapers or whatever. Back in the States, the great majority of kids went from high school to college. If you did not you were considered a dropout. The other conspicuous aspect of the Aussie men was that kindred mateship was the main priority. When it came to meeting girls the mateship factor would still be evident and he would try and blend the two, which sometimes did not work. In America, the young men had guys and girls who he called buddies. The co-ed high schools encouraged social familiarity between boys and girls.

If an American boy called on a young lady, he would invariably bring some flowers or some other gift, and always with respectful manners and courtesy. The custom did not change when the boys were overseas. Some Australian boys would do likewise, but to the great majority gifts and overt courtesy were deemed to be gestures of a sissy. Bill Bentson and other Americans had noticed in some of the dances that the Aussie boys congregated on one side of the orchestra, the girls on the other. The Red Cross organised such functions for servicemen and young women. Joan Staines remembered when the representatives from the Red Cross came to her place of work and asked if the girls would like to attend a dance at the City Hall. The American dance band was really swinging when Bill Bentson walked up to a group of women and asked one of them, a girl called Joan, to dance. Bill took her home in the tram and asked if he could kiss her goodnight. 'Goodness no,' said Joan. 'My mother might see us.'[42]

After a few weeks of constant courtship, Bill and Joan decided to get married. The procedures required for a couple to share their name were formidable. Bill had to present a request in writing to an officer with the rank of major general or higher; Joan had to write to the archbishop. Bill, who worked daily in the office of the Supreme Commander, knew about red tape. He also understood the initial reservations from family, friends, buddies and the army. After all, Joan was only seventeen. However, Bill Bentson and Joan Staines — and 5000 other Allied couples — were married in the gloomy garrison town of Brisbane, aka Base Section 3, during World War II.

There were no girls, dances or trams in a place called Logan Village, south of Brisbane. This railway siding was the perfect example of a bush town. There was a pub, a post office and a few scattered homesteads. Soon this area was transformed into a bush camp that became the new home for the American 32nd Division. Known as the Red Arrow, this division had been in Australia since April and had been stationed in Adelaide before being ordered north. The camp had to be built before the 32nd arrived. Forward units including engineers, tradesmen and civilian workers from the Queensland Main Roads Department arrived to construct a camp large enough to billet over 15 000 men and equipment. The usual American resourcefulness was apparent as the 76 acres were transformed into Camp Tamborine, named after a mountain range a few miles further south. Roads were built, the railway facilities enlarged and before long the camp was ready, complete with water tanks, generated electricity, mess huts and even a post office which also doubled as a pay office.[43]

The 32nd left Adelaide in July. Most of the personnel went by train, while others and their equipment sailed to Brisbane on a convoy of five Liberty ships. Three days later, off the coast of New South Wales, one of the ships was torpedoed by a Japanese submarine. There was only one fatality — a 25-year-old sergeant from Michigan, Gerald O. Cable.[44] This young man became the first 32nd Division battle fatality of the war and the camp at Tamborine would now be called Camp Cable.

It was not only the 32nd Division that occupied the camp during the war. The 1st Marine Division, famous for their heroic defence of Guadalcanal, was billeted there in 1943, and an Australian unit later found a home in the bush near Logan Village. From late July 1942, the Red Arrow Division lived and trained there while its senior officers awaited orders.

In his office in the AMP building in Brisbane, MacArthur contemplated the forthcoming campaign in New Guinea. This, he believed, was his destiny; the start of his crusade to return to the Philippines.

MacArthur's plan was to use an existing airstrip at Buna to support his offensives in New Guinea. The recently formed Port Moresby-based 39th Australian Militia Battalion, known as the Maroubra Force, was chosen to protect the airstrip. In order to reach their objective they would cross the Owen Stanley Range and walk along the tortuous Kokoda Trail.[45] The 39th Battalion was inexperienced, poorly equipped and had little training for what lay ahead. The average age of the soldiers was eighteen. In contrast the officers were of a mature age, many of them veterans of World War I.[46]

The Kokoda Trail crosses some of the most inhospitable terrain on Earth. In some areas you could only walk single file. Men walked with full packs and equipment totally unsuitable for jungle warfare. Long sticks, whittled from the bush, were obligatory to keep from slipping further in the mud or off the trail. Foul-smelling and harbouring disease, it is a terrain that favours no-one, characterised by vines, swamps, spiders, leeches, mud and more mud — it was always wet. It was a godforsaken place, difficult enough to survive in let alone fight a battle.

On 15 July the 39th Battalion reached the village of Kokoda. Six days later the Japanese landed in force in the Gona-Buna area of north-west New Guinea. On 23 July a company from Maroubra Force encountered an advanced attachment of Japanese troops from the South Seas Detachment estimated to be 2000 strong. These were crack troops, veterans from the campaigns in China, Malaya and the Philippines. Under the command of General Horii, they planned to capture Port Moresby by a land assault over the Owen Stanley Range. The battle for New Guinea had begun.

Two thousand kilometres from the battlefields in New Guinea, MacArthur, Blamey and other senior staff officers had no strategic appreciation of the conditions prevailing there. It gave MacArthur no joy to hear that the Japanese had seized the initiative in New Guinea, and when he heard reports that the Australians were retreating he castigated Blamey for their performance. Unconvinced about the worth of the Australians, MacArthur had told a visiting Congressman, a lean, tall Texan called Lyndon Baines Johnson, that Australia was 'totally unprepared to face war, even more unprepared than our own beloved country'. MacArthur also told Johnson that the Australians were undisciplined and were led by a former chief of police who had no professional experience.[47] The former lawman was Blamey. Although he had the rank of General of Allied Land Forces, he would seldom command American troops. Blamey was as anxious as MacArthur that the Australians put up a good fight in New Guinea. He had despatched the 21st Brigade from the 7th Division to Port Moresby to reinforce the units on the Kokoda Trail, but there still appeared to be a stalemate.[48]

Blamey had no doubt that MacArthur believed the Australians were not fighting. The situation changed weeks later when the Japanese suffered their first decisive defeat on land — at Milne Bay, on the eastern tip of New Guinea.[49] Although there were a few Americans in the area, this was undoubtedly an Australian victory. MacArthur was aware that the American 1st Marine Division had also started the first Pacific offensive by landing at Guadalcanal on 7 August. Desperate for a successful offence in New Guinea by his own forces, the Supreme Commander issued an order to call to arms the division at the bush camp south of Brisbane.

On 15 September 1942, the first units of a still untrained and inexperienced 32nd Infantry Division arrived at Port Moresby.[50]

CHAPTER FIVE

WHAT A DIFFERENCE A DAY MADE

While many of the Americans who were posted to Australia during the war experienced combat, many of them did not. In contrast, some Allied personnel would be immediately involved in desperate offensive and defensive actions in the area of northern Australia often referred to as the Top End.

Between the wars Darwin was a crude, ugly, isolated outpost, with corrugated-iron shacks and muddy streets. As late as 1936 the town had no electricity, guttering, running water or sewerage. A visiting politician called it 'the most squalid, contemptible place I ever saw'.[1]

Communication was usually by sea, with coastal steamers and ships running interstate and between Indonesia, Malaya and the Far East. In 1939 there was a rail link south to Katherine, but Darwin had no all-weather road link with the southern centres. The town was Australia's Lost Horizon, but with squalor instead of splendour, and for the men who were stationed there it was anything but a Shangri-La. Dudley Voce arrived in Darwin in December 1940 with the 14th Anti-Aircraft Battery: 'It seemed a very isolated, unreal sort of place. Some men couldn't believe that they were still in Australia, it seemed so different and exotic.'

In 1938 the town's non-Aboriginal population was 3653. In the next two years that population increased considerably due to the influx of military personnel.[2] There was also a busy works program with the construction of oil tanks, a hotel, commercial banks, a public hospital and a dam providing piped water for the town.[3] Military installations were even more evident, including hangars, barracks, gun emplacements and airfields.

Few people in Australia, let alone the rest of the world, knew anything about Darwin. One of the few instances of the town being in the international spotlight occurred when the American aviator Amelia Earhart used it as a refuelling stop during her ill-fated attempt to fly around the world. Earhart with her navigator Fred Noonan landed their Lockheed Electra at the RAAF Station on 28 June 1937. 'Pearl fishing is the main industry of Port Darwin,'[4] she speculated. The pearl fishing craft Earhart saw from her Electra may well have been Japanese. They were familiar prewar visitors to northern Australian waters. Officials warned of the 'subversive activities of Japanese pearlers'[5] which became another factor in the military build-up of Darwin. Of course, Earhart knew nothing of this as she gazed at the vastness of the Top End. She conveyed her impressions in a diary:

The country of this northern coast of Australia is very different. Here, as far as one can see, were endless trees on an endless plain. At Darwin we left the parachutes we had carried that far, to be shipped home. A parachute would not help over the Pacific.[6]

Sadly, Earhart was correct. Parachutes would have been of little use to herself and Noonan two days later as the Electra disappeared forever into the vast expanse of the South Pacific.

In 1939 Darwin had only a few basic port facilities including an L-shaped wharf which was limited to the berthing of only two medium-sized ships. Shore cargo handling equipment was elementary and slow. Some ships were unloaded into lighters and other harbour craft for transfer to the boom jetty or to select beach areas. The process was laborious and many ships were required to sit patiently at anchor in the vast harbour inlet.[7]

Although the military build-up was considerable, the area was ineffectively defended. More shore and anti-aircraft weapons were needed, as were at least four fighter squadrons. With the Japanese threat to Darwin obvious, the town's women and children were evacuated to the south, many of them by sea. Over 1900 left between 19 December 1941 and 15 February 1942.[8] Fewer than 2000 civilians remained, amongst them 63 women who were employed in essential roles as nurses, telephonists, stenographers and government workers.[9]

The Administrator for the Northern Territory, Mr C.L.A. Abbott remained, as did his family and servants. The postmaster Hurtle Bald also stayed, and contrary to the evacuation decree his wife Alice and daughter Iris remained also. The 48-year-old Bald, who had been in Darwin since 1928, did not want his family to leave. Besides, there was a slit trench beside the post office that would be a safe shelter in the unlikely event of an air raid.[10]

In January 1942 the Australian Army personnel in and around Darwin constituted a brigade and other units. There were also 1100 naval officers and ratings and approximately 2000 air force personnel. After the first few weeks of the war in the Pacific, Japanese expansion had impacted on the Pacific Allies — America, Britain, the Netherlands and Australia. Collectively, an alliance was formed called ABDA. Command was given to the Englishman, General Sir Archibald Wavell, who had been appointed Supreme Allied Commander at the start of the Pacific war. The areas covered by ABDA were Burma, the Philippines, Malaya, Singapore, the Netherlands East Indies, northern Australia and New Guinea. The arrangement was ineffective and indecisive and by February 1942 most of the designated areas had been overrun by the Japanese.[11]

In the early days of the Pacific war the Northern Territory was congested with air and naval traffic to and from the Philippines, Java, Ambon and Timor. Only ten days after Pearl Harbor, the desert strip of Batchelor, 80 kilometres from Darwin, had American B-17 bombers on the tarmac preparing to mount an offensive. MacArthur had ordered several Fortresses back to Australia and on 22 December nine of them left Batchelor to bomb Japanese forces in Davao on the southern tip of the Philippines.[12] The sortie may not have been decisive, but it was the first American offensive

Brisbane, 25 March 1941. The largest crowd in the history of the city greets the American naval squadron. *(Courier-Mail)*

Early visits from the American Navy

Above: The Great White Fleet visits Australia, 1908. The USS *Wisconsin* receives stores and visitors.

Below: A tragedy about to happen. A large crowd aboard the ferry *Rodney* bids farewell to the USS *Louisville* on Sydney Harbour, 15 February 1938. Moments later the ferry overturned with the loss of nineteen lives.

John Curtin, Australia's wartime Prime Minister.

Franklin Delano Roosevelt, 32nd President of the United States.

The Australian soldier, fearless and formidable but no winner in the fashion stakes. *(John Oxley Library, Brisbane)*

The *Pensacola* convoy at sea.

New recruits pose for the camera. The lucky service would be the Women's Royal Australian Naval Service (WRANS).

'I can see it. It's Os-tral-yah.' December 1941.

The Yanks are here. Sydney, 11 April 1942. *(Courier-Mail)*

Yankmania — Brisbane 1941. *(John Oxley Library, Brisbane)*

Two girls in every port. *(Courier-Mail)*

All bets off. Camp Ascot, temporary home for the men of the *Pensacola* convoy, December 1941. *(Courier-Mail)*

The construction of Camp Cable, near Logan Village, Queensland, 1942. *(John Oxley Library, Brisbane)*

The wharfies in the war years — seventeen men and one empty hand barrow. *(John Oxley Library, Brisbane)*

The P-40 Curtis Kittyhawk, similar to the aircraft of Major Pell's 33rd Pursuit Squadron.

of the war from an Australian base. Sergeant James Cannon, who was killed on this raid, most likely has the unfortunate distinction of being the first American battle fatality of all those who passed this way. He was buried in Darwin on 26 December 1941.[13]

In early January 1942, General George Marshall the US Army Chief of Staff in Washington, directed that Darwin would become an American army and naval base. On 5 January, the United States Armed Forces in Australia under the command of Major General George H. Brett designated Darwin as Base Section 1. Brett immediately ordered the 147th and 148th Field Artillery regiments which had recently arrived with the *Pensacola* convoy in Brisbane, to proceed there.[14] The *Holbrook* arrived in Darwin with the regiments and their equipment later that month. In addition, new aircraft squadrons were formed and also deployed to the Top End. Another convoy vessel, the *Republic*, carried factory shipping crates of P-40 Kittyhawk fighter aircraft, along with the enthusiastic, but inexperienced pilots to fly them. Shortly after arriving in Brisbane this group of pilots and their aircraft were ordered to form a new combat unit — the 33rd Pursuit Squadron (Provisional).[15] Although most of the pilots were novices, they were placed under the command of a much respected and experienced officer.

Captain Floyd Joaquin Pell was a 28-year-old career officer from Ogden, Utah, who had graduated from West Point, Class of '37. In June 1940 Pell was transferred to the Philippines and assigned to Nichols Field. In September he was promoted to captain. One year later he arrived in Australia with General Brereton to conduct a survey of airfields and to assess the logistics for potential air traffic from Australia to MacArthur's forces in the Philippines.[16]

Pell was in Brisbane when the *Pensacola* convoy docked and soon became an obvious choice to form, train and lead the new squadron. He was well aware that intensive training would be crucial to the squadron's effectiveness. The RAAF gave permission for the new American squadrons to use the facilities at the base in

Amberley [17] 65 kilometres south of Brisbane. RAAF crews would also assist in uncrating and assembling the 34 P-40s, and other Kittyhawks that had arrived on another convoy. The American pilots included Lieutenant Robert Oestreicher. 'There was one other and myself who'd ever flown the ... P-40 before,' he noted. 'The rest were right out of flight school — and they had no tactical training.'[18]

Robert F. McMahon was also in the fledgling squadron:

None of us had any qualifications for test flying, I had fourteen hours in all, most of it logged in Hamilton Field, California, in training aircraft. Captain Pell then chose the pilots who had over fifteen hours of flying time on the P-40s and transferred them into the old Philippine 17th Fighter Squadron to send to Java, with Captain Boyd 'Buzz' Wagner in command.

After many days of assembling, training and test flying, the aircraft were finally made operational in the first week of February.[19]

The 33rd squadron was deemed ready for combat. Its 25 aircraft were led by Pell, who in February was promoted to major.

The air route from Brisbane to Darwin, encompassing Charleville, Cloncurry and Daly Waters, was arduous and primitive. Lieutenant Oestreicher made the trip several times, usually as a guide for inexperienced pilots: 'We had no maps ... or any navigational aids to speak of, but I'd been given some information about roads and telegraph wire. This was pretty much how we navigated.'[20] It was a war within a war. In mid-January, sixteen Kittyhawks of the 17th Pursuit Squadron had left Brisbane. Due to accidents and equipment failures en route, only fourteen would reach Darwin and then Java. Another squadron, the 20th Pursuit, left Brisbane and arrived in Darwin with the loss of only one aircraft. The 3rd Pursuit Squadron, under Captain Grant Mahoney, flew into Darwin with another eighteen Kittyhawks.

Timor and Java, then under Japanese threat, were in desperate need of fighter aircraft. The flight from the Australian south-east coast was only the first leg of an ever increasingly dangerous journey. Captain Mahoney's aircraft were split into two groups. While one left for Java, nine planes departed for Koepang in Timor but were unable to find the airfield. The pilots baled out, or crash-landed their aircraft on the Timor coast. One was killed and the remainder rescued by the RAAF.[21]

The journey to Darwin and beyond was becoming as challenging as the Japanese foe. The tragedy of the 3rd squadron in Timor prompted General Brett to direct the next squadron of P-40s to be flown direct to Perth and then transported to Java by sea. The first group to be ordered west was Major Floyd Pell's squadron — the 33rd. The route was through Sydney, Melbourne, Port Pirie and then the long haul to Perth where the old carrier *Langley* awaited to take the squadron to Java. While at Port Pirie, Pell's orders were changed. He was to proceed to Darwin with fifteen aircraft and provide air cover for an Allied convoy to Timor.[22] The remaining nine Kittyhawks were to continue their journey to Perth under the command of Lieutenant G. W. Keenan. It must have been an ongoing strain for Pell, with his orders being constantly changed.

The last day in Port Pirie was an ordeal for the men of the 33rd Squadron. Lieutenant Richard E. Pingree, while test flying his recently repaired Kittyhawk, crashed on the outskirts of the town and was killed. Like his squadron leader, the 21-year-old Pingree was from Ogden, Utah. One hour after his funeral service the squadron took off from Port Pirie and in a tight formation disappeared over the northern horizon.[23]

At about the same time that Pell and his Kittyhawk squadron left Port Pirie, Vice-Admiral Chuichi Nagumo and a Japanese carrier task force left Palau Island heading south. The force included the majority of the ships that had devastated Pearl Harbor a few weeks before. The carriers *Akagi, Kaga, Soryu* and *Hiryu* had all enjoyed glory in the operation that started the Pacific war. The heavy *cruisers Tone, Chikuma, Takao* and *Mayo* were on point duty. Nine destroyers completed the task force.[24] Nagumo was complying with a Southern Area Fleet telegraphic order of 9

February. The port of Darwin was to be neutralised prior to the invasion of Timor. Admiral Kondo had set the date of 20 February for the attack. Reconnaissance aircraft had confirmed that Darwin was full of shipping.[25]

Timor was garrisoned by the 2/40th Battalion and the 2/2nd Independent Company. These Australian units were under the command of Brigadier WCD Veale.[26] It was deemed crucial to reinforce Timor as the Japanese, who had just captured Ambon, would be certain to launch an attack on the island. The airfield at Koepang was not only essential to the defence of Timor but was an important base for men and supplies to MacArthur's garrisons in the Philippines.

The Australian 2/4th Pioneer Battalion, AIF, together with a battalion of the US 148th Field Artillery and specialist units, boarded the transports *Meigs, Mauna Loa, Tulagi* and *Portmar* in Darwin harbour. The escorts were the heavy cruiser *Houston*, the American destroyer *Peary,* and the Australian sloops *Swan* and *Warrego*. The convoy was bound for Timor some 800 kilometres away. The ships had waited in vain for air escort before departing early in the morning of 15 February.[27] A few hours later Captain Rooks of the *Houston* radioed Darwin for urgent air support. A Japanese Kawanishi-type 'Mavis' 97 flying boat from Ambon had discovered the convoy.[28]

On that morning there were two Kittyhawks in Darwin. Both had been left behind with engine trouble when the 3rd Pursuit Squadron had flown to Java. Lieutenants Oestreicher and Buel had mixed feelings about being left behind, but both hoped to catch up with the squadron.

With Oestreicher out on patrol, the only available aircraft was the Kittyhawk belonging to Buel. The ground crew prepared it, removed the wheel chocks, and the American took off alone on an interception course. Less than an hour later *Houston* crew members cheered as they saw a lone P-40 fly in the direction of the Japanese aircraft. After a few minutes some of the ship's company saw a flash on the horizon and then there was nothing. Lieutenant Robert J. 'Blackie' Buel and his aircraft were never seen again.[29]

The casualty rate of the American fighter pilots was severe. At Christmas 1941, Lieutenants McMahon, Buel, Metsler and McLean were sharing a pyramidal tent at Camp Ascot in Brisbane. By the second week in February, McLean had been killed in Java, Metsler had broken his neck while baling out over Koepang and Buel had disappeared into the Timor Sea.[30] Only McMahon remained and his future was decidedly uncertain as he flew with the 33rd Pursuit Squadron across the centre of Australia towards the Top End. Early in the afternoon of 15 February 1942, Oestreicher and his Kittyhawk constituted the only fighter presence on the northern coast of Australia.

★   ★   ★

In 1942, the destroyer USS *Peary* (DD226) was already obsolete. It was named after Rear Admiral Robert Edwin Peary, a noted Arctic explorer, and launched at the William Cramp and Sons shipyard in Philadelphia in April 1920, two months after the admiral's death. Mrs Edward Stafford, daughter of the explorer, christened her.[31] The ship was a member of the four-stack 'Flush-Deck' class. Constructed before the threat of air attack, they had a puny armament of four 4-inch and one 3-inch guns and twelve torpedo tubes.[32] They had an impressive turn of speed and were good sea boats but in 1940 they were considered so expendable that Roosevelt provided 50 of them to Churchill for convoy duty.

Their crews referred to the destroyers as 'four-stackers' and quipped that they were 'old enough to vote'. The *Peary* and twelve other Flush-Deckers were attached to the Asiatic Fleet under the command of Admiral Thomas C. Hart. Since 1940, the fleet had been based at the Cavite naval base in Manila Bay. In December 1941 this comprised the heavy cruiser *Houston*, two light cruisers, 13 Flush-Deck destroyers, 28 old submarines and an assortment of small minesweepers and fleet auxiliaries. The fleet was too small and obsolete to match the Japanese Navy in battle and on 20

November Hart had been ordered by the Navy Department to withdraw and deploy his fleet to southern areas. The submarines would remain in Philippine waters to repel any Japanese invasion forces.[33] Still remaining at the Cavite naval base on 10 December were four destroyers, five minesweepers, two fleet oilers a floating dry dock and a flotilla of PT boats under the command of Lieutenant John D. Bulkeley. One of the destroyers undergoing repairs at the base was the *Peary*. Everyone knew that a Japanese air strike was imminent. The Iba, Nielson and Nichols airfields north of Cavite had been destroyed by the Japanese two days before.[34]

The navy knew that Cavite was next. Fortunately Admiral Hart was given two hours warning that Japanese aircraft were flying from Formosa and in the direction of Manila across Northern Luzon. Decks were cleared, crews leapt to action stations, guns were primed and Bulkeley took his boats into Manila bay.[35]

Early in the afternoon, the Japanese attacked. Fifty-four bombers flying in a V formation at 20 000 feet proceeded to bomb both the town and the naval base. 'It was a beautiful clear day,' wrote Bulkeley, 'and I remember the sun made rainbows on the waterspouts of their bombs. They were from a hundred and fifty to two hundred feet high and it made a mist screen so dense you could hardly tell what was happening to the ships.'[36]

The altitude of the bombers was beyond the effective range of the 3 inch anti-aircraft weapons on the ships and shore. 'Where in hell is our air force?' shouted one of Bulkeley's crew on PT 34. 'Why in Christ's name don't they do something?'[37]

The answer lay in the ashes on the tarmac of the Clark and Iba airfields, where the Japanese had destroyed MacArthur's air power — caught on the ground — in the first hours of the war. The 56 fighter aircraft lost in the debacle could well have made a difference to the fate of the Cavite base on 10 December. However the Japanese aircraft, operating with total impunity, began to destroy the Cavite base ships and facilities.

The *Peary* was soon engaged. A bomb struck her amidships,

killing eight men and wounding Commander Harry H. Keith, but the ordeal had just started. Flying shrapnel and steel punctured the two forward smokestacks and splinters sprayed the open decks.[38] Fires from the adjacent torpedo workshop had also spread to the *Peary*. The old S-class *Sealion* was the first American submarine to be lost in the war. It had also been bombed and was a mangled mess, still attached to the wharf with her stern on the bottom.[39] The old, powerless, stationary Flush-Decker was facing a similar fate.

'The Whip is coming in to take you out,' radioed Lieutenant Commander Feriter from the USS *Whippoorwill* — a diminutive, 840-ton craft from the Bird class of minesweepers that were even older than the *Peary* and her sisters. As the little ship towed the *Peary* away from the pier, the crew hosed the fierce fires on the destroyer's decks. Later, when the destroyer was out of danger, the fires were extinguished and the wounded, including Captain Keith, were transferred to hospital. The ship with a new captain, the former executive officer Lieutenant John M. Bermingham, lived to fight another day.[40]

Cavite was left a burning shambles. All of the naval repair facilities, a transmitting radio tower, the torpedo overhaul shop and 233 torpedos were destroyed.[41] Five hundred American servicemen and 1500 Filipino had been killed.[42] The only joy for the Americans was that two of Bulkeley's boats, PTs 31 and 34, shot down three Japanese aircraft as they attempted to strafe the boats in the harbour.[43]

After the attack the Asiatic Fleet was further dispersed. The *Peary* was ordered to sail to Darwin. It was a perilous journey, Bermingham thought, as he gazed at his charts and plotted his course, and the more so in daylight. The first stop for the charred destroyer was at Negros island at the entrance of the Mindanao Sea. Some of the crew looted stores and painted the ship green. Others draped it with some palm fonds and other foliage from the stores and from the jungle. Although crude and improvised, the ship now had a form of camouflage. It proved to be effective as several Japanese aircraft flew close, but evidently did not sight the ship. But would their luck hold? At nightfall the old vessel set course for Ambon.

In daylight it was obvious that *Peary* was being shadowed by a Japanese aircraft. Early in the afternoon, three Japanese flying boats attacked the old destroyer. For two hours Captain Bermingham and his crew skilfully evaded and fought the Japanese, who eventually withdrew. It was a remarkable effort by the pugnacious destroyer, but something even more remarkable was about to happen. Just before dark, the *Peary* was attacked once again, this time by Lockheed Hudson bombers that displayed red, white and blue roundels. They were either Australian or British, concluded the captain of the *Peary*, but it made little difference as the ship was forced to defend itself against this 'friendly fire' until, mercifully, night fell. It may have been due to the camouflage that an identification error was made, or perhaps over-enthusiasm by the Allied pilots. Whatever its cause it was a tragic mistake as the *Peary* suffered several casualties, including one man killed and another lost overboard.[44]

On 3 January 1942 a worn and weary USS *Peary* crawled into Darwin harbour. Its condition was so poor that until such time as it was once again battle ready, it would only conduct local escort and patrol work.[45]

★　★　★

As his squadron flew cautiously through the heart of Australia, Floyd Pell's thoughts must have been mixed. He would doubtless have been in awe of the vast size and desolation of the country beneath him. It was so hot, so dry, and the horizons seemed endless. The thought of his pilots coming down in this place filled him with trepidation. Even when fitted with extra removable belly tanks a Kittyhawk can only fly a few hundred miles before refuelling. It was a feat of navigation even to find the fuelling stops on the way.

The stops themselves were primitive and barren. Some had no

ground crew, so the pilots had to roll drums to the aircraft and pump their own gas into the tanks. The dust was thick, red, and always swirling and blowing in your face, causing stinging and asphyxia. Two of the Kittyhawks made forced landings at Daly Waters. Blinded by the dust Bob McMahon's P-40 ran into a tractor.

The Aussie driver was scared out of his wits and jumped off his machine as I gunned my ship to gain altitude in order to miss him. I didn't and I bounced off him like a rubber band, breaking the main spar on the wing of my P-40.

I was airborne and I signalled to my wingman. I told him to fly under me and inspect the damage. He mentioned that I should land as quickly as possible, but to hell with it, we were getting close to Darwin and I was not going to turn back now.[46]

McMahon and his 'Barhootie the Cootie' flew on.

Shortly after the stop at Daly Waters Pell saw another P-40 go down. It performed a good three point landing on level ground near a billabong. Lieutenant Richard Suehr (pronounced Sear) was the pilot and a popular member of the squadron. Pell had teased him at a Brisbane briefing by calling him 'Sewer'. 'It's Sear, not sewer, Sir,' retorted Suehr. Pell replied, 'Okay Stinky, sit down.'

The name stuck and now 'Stinky' Suehr had landed in the middle of nowhere. Fortunately for the American, his position was noted and an aircraft fitted with survival gear was despatched to pick him up. Suehr would not easily forget his ordeal.

Somehow after the crash landing he had lost his boots. While limping and cursing his luck he was chased by a scrub buffalo. Such situations are not covered in basic training. An American rescue aircraft arrived to save his life and a few days later, in a Brisbane hospital, doctors saved his badly injured feet.[47]

The 33rd Pursuit Squadron lost five aircraft on the journey through the centre of Australia. For Pell and his pilots it became a battle of attrition just to reach Darwin, where perhaps another battle would await. There were also rumours from other guys who had previously flown into Darwin that the Aussie gunners shot first and asked questions later. Pell would have been even more concerned had he known that the Darwin defences had not been notified of his pending arrival.

The 33rd Pursuit Squadron's arrival in Darwin resulted in the air-raid sirens alerting the defences, but fortunately for Pell and his pilots the anti-aircraft batteries recognised the Kittyhawks as being friend and not foe. It was just as well. The 33rd Pursuit Squadron landed on the RAAF base in Darwin with only ten aircraft of the fifteen that had left Port Pirie.[48] The bad news for Pell was that the convoy had departed for Timor, on time and unescorted, some hours before. Although the remaining aircraft were in desperate need of maintenance, Pell ordered three of them to catch and watch over the convoy for as long as possible before returning to Darwin.

Floyd Pell was a robust, spirited man who seemed fearless. He had painted on the nose of his Kittyhawk a caricature of a boxer taking a swing at a Japanese with the caption, 'Slugger'. The name stuck. Slugger Pell subsequently divided his aircraft into A and B flights and began preparations for the next leg of this odyssey. He had received another order for the squadron to fly to Java. Surely, he thought, the aircraft would be of more use here in Darwin, which had virtually no air support.[49]

Darwin dock workers and ships' crews were astonished to see the *Houston* convoy sail back into the harbour. It had been attacked by over 30 Japanese land-based aircraft. In spite of the ships suffering little damage, the ammunition stocks of the escorts had been seriously diminished and the convoy was ordered back to Darwin. No sooner had the ships dropped anchor than the *Houston* and *Peary* were raising steam to join an ABDA naval force at Tjilatjap in Java. More than one onlooker realised that the return of the convoy and the huge amount of shipping in the harbour would make a tempting target for the Japanese.[50]

Out to sea, the *Houston* and *Peary* soon encountered more adventure when a submarine was detected. In an inconclusive action, the *Peary* used up so much fuel that Captain Rooks of the

Houston ordered her back to Darwin. On the morning of 19 February the *Peary* was anchored in the harbour with 44 other ships, many of them waiting for unloading.

The American ships included the *Peary, Meigs, Portmar, Admiral Halstead, Mauna Loa* and the *William B. Preston;* RAN ships included *Swan, Gunbar, Kara Kara, Kookaburra, Kangaroo* and *Deloraine*. HMAS *Katoomba*, a corvette, was also in Darwin, but in a floating dry dock undergoing repairs after a collision. With her stern in the air, she was an ungainly sight. Other Australian ships included *Neptuna, Zealandia, Barossa* and the hospital ship *Manunda*.[51]

Although the ground defences were barely adequate, the air cover for Darwin was virtually non-existent. At the RAAF station were Pell's eleven Kittyhawks (which included Oestreicher's now damaged P-40), six Hudson bombers and five unserviceable, obsolete Wirraways. Batchelor airfield had nine Wirraways and at Daly Waters there were eight Hudson bombers with no crews.

The day was bright and clear, there was a light westerly breeze and Floyd Pell was agitated. He had planned for the squadron to leave for Java at dawn, but yet again there was more delay. His Kittyhawk had a coolant leak. The American pilots had become very resourceful. Bob McMahon spent a whole day robbing a disabled Kittyhawk, and switching the engine, propeller and carburettor with his 'Barhootie the Cootie'. However, the problem with the squadron leader's aircraft was proving difficult. While Pell and his radiator fumed, the rest of the pilots sat strapped in their cockpits awaiting the skipper to lead off. At 9.15 am, Pell had had enough. He dismissed the mechanics from his aircraft and ordered Lieutenant Vaught to surrender his aircraft and fly the other back to Brisbane when possible. Fifteen minutes later the 33rd Squadron was airborne in two groups heading for Java via Timor. They were to follow a converted B-24 Liberator which would navigate and lead the flight to Koepang. 'A' flight included Major Pell and Lieutenants Hughes, McMahon, Rice and Glover. 'B' flight included Flight Leader Lieutenant Oestreicher, and Lieutenants Peres, Perry, Wiecks and Walker.[52]

Thirty minutes before the ten aircraft left for Java, a Japanese force of 188 aircraft from the *Akagi, Kaga, Soryu* and *Hiryu* flew in formation towards the northern coast of Australia. The attack leader was Commander Mitsuo Fuchida. Under his command were 36 Zero fighters, 71 Val dive bombers and 81 'Kate' high level bombers. Fuchida and most of the men and aircraft had been responsible for the Pearl Harbor raid the previous December. Fuchida set a course of 148 degrees, which would lead the armada to the town and port of Darwin. The flight was expected to take a little over an hour.[53]

Shortly after leaving Darwin, Pell and the 33rd Pursuit were ordered back to base. Poor weather was causing concern. The long flight was dangerous enough in good conditions, but with the prospect of storms and with inexperienced pilots it could be fatal. Forty minutes after take-off, Pell and his group were taxiing back to the dispersal point at the RAAF Station.

After ordering Oestreicher and 'B' flight to climb to 15 000 feet and remain on patrol for two hours, Pell climbed out of his aircraft and started to walk towards the RAAF tower. Then all hell broke loose.[54]

The level of disaster at Pearl Harbor ten weeks before could have been minimised had the warnings been heeded. Tragically, the raid on Darwin was no different in this respect. Father John McGrath was at a mission on the southern tip of Bathurst Island about 80 kilometres north-north-west of Darwin. At 9.30 am on the morning of 19 February he noticed a commotion amongst the islanders, and looking towards the sky he saw a large formation of aircraft flying in the direction of Darwin. They were difficult to identify, but almost immediately the mission's transceiver was being tuned to VID, the Amalgamated Wireless coastal station in Darwin.

'Eight-S-E to V-I-D, I have an urgent message. An unusually large air formation bearing down on us from the north-west.

Identity suspect. Visibility not clear. Over.'

'Eight-S-E from V.I.D Message received. Stand by.'

It was 9.35 am when the message was logged. The people on the mission had their doubts dispelled about the formation as several Japanese aircraft strafed the area. The messages did create some interest with the intelligence staff at navy headquarters. Lieutenant Commander McManus telephoned his counterpart at the RAAF base and reported the sighting.

'Don't worry, it's the American Kittyhawks, they just left for Java,' was the reply.

McManus gazed at the map. The sighting was north of the route that Pell's much smaller group would have taken. This was a large formation coming in the opposite direction. McManus later remarked: 'I wanted to sound the alarm at once but was overruled. There had been a series of earlier false alarms which it was undesirable to repeat.'[55]

The reluctance to sound the alarms was understandable. Since January there had been false alarms whenever American ships entered the harbour. There was another when Major Pell flew in unannounced. The RAAF then received a report from the 2/14th Field Regiment at Nightcliff that a P-40 had crashed into the water and a parachute was seen. Five minutes later there was a further report that an aerial dogfight was taking place. The reply from the RAAF did not inspire confidence: 'If this is an air raid we know nothing of it'.[56] Cecil Burns was a member of the 19th Machine Gun Regiment, stationed at Casuarina beach, fifteen kilometres north of Darwin. He immediately recognised the formation as hostile. In a matter of moments he was reporting to Sergeant McDonald, 'The Japs are here! The Japs are here!' 'What makes you think they're Japs?' he was asked.

'They've got bloody great red spots on 'em.'

McDonald reached for the direct-line telephone to Captain Brown at brigade headquarters. 'We've got Japanese planes.'

'What makes you think they're Japs?' 'They've got bloody great red spots on 'em'. Without delay, Brown contacted Army Headquarters. 'What makes you think they're Japs...'

It was at that moment that the first bombs fell on Darwin. A moment later Captain E. Penry Thomas broke the glass covering the alarm button. The sirens sounded in unison with the explosions.[57]

Lieutenant Oestreicher, aloft with 'B' flight at 8000 feet, was the first to see them: 'I spotted a plane diving on us from about 2000 feet above and in an eight o'clock position. I saw the red roundels on the fuselage and yelled, Zeros, Zeros, Zeros.' Oestreicher climbed his aircraft towards the sun and managed to fire a burst at a Zero.

At 12 000 feet I counted eighteen more enemy planes at around 20 000 feet. I called 'B' flight on the radio and advised heading for the clouds about five miles south of Darwin. After flying among the clouds for about half an hour I spotted two Series 97 dive bombers with fixed landing gear on a course heading for Batchelor field.[58]

Lieutenant Max Wiecks was typical of many young American servicemen in the early stages of the war who found themselves unprepared, inexperienced and in a desperate situation. Although 27, he had been a pilot for only a month and had fewer than 50 hours in the cockpit of a fighter — all but twelve of them had been accumulated flying to Darwin.[59]

On the morning of 19 February, Wiecks had a faulty radio and did not hear the alarm. The others were occupied with dozens of Japanese planes, 'swarming like bees' said one of the American pilots. The sight of Lieutenant Peres's Kittyhawk being shot down was Wiecks first awareness of the raid. He did not know that Lieutenant Perry had also been hit and had plunged into the bay. In a matter of moments, Peres and Perry were dead, Lieutenant Walker in the remaining Kittyhawk had his aircraft shot up, his left shoulder shattered and was limping back to the airfield with his right hand on the controls.

In 1942, the Japanese Zero was the superior fighter aircraft in the Pacific theatre. Designed to meet a 1937 Imperial Navy specification for a carrier-based fighter, it was armed with two 20 mm cannon and two 7.7 mm machine-guns. The Mitsubishi A6M Zero first appeared in 1939 and was in action in China the following year, dominating any fighters that opposed it. Fast, powerful and manoeuvrable, it was skilfully handled by experienced Japanese pilots. During the war, 10 937 Zeros were built, and on 19 February 1942 the skies over Darwin were full of them.

The Curtiss P-40 Kittyhawk first flew in 1938. It was a robust, sturdy and adaptable aircraft, but compared to the Zero it was underpowered and undergunned. Although 13 738 Kittyhawks were built during the war, on that morning there were only ten of them in Darwin — five of them were stationary on the tarmac at the RAAF Station.[60]

Max Wiecks was now fighting for his life as swarms of Zeros closed in. He did not have time to fire his guns before the aircraft was plunging towards the sea.

I was close to the water and I knew I had to jump. I jettisoned the canopy and unbuckled my seat belt. Immediately, I was catapulted out of the cockpit and had just opened my parachute when I heard the plane hit the sea.

When he arrived in Brisbane, Wiecks did not have a parachute. Prior to leaving for Port Pirie, he had stolen one from the RAAF operations room in Amberley. It was now saving his life as it gently lowered him into sea, fifteen kilometres from the Australian coast.

Floyd Pell was talking to an operations officer about the aborted flight to Java when he heard Oestreicher's alarm. The aircraft of 'A' flight were on the ground, but Pell had left his radio on. Looking to the skies he saw masses of aircraft, many of them approaching the airfield and preparing to attack.

'Pilots to your planes', Pell shouted. 'Get the belly tanks off, let's get airborne.' Pell ran to his machine, started his engine and began to taxi through grass and bushes in an attempt to reach the dispersal area as quickly as possible. For the Japanese, who had begun strafing potential targets, none was more inviting than the grounded 'A' flight. As Pell accelerated along the tarmac, he needed only seconds to arrive at take-off speed. The seconds seemed like hours. He could see the Zeros in his rear-vision mirror and feel the impact of the cannon striking his aircraft. The Kittyhawk shuddered, choked, and began to fall. Pell baled out and pulled his ripcord at a height of less than 100 feet. He hit the ground with a thud. Temporarily stunned, he was helpless as his parachute started to drag him slowly along the ground. A Zero manoeuvred for a strafing run and its 20 mm cannon tore into Pell's body, killing him a few feet from the safety of a slit trench.

Lieutenant Hughes was behind Pell. He saw the major get airborne before he too was killed and his aircraft destroyed. Lieutenant Robert McMahon had just turned 21. He had been sitting in his aircraft when Pell shouted the order to take-off. An American mechanic ran towards him and with commendable restraint exclaimed: 'Excuse me Lieutenant, The Japanese are here.' McMahon started his engine and started to follow Pell and Hughes. Almost at the point of take-off, McMahon had to brake urgently to stop running into another Kittyhawk. It was Walker from 'B' flight. McMahon noticed that the P-40 was a mess and that the pilot was flying with one hand, the other being limp. Virtually incapable of flying his aircraft, Walker was landing so Vaught could use the aircraft against the Japanese. Fortunate that the Zeros had not seen him, McMahon was airborne before he drew their attention.

I was heavily engaged over the water north of the field and was getting some hits from the rear, so I tried to execute a vertical, away from my turn to the right. When I pulled out, I was only 100 feet or so above some shore-line trees. I saw another large flight of Japs ahead, so I turned and headed for town and the smoke from the harbour. The Zeros broke up their tightly pressed attack and I got one in my sights and fired. Then the Zeros got on top of me.

I must have been hit more than 100 times by machine-gun bullets. I was wounded slightly in the leg.

McMahon flew over the harbour, where he saw life rafts in the water and men swimming. As if he did not have enough troubles, he had to endure the harbour defences and ships firing at him. 'My old crate was like a sieve. I tried to fire at a Zero but I was out of ammunition.'

McMahon had no option other than to bale out. Hanging helpless and drifting towards the ground, he was fired on and some shroud lines were shot away before he landed in a swamp and mangrove area on the west side of the harbour. Sitting in a crocodile haunt on his rubber parachute seat with his boots full of blood, his mind in shock, he should have been terrified, but not after what he had been through. He was alive and safe — at least for the moment.

Lieutenants Rice and Glover were the last of 'A' flight to get airborne. Rice was in trouble from the start. At 5000 feet he found his controls shot away. With his aircraft spinning toward the ground, Rice exited the cockpit but not before hitting his head on the frame of his windshield.

Before losing consciousness he pulled his ripcord, but like a puppet on a string he was easy prey for Zeros moving in for the kill. Rice owes his life to Glover who shot down one Japanese aircraft and protected his buddy while he drifted earthwards.

I got one of the little sons of bitches — just blew him up. Then they got me. I was diving away from them, levelled out and looked back and they seemed to be closing up, so I started to put the stick and throttle forward and then I was in the trees.

Glover's aircraft cartwheeled several times before smashing into pieces in a cloud of dust and fire. Ground staff who had watched the battle and were impressed by Glover's valiant efforts were dismayed to witness the crash and the apparent death of the pilot. It came as a real shock when they saw a figure walk from the dust and smoke. Glover was limping, but he was alive. It was a miracle. Oblivious to all, Glover walked a few paces, then sat down on the tarmac and buried his face in his hands.

Meanwhile, Lieutenant Walker had somehow managed to land his Kittyhawk with his arm shattered. Taxiing towards the RAAF tower, he climbed out of the cockpit and jumped into a slit trench. Vaught was waiting to replace him in the cockpit, but at the last moment decided to retrieve his parachute from Pell's faulty Kittyhawk in the No. 12 hangar. The action saved his life, for in the interim, the Japanese turned Walker's Kittyhawk into a charred wreck.

Rice had also fallen into the mangroves, wounded but alive, and McMahon and he were rescued from the mangroves later in the day. Wiecks eventually reached shore, climbed into a tree for the night and early the next morning followed a track leading to an Australian position.[61]

★   ★   ★

Early on that morning of 19 February, many of the crew of the USS *Peary* were told to rest by Captain Bermingham. The previous day had been a long one and the crew were fatigued. At 9.58 am, Bermingham was seen pacing the bridge. Everyone knew that the dock was slow and the refuelling behind schedule. The way things were going, the *Peary* would never catch up to the *Houston*. Mel Duke looked up from the ship and saw the armada of aircraft.

Someone looked up and said 'Oh, well, Roosevelt hasn't let us down. He promised us air supremacy in the southwest Pacific in 30 days. There it is'. Somebody else looked up and said 'That's not bloody our planes, those are Japs'.[62]

Bermingham knew that, unless he could get under way, the ship would be helpless. 'Weigh anchor, on the double,' he ordered. The crew rushed to their action stations and the old ship struggled to get under way. But there was no time. The first bomb hit the stern, destroying the propellers and damaging the engine room. Depth-charges and men were thrown into the air and into the sea. Another bomb exploded in the galley and fires and smoke were soon raging through the ship.

Bermingham and his crew were still trying to evade other ships and reach for the open sea. The *William B. Preston* was a converted seaplane tender about the same vintage as the *Peary* and now she too was fighting for her life. While the men on the *Peary* fought the fires and flooding, a third and fourth bomb struck, buckling her plates and rupturing fuel and oil tanks. Then the forward magazine exploded, killing Captain Bermingham and many men on the bridge. The destroyer was without power and drifting, its decks littered with the dead and wounded.[63] A fifth bomb exploded in the engine room and the ship began to break up. The chief officer of the Australian hospital ship *Manunda* witnessed the last moments of the *Peary*:

The American destroyer was on our port side, a solid mass of flame with burning oil all around her and what was left of the crew jumping into the burning oil. We manned our motor life boat with four of the crew and went to their rescue and eventually picked up over 30 badly burnt and wounded men.[64]

The *Peary* was doomed, but men manned the weapons that could still fire until the ship slipped beneath the surface — stern first with her bow gun still firing. Ninety-three men from the *Peary* were lost with the ship. Only one officer, Lieutenant W.J. Catlett, survived. One of the boys from the *Peary* who died that day was called Darwin.

The *Manunda* had been in port since mid-January. There had been delays unloading her and although she was destined for Singapore, the ship was still sitting in the middle of Darwin harbour on 19 February. The *Manunda* was lowering boats to pick up the many wounded in the water when the Japanese attacked, apparently deliberately. A near miss resulted in shrapnel killing four personnel and damaging the upper decks. Then a bomb exploded between B and C Decks, causing many casualties and destroying the medical and nursing staff quarters. It was here that AANS Sister Margaret de Mestre and Sister Lorraine S. Blow were seriously injured. The *Manunda* soon resembled other ships in the harbour, on fire and with dead and wounded on decks. In all, twelve crew died and a further 58 were wounded. Sister de Mestre was among the wounded in the operating theatre. It was here that she would have served, but now she was being treated by her colleagues as they fought to save her life.

Margaret de Mestre was a country girl, born in Bellingen, New South Wales. Her Aunt had been a nursing sister in the Great War and Margaret did not hesitate to continue the family tradition. After training in Sydney she joined the Australian Army Nursing Service in 1940. That day in Darwin, aged 26, she was the first and only Australian nurse to die on active duty in Australia.[65] The Australian people would not know for many years that only three days earlier, 21 nurses from the 2/13th Australian General Hospital (AGH) were shot to death by the Japanese in the sea off Banka Island.[66]

Other ships suffered the full force of an attacking armada of nearly 200 aircraft. The Australian ship *Neptuna* was filled with a cargo of 200 depth-charges. She blew up at the wharf, killing 45 men. The explosion was enormous — nobody there that day would ever forget it; it was as if the earth shook — and debris fell over the harbour and on to the town.

HMAS *Deloraine* was a new corvette, only eight weeks old, and had achieved the distinction of being the first to hit back at the Japanese. On 23 January, just east of Bathurst Island, the *Deloraine* depth-charged and sank the Japanese submarine I-124 in only 25 fathoms.[67] *Deloraine* was in Darwin the day that the Japanese attacked and was lucky not to be damaged, but debris from the *Neptuna* did fall on her. While the raid was in progress, Leading Signalman Douglas Fraser calmly took photographs of the action.

At nearly 13 000 thousand tons, the American ship *Meigs* was the biggest vessel in harbour that day. She was a member of the *Pensacola* convoy and should have been back in the States after a trip to Manila. Instead, she lay at the bottom of Darwin harbour. Another American ship, the *Mauna Loa*, was also sunk. The seaplane tender *William B. Preston* was severely damaged, as were the *Portmar* and another *Pensacola* convoy veteran the *Admiral Halstead*.

Many civilians also died. The habitual 'smoko' routine cherished by the wharfies resulted in 22 of them being killed as they were brewing up their morning cuppa.[68] A huge bomb destroyed the post office and the adjacent slit trench. Postmaster Bald, his family and staff — nine in total, died instantly. Abbott, the town's administrator, hid with his family under his sturdy office at Government House, narrowly missing death as a bomb exploded nearby. Abbott was slightly injured but an 18-year-old Aboriginal maid, Daisy Martin, died under a collapsing block of concrete.[69]

Aircraft from the Japanese carriers were responsible for the first raid on Darwin. Shortly before midday, another 54 aircraft from Ambon and Kendari also attacked the town and harbour.

The day was full of minor incidents and personal dramas. Lieutenant Thomas Moorer and his crew of the Darwin-based American Catalina of the navy's Patrol Wing 22 were cruising near Bathurst Island on that morning when nine Zeros from the Japanese carriers sighted and attacked Moorer's flying boat, 'setting my plane afire, destroying the port engine and shooting large holes in the fuel tanks and fuselage'. The Catalina was quickly forced into the sea where the crew, of whom four were injured, managed to escape in a dinghy and were subsequently picked up by a merchant ship, the *Florence D*. A second ship, the *Don Isidro*, was also nearby. These vessels were maritime mercenaries commissioned by the Americans in cash to run the Japanese blockade and take supplies to MacArthur. En route to Mindanao, they concluded that the trip would be too risky and had decided to make for the safe port of Darwin. The Japanese aircraft returning to their carriers attacked both the *Florence D.* and the *Don Isidro*, sinking them in shallow water. Another fourteen men died. Moorer and his crew were once again in a lifeboat and once again in the water. It had been a long day and one to forget, thought Moorer, as he and 40 other survivors paddled in the direction of Bathurst Island and the sanctuary of the Catholic mission.[70]

An odd cultural confrontation occurred when a damaged Japanese Zero crash-landed in a lightly timbered valley on Bathurst Island. The pilot, Petty Officer Hajime Toyoshima, wandered aimlessly around the island until he was captured by a young Tiwi tribesman, Matthias Ngapiatilawai, who knew little of the outside world other than the occasional Western film shown on Father McGrath's projector. 'Stick 'em up,' he shouted at the startled Japanese, before relieving him of his clothes and revolver and marching him to the mission.[71] Toyoshima was the first Japanese prisoner of war to be taken on Australian soil. Ashamed of his capture, he was sent to the Cowra prisoner of war camp in New South Wales. He ultimately had his moment of glory, dying with 233 other Japanese as they rushed the Australian machine-gunners in a mass-escape attempt on the night of 4 August 1944.[72]

The Japanese had succeeded with their mission to neutralise Darwin. But the attack was unnecessary as Darwin had little offensive capability and posed no threat to the Japanese and their Timor invasion. The analogy attributed to Commander Fuchida of 'smashing an egg with a sledgehammer' is here appropriate. The Japanese used 243 aircraft in the two raids that day, dropping 114 620 kilograms of ordnance consisting of at least 683 bombs. Ten weeks before, the Japanese had used 350 aircraft to attack Pearl Harbor, dropping 271 bombs and torpedos for a total ordnance of 146 400 kilograms.[73]

The damage in Darwin was extensive. The harbour was littered with sunken and burning ships. The wharf was wrecked and burning. Much of the town was demolished, with raging fires and tons of rubble from the bombing. There were dead and injured on the ships, in the town and along the foreshores. The final death total for the Darwin raid was 243. Twenty-one ships were sunk or damaged. The Japanese lost between seven and eleven aircraft, most of them shot down by Major Pell's 33rd Pursuit Squadron.[74]

The scale of the disaster at Darwin was suppressed by the authorities. The *Sydney Morning Herald* told its readers that fifteen were killed and that the town had suffered some damage. It was not until the end of March that the Brisbane *Courier-Mail* revealed the full extent of the disaster.

Darwin provided the first opportunity for Australian and American forces to fight together in defence of the mainland. However when the attack came, confusion and incompetence meant it was a complete surprise. If only a few minutes warning had been given, many of the crew in the *Peary* would have been saved and Major Pell's squadron would have been better prepared and a more formidable foe.

A third of the deaths that day were Americans, many of whom showed selfless devotion and gallantry. All ten of Pell's 33rd Squadron were awarded the Distinguished Service Cross. Major Pell's DSC was presented to his father, Wesley Orr Pell of Ogden, Utah, on 1 September 1942.[75] Floyd Pell had no luck that month. Even if his flight had reached the *Langley* in Perth, he and his men would have been on board when the ship was sunk by the Japanese en route to Java on 27 February.[76]

Camp Pell in Melbourne, soon to become a temporary home for thousands of American servicemen, was so named in honour of the squadron leader.

The USS *Houston* lived to fight another day, but only just. She was member of an Allied force that met the Japanese in the Java Sea, the battle being another defeat in a long series of disasters for the Allies. *Houston* and HMAS *Perth* attempted to reach Australia through the Sunda Strait, but early in the morning of 1 March they confronted the entire Japanese task force preparing to land on Java. In a memorable action of defiance against overwhelming odds, both cruisers were sunk. Captain Waller of the *Perth* and Captain Rooks of the *Houston* and 700 of their crews were lost, while the survivors were interned in Japanese prisoner of war camps.[77]

The Japanese carrier force that attacked Darwin would have few further moments of glory. Ten weeks later, all four carriers were sunk by the American Navy in the Battle of Midway.

The USS *Peary* and other Allied ships sunk in February 1942 lay in Darwin harbour until 1959 when the salvage rights were tendered. The winner was the Japanese Fujita Salvage Company.[78]

CHAPTER SIX

TOO MARVELLOUS
FOR WORDS

A Digger is in a hotel with a Yank. Says the Aussie, 'Fair dinkum, mate, who does this MacArthur think he is — Jesus Christ?'

'No, buddy,' replies the Yank, 'Jesus Christ thinks he's MacArthur.'

This story adequately describes the sometimes ironic reverence accorded by many to Douglas MacArthur, the Supreme Commander of the South-West Pacific Area during the war.

MacArthur possessed a brilliant mind, an iron will, enormous courage and charismatic star quality. Equally obvious were a rampant arrogance, colossal conceit, obstinacy and vanity. In Australia's darkest hour, with the Rising Sun of Japan on the horizon, MacArthur arrived to extinguish the flame. He was regarded almost as a military messiah, though he did not arrive on a donkey but on a train and it was not Jerusalem he entered but Melbourne. Blessed is he who comes in the name of America. Douglas MacArthur was the chosen one.

To many, his image is the image of the Pacific war. A great man who performed great deeds. The legend of the fearless, defiant leader with his braid cap, leather jacket and corncob pipe, battling overwhelming odds was born in the ruins of Corregidor island. By the time he accepted the Japanese unconditional surrender on the USS *Missouri* in Tokyo Bay four years later, he was an icon.

The great man was born in 1880. His father was a Civil War hero who won the Medal of Honor for leading a charge in the Battle of Chattanooga. The life of a soldier was always destined for Douglas and he became the quintessential army brat, raised on discipline, with the sound of bugles and cannons ringing in his ears. He graduated from West Point in 1903, first in his class. The ambitious MacArthur became an aide to Theodore Roosevelt, but the 26th president was not the first who would have to contend with the stubborn, ambitious, assertive young officer. During World War I MacArthur became one of America's most famous commanders. He pleaded with President Wilson for the formation of an elite force, called the Rainbow Division, and the 37-year-old MacArthur was then assigned to it as chief of staff.

With his striking attire and equally striking refusal to bear a side-arm, MacArthur became a familiar figure in the front line. Although gassed and injured, he was decorated nine times for heroism — sometimes for being foolishly fearless. It came as no surprise that, at age 38, MacArthur became one of the youngest generals in the United States Army. The traits, style and qualities that were to be synonymous with his legend were evident even in the early stages of his career. A serving American general in World War I, Enoch Crowder, said of the young general: 'Arthur MacArthur was the most flamboyantly egotistic man I had ever seen; until I met his son.'[1]

MacArthur returned from the Great War in glory and accepted the post of Superintendent of West Point. His career success, both militarily and politically, was spectacular. At the age of 44 he was promoted to major-general — the youngest appointed in peacetime. In 1930, at the age of 50, MacArthur was promoted to Chief of Staff of the United States Army.

His friend/foe relationship with the government became even more notable with the arrival of Franklin Roosevelt. The new president and his New Deal were focused on rejuvenating the domestic economy. MacArthur's eloquent and impassioned arguments for new weapon development enjoyed a sympathetic hearing, but they did not have a priority over an economy with 14 million unemployed. It caused little grief to the Roosevelt administration when, in 1936, MacArthur announced that he had accepted an invitation from President Manuel Quezon in Manila to become his military adviser and to take command of the Filipino Commonwealth Army.

The MacArthur name was already a familiar one in the Philippines. Arthur MacArthur had been the military governor at the turn of the century, and Douglas had served there as a young officer in 1903. It was then that he had met the young law school graduate called Manuel Quezon.[2]

The Philippines had been an American protectorate since America's victory over the Spanish in 1898. A democratic government was introduced and the chain of islands was patrolled by the American fleet, which had a large base at Cavite. Washington had promised the Philippines total independence by 1946, although it would then need to be self-reliant, both politically and militarily.[3]

President Quezon undoubtedly saw the military acumen of MacArthur as particularly useful in training and preparing his hordes of untrained soldiers for the prospect of countering foreign aggression. So senior an American officer serving in the Philippines government could only enhance the potential of American military aid. MacArthur had resigned his senior post to relocate to Manila, and he was not alone. During the voyage to the Philippines from San Francisco he met Jean Marie Faircloth, a wealthy 37-year-old woman from Murfreesboro, Tennessee. She became his second wife, and at almost 60 MacArthur welcomed Arthur IV to the family.[4]

Moving in to a six-room air-conditioned penthouse that Quezon had built for him on top of the Manila Hotel on Dewey Boulevard,[5] MacArthur was ready to become the Napoleon of Luzon. 'President Quezon is going to make me a field marshall and I'll make you a General,' MacArthur said to his aide, Major Dwight Eisenhower. 'You see,' explained MacArthur, 'the Filipinos' mentality is impressed with such exalted titles.'

Dressed in a self-designed uniform with much gold braid, MacArthur told an anxious Quezon, 'I don't think that the Philippines can defend themselves. I know they can.'[6]

By July 1941 it appeared that hostilities with Japan were imminent. Roosevelt returned MacArthur to active duty as commander of United States Army Forces in the Far East, and while reinforcements started flowing into the Philippines MacArthur now proceeded to construct a senior staff unit which was soon to become a coterie. The criteria for membership have always been puzzling. Some of his staff were obviously of outstanding quality, but many were chosen for their loyalty alone, their personality, or for other non-professional qualities that endeared them to 'the General'.

Sidney L. Huff was the first to be honoured. He was a naval lieutenant when MacArthur first met him in 1935. Although there were many more senior experienced officers available, Huff become a naval adviser before being transferred to the army with the rank of lieutenant-colonel. He later became the General's aide and assisted Mrs MacArthur, eventually becoming almost indispensable to her.

Richard K. Sutherland replaced Eisenhower as Chief of Staff. According to his colleagues, he was efficient, ruthless, short-tempered, autocratic and antagonising. What it was that endeared Sutherland to MacArthur is uncertain; however, the two men were virtually inseparable during the Pacific war. Lieutenant Colonel Richard J. Marshall became deputy Chief of Staff, Colonel Hugh Casey was an engineer, Major William Marquat an anti-aircraft officer and Colonel Charles A. Willoughby — a huge man and German by birth; Sir Charles, as he was called — was in charge of intelligence. Colonel Spencer B. Akin was involved with signals and communications, Colonel Harold 'Hal' George looked after aviation matters and Colonel Charles P. Stivers was involved with administration.

There were others as well. Fortune smiled brightly on Captain LeGrande A. Diller. He had served for two years with the Philippine Division before he played a fateful game of golf with Sutherland. Diller was formerly an engineer and Sutherland thought that the General would approve of him. At Sutherland's instigation, Diller was soon in MacArthur's office. The 40-year-old had not even seen the C-in-C previously in those two years, but 'You're a member of my family now,' MacArthur told him. Career prospects with MacArthur's 'Bataan Gang' were dynamic. Three months later, Diller was a lieutenant-colonel and in charge of MacArthur's public relations.[7]

In December 1941, MacArthur could boast of a sizeable force of 12 000 Filipino regulars and 100 000 conscripts, with 20 000 Americans. The Far East Air Force under the command of Major General Lewis Brereton had a strong contingent of the new B-17 Fortresses, fighter and miscellaneous aircraft, the majority of them based at Clark and Iba airfields. The total aircraft available to defend the Philippines was in excess of 200. General Marshall called it 'an immensely strong offensive and defensive force'.[8]

Admiral Thomas Hart had only a small group of surface ships in his Asiatic fleet, but the main deterrent was a force of 29 submarines based at the Cavite naval base in Manila.

It was 3.40 am on 8 December 1941 when MacArthur learned about the Japanese attack on Pearl Harbor. There had been many warnings about Japanese intentions since late November, but no-one knew where and when they would strike. 'It should be our strongest point,' MacArthur said of Pearl Harbor. 'Surely they will be repulsed.' He asked Jean to bring him his Bible and after some spiritual inspiration proceeded to prepare for the attack that Washington had told him was highly probable.[9]

Other officers knew about the attack as well. Brereton had been informed by General Arnold, who immediately told him not to let his aircraft be caught on the ground as they had been at Pearl Harbor. Admiral Hart was informed of the attack by his counterpart, Admiral Kimmel, who had witnessed his Pacific Fleet being decimated.[10]

What happened next is a mystery that will never be solved. Each of the participants gave a contrary account, but the common element concerns a proposed bombing raid on the Japanese base at Formosa by Brereton's B-17s, seventeen of which were on the tarmac at Clark Field. Brereton went to headquarters to discuss details and obtain approval, but Sutherland would not let him see MacArthur and told him to return to Clark Field and await instructions. A reconnaissance mission to Formosa was thought prudent before the attack. There was much procrastination and confusion before the Japanese rendered the issue academic by attacking Clark and Iba fields and destroying the majority of the Far East Air Force — all stationed on the ground. Eighteen B-17s, 53 P-40s and 30 other aircraft were lost. There were also 80 dead and 150 wounded. The Japanese lost only seven aircraft. MacArthur's staff had had over eight hours to take preventative measures. It was a military fiasco.[11]

'They caught them on the ground!' screamed Roosevelt. 'On the ground!' Stores, munitions, facilities, ships and men were also destroyed at Cavite. There were very few American aircraft remaining to challenge the Japanese aviators.[12]

MacArthur lost the Philippines in that first hour. It was a disaster, strategically far worse than the Pearl Harbor raid. Many men died during the raids and many more were to die as a consequence of them.

It is possible that MacArthur and Quezon saw the possibility of the Philippines gaining neutrality in the Pacific war. MacArthur had often referred to the prospect of the country becoming a Pacific Switzerland. It would have been prudent, he thought, that his forces should not strike the first blow. Roosevelt was aghast and reminded MacArthur that an American flag flew over the Philippines.[13] MacArthur did not have to wait long for the Japanese invasion. On the day that Roosevelt awarded MacArthur his fourth star, the 14th Army, under General Homma, landed its 48th Division at Lingayen Gulf and the 16th at Lamon Bay. In the middle was the city of Manila and the bulk of MacArthur's forces.[14]

In prewar planning, MacArthur planned to stop the Japanese on the beaches. Although he had ten divisions for the defence of the Philippines, only one was American — the Philippine Division.

The remainder were poorly trained and ill-equipped Filipinos, who were no match for experienced and aggressive Japanese. In direct contrast to the adopted plan to stop the Japanese on the beaches, MacArthur had also devised a contingency plan for a withdrawal to the Bataan peninsula. There they would make a stand until the American fleet arrived.

Although the American and Filipino forces outnumbered the Japanese by almost two to one, they were routed. Manila was declared an open city four days after the Japanese landings.[15]

MacArthur cabled Washington incessantly for reinforcements and supplies. He was furious when he learnt that a large convoy of men and equipment had been diverted to Australia while in the middle of the Pacific. MacArthur cabled Marshall: 'What can I expect in the way of fighters to strafe the Japanese?' He was told that the nearest ones were in Brisbane, Australia, not counting the charred wrecks on the Clark and Iba airfields.

If the defence of the Philippines was conducted poorly, then the retreat was conducted brilliantly. The Northern Luzon Force under Lieutenant-General Jonathan Wainwright and the South Luzon Force under Major-General George Parker merged in the Bataan peninsula.[16] However it was during the withdrawal that another major blunder occurred. For a variety of reasons, essential provisions were not shipped to Bataan. Despite the availability of transport, 50 million bushels of rice — enough to feed MacArthur's army for four years — was left for the Japanese at Cabanatuan, a few miles north of Manila. When the 'Battling Bastards' of Bataan made their stand, they were on half rations from the first day. An American commander in the Cabanatuan area later stated:

Not one grain of rice on Cabanatuan was touched. Although a vital part of the war plan, none of it reached Bataan! Perhaps it was fortunate that as we bivouacked amid the smoking ruins of Clark Field on that first day of war, we could not see these things that were yet to come — food and material of war sabotaged by the same mismanagement and indecision which has destroyed our air power.[17]

'I hope you will tell the people outside what we have done and protect my reputation as a fighter,' said MacArthur to Major General Brereton. 'General, your reputation will never need protection,' replied Brereton, who was leaving Bataan for Australia to organise air power for use in the Philippines.[18]

MacArthur, his family and aides boarded a steamer for the short trip to Corregidor — the 'rock' that was to be the Gibraltar of the Pacific. A small mass, it had the appearance of a tadpole, but there were barracks, a hospital, an airfield and the Malinta Tunnel.[19] The Japanese had a naval blockade around the Philippines and only ships prepared to run the gauntlet got through. Before long American submarines were the only source of supply, but their capacity was minute in relation to the essential requirements. Efforts to supply MacArthur were allotted to the War Plans Division of which Dwight Eisenhower was the main architect. 'Ships, ships, all we need is ships,' he wrote in his diary. 'Also, ammunition, guns, tanks, airplanes — what a headache.' It was a desperate situation and Eisenhower despatched Lieutenant-General George Brett and Patrick Hurley to Australia with a slush fund of $10 million dollars to organise blockade runners to ferry supplies from Australia.[20]

'They were filthy, and they were lousy, and they stank. And I loved them,' said MacArthur of the men facing the Japanese hordes on Bataan. He may well have loved them, but he seldom displayed any affection. Douglas MacArthur was confined to his tunnel headquarters for a period of 77 days. Only once did he make the three mile journey across the bay to visit his men. On 10 January, he ventured to the front and told anyone who would listen that, 'Help is definitely on the way. You must hold on until it comes. Help is on the way.'[21]

MacArthur never returned to the front line. He never experienced the ordeals of the front-line soldiers who called him 'Dugout Doug'. The next they heard of him he had left with his entourage for Australia and they hated him for it.

Darwin in the war years — isolated and vulnerable.

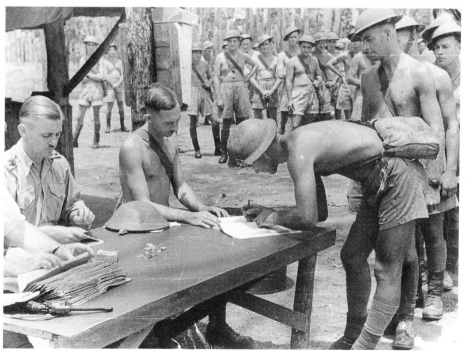

Payday in Darwin. Only the officer wears a shirt. *(Courier-Mail)*

The USS *Peary* — an ancient four-stacker, old enough to vote.

The defiant *Peary* sinks stern first. *(Courier-Mail)*

Sister Margaret de Mestre, AANS, killed in Darwin, 19 February 1942.

Lieutenant Walker's Kittyhawk at the RAAF drome, Darwin, 19 February 1942.

Second Lieutenant Robert J. Buel, 21st Pursuit Squadron, who died defending Darwin.

MacArthur and Sutherland, Corregidor, March 1942. What now?

MacArthur inspecting artillery of the 1st Calvary Division with Major-General Swift, Strathpine, Brisbane, late 1943.

Sleepy, sombre Brisbane, 1941.

The aftermath of a collision between a crowded tram and an alcohol-affected US Army truck driver, Moorooka, Brisbane, 6 September 1943. Five women died.

Private Eddie Leonski's lethal smile. Three Melbourne women died by his hands in 1942.

A day at the races. John Wayne with Lieutenant Colonel Blackween, Brisbane, December 1943. (*John Oxley Library, Brisbane*)

Mr Deeds goes to Brisbane. Gary Cooper with Phyllis Brooks and Una Merkel.

The Artie Shaw Navy band arrives in Sydney, September 1943.

Standing room only at the Trocadero in Sydney.

On 3 January 1942, President Quezon transferred $500 000 from the Philippine Treasury to a private account in the American Chase National Bank. This was a monetary contribution to MacArthur and his staff and was created as Executive Order No 1 of the President of the Philippines, 'in recompense and reward, however inadequate, for distinguished service rendered between 15 November, 1935 and 30 December, 1941'. One of the conditions of this 'reward' was that President Roosevelt and the Secretary of War would be informed. The other recipients of 'recompense and reward' were Sutherland, Huff and Marshall, who shared an extra amount of $140 000.

This financial bonanza was deemed a bonus, initially agreed to while MacArthur was serving as a mercenary and training the Filipinos. But in July 1941 MacArthur had been reinstated on the active list and was once again working for Uncle Sam. MacArthur should have been aware that United States Army regulation 600-10, Part 2C, December 1938, forbids serving officers of the United States Army to accept 'a substantial loan or gift or emolument from a person or firm with whom it is the officer's duty as an agent of the government to carry out negotiations'.

On 28 December, with the Philippines in ruins, MacArthur demanded a further $35 000 in expenses. There was a directive for Quezon's deputy, Jorge Vargas, to purchase New York stock certificates for this amount and the transaction was supported by the New York manager of the Philippine National Bank. It is believed that after the war Douglas MacArthur earned a million dollars on this scheme alone.[22]

Meanwhile, the sick and exhausted men on Bataan composed this parody to the tune of 'The Battle Hymn of the Republic':

Dugout Dug MacArthur lies a-shakin' on the Rock,
Safe from all the bombers and from any sudden shock.
Dugout Doug is eating of the best food on Bataan
And his troops go starving on...

Douglas MacArthur's performances as a military leader would always divide opinion, but no-one could suggest that he did not possess an abundance of courage. There is no question that MacArthur was prepared to die on Corregidor; he had asked Huff to obtain him a firearm. 'I fully expected to be killed,' MacArthur told a confidant after the war. 'I would never have surrendered. If necessary I would have sought the end in some final charge.'[23]

It never came to that. Roosevelt knew that although the Philippines were lost, the American public had been delivered a new hero. The media had created a modern gladiator, defiant in the rubble of Corregidor, cheering his men for a glorious last stand. MacArthur as the knight of the free people, standing alone against the yellow hordes. Roosevelt also knew that Australia would be the bastion for any new offensive. To have MacArthur down-under would be useful; to have him captured or killed in what had become a lost cause would be a public-opinion disaster.

On 22 February 1942, MacArthur was ordered to leave the Philippines. It was initially arranged that only he would be leaving, but the loss of his wife and son would also be a PR disaster for the Roosevelt administration. The directive was changed so that the General's family would leave with him.

'Jonathan, if I get through to Australia you know I'll come back as soon as I can with as much as I can,' MacArthur told Wainwright. 'In the meantime you've got to hold,' he added, patting the frail, undernourished officer on the back and rewarding him with two jars of shaving cream and a box of cigars. 'Oh Jonathan, I want you to know that when I get back, if you're still on Bataan I'll make you a lieutenant general.'[24]

It was pitch dark on the night of 11 March 1942, when General Douglas MacArthur, his family and an entourage of 20, boarded a fleet of four PT boats on Corregidor's south dock. The boats, under the command of Lieutenant John D. Bulkeley, were to transport the group to the island of Mindanao, from where four B-17 Fortresses were to fly them to Darwin.

The daring escape through the Japanese-held Islands has become legend and the feat itself was well executed and effective, but MacArthur's actions seemed personally motivated. In defiance of his orders, he evacuated all of his senior staff officers. Sergeant Paul Rogers, a staff clerk, also found a seat in one of the boats, as did young Arthur's nanny.

The destruction of the United States Far East Air Force and damage to the navy during the Philippines campaign meant that many technicians and specialists were left to shoulder arms in the garrison in a futile effort to stop the Japanese. These soldiers in particular would have been invaluable for the forthcoming counter-offences from Australia. However, there was never any competition for the vacant seats on Bulkeley's PT boats.[25]

MacArthur's defence of the Philippines was, at the very least, disappointing. He had made major blunders; he had no air force and his troops were starving; it would not have been unreasonable for MacArthur to have been relieved of his command.

Instead, he was awarded the Congressional Medal of Honor for his heroic defence of the islands. His face and features were on the front covers of almost every magazine and newspaper in America, he was nominated Father of the Year and many a new-born baby would be called Douglas. Many Americans also wanted him to stand for public office.

The Congressional Medal of Honor is a noble and proud decoration and only 433 were awarded during the war. However it has had some unlikely recipients. Charles Lindbergh received a Medal of Honor for staying awake in an aeroplane for 37 hours, and George M. Cohan got his for writing a song.[26]

MacArthur's award had as much to do with politics as valour, and General Marshall had a pragmatic reason for recommending it. He knew that a decoration to MacArthur would be a useful counter measure to Japanese propaganda; it would meet with popular approval and also prove a useful morale booster.[27] The image of the indestructible and courageous general was also perpetuated in the media. The book, *They Were Expendable*, by William White, depicted the adventures of the PT boats in the Pacific. It included an account of Bulkeley's mission taking MacArthur's entourage off Corregidor. Metro Goldwyn Mayer wasted no time in releasing a film inspired by the book. John Wayne starred and John Ford directed. The film conveyed an image of MacArthur that thrilled the world. For the scene at south dock, Ford portrayed MacArthur with almost a Christ-like reverence as he walks towards the boats to the strains of 'The Battle Hymn of the Republic'. Although it is night, Ford's MacArthur wears sunglasses; he has his cane and corncob pipe. The enlisted men on the boats freeze in awe; some remove their hats; one asks for an autograph. 'Why sure, son,' replies the General.

This was the perception that the American public had of MacArthur. He had become a living legend. It may well be to his credit that MacArthur developed this majestic sense of presence, but if John Ford had shot his film on location, he could have used the latest Bataan chant on the soundtrack:

> Our leader has vanished like last summer's rose.
> 'Gone to get help,' he would have us suppose.
> Let him go, let him go, we are the braver.
> Stain his hands with our blood, dye them forever.[28]

The PT boats arrived at Del Monte in Mindanao on schedule. MacArthur thanked the crews and awarded all of them Silver Stars. The Japanese had yet to take the island so the airfields were intact. It was difficult to find spare aircraft, but eventually a well-worn B-17 was located to transport the group to Darwin. 'Under no circumstances would I allow anyone to board such a dangerously decrepit aircraft,' said MacArthur. 'To attempt such a desperate and important trip with inadequate equipment would amount to consigning the whole party to death and I could not accept such a responsibility.' MacArthur demanded the three best planes in the United States or Hawaii, crewed by experienced airmen and quickly; the war would not wait. The demand was cabled to Washington. Some hours later two Fortresses arrived after a 2275 mile non-stop flight from Australia.

Lieutenant Frank P. Bostrom told MacArthur that he could take everybody, providing the luggage was left behind. MacArthur concurred and told Bostrom that he had just won himself the Silver Star. It is not every day that a four-star general sits in the operator's seat in a B-17, but MacArthur strapped himself into the seat as Bostrom battled to keep the sputtering, overweight Fortress in the air. MacArthur opened a case of apples, munched on one and passed the remainder to crew and passengers.

After nine hours in the air, the two aircraft were nearing the northern coast of Australia. Darwin could not receive the aircraft, as an air raid was in progress. There would need to be a detour to Batchelor, about 60 kilometres to the south. No-one could have selected a more barren, desolate, primitive location for the esteemed visitors to experience their first contact with Australia. There were some servicemen there, those who did not have a choice, a couple of shacks and open latrines.

MacArthur was one of the first out of the aircraft. 'We made it, Dick,' he said to Sutherland. 'It was close, but that's the way it is in war. You win or lose, live or die — and the difference is only an eyelash.' Several confused ground staff approached the unexpected aircraft. MacArthur spotted an American officer and called him over. 'Where is the troop build-up in this country?' asked MacArthur. 'The forces to reconquer the Philippines.'

One can only imagine the trepidation felt by this officer as he was confronted by one of the highest ranking generals in the United States Army with a whole planeload of senior officers behind him. 'So far as I know, Sir, there are very few troops here.'

MacArthur turned to Sutherland. 'Surely he is wrong.'

The weary travellers gathered in a tin shack with a mess sign nailed above the door. The group indulged in a breakfast of canned peaches and baked beans. 'Never, never again, will anyone get me into another airplane,' exclaimed Jean MacArthur. 'Sid, please find some way we can get to Melbourne without getting off the ground.' MacArthur demanded a motorcade to get to the railway station in Alice Springs. When told about logistical problems, MacArthur lost his cool under the hot sun. 'They're just too damned lazy to do what I want!' he told Major Charles Morhouse, his medical officer. 'Mrs MacArthur is tired of flying and these damned flies are driving her crazy.' Morhouse explained that young Arthur and some of the others were not up to an automobile journey of 1000 miles through the desert. The reluctant and frustrated group eventually boarded two C-47s for the flight south.

Alice Springs was the next stop on the MacArthurs' unexpected tour of the outback. In early 1942, Alice Springs was a major staging point for men and munitions to Darwin and other centres. There were over 8000 troops and 3000 vehicles in the town. The few remaining civilians were merged into what was a large military camp. No-one knew that the most senior officer in the Pacific theatre of war had landed on the drome. 'This is a flat, arid and uninviting region of scrub and sand,' MacArthur said of Alice Springs. The party believed a train would be available to transport them south.[29] There was a regular train, but MacArthur had just missed it; the next one would be along in a week. A nurse in Alice Springs, Sister Geisler, who joined the group for the journey, recalled the next development:

Mrs MacArthur was exhausted and refused to fly any further. The train had left a few hours earlier, so a signal was sent down the line for an engine, sleeping car and a dining car to come up to Alice Springs. It arrived the next day.[30]

Alice Springs at that time was not exactly a thriving metropolis. It must have been bemusing for locals and servicemen — as they lined up to purchase tickets for the Western double feature at the Pioneer picture theatre — to witness an entourage with the central figure being a four-star general who they believed was in Bataan resisting the Japanese hordes, walk down Leichhardt Terrace and into the theatre without even paying admission.

With Douglas MacArthur literally in the middle of the country, it was time to make the epoch-making announcement. The Commander of United States Forces in Australia, Lieutenant-General George Brett, telephoned Prime Minister Curtin to inform him that General MacArthur had arrived. He then read a prepared statement from Roosevelt:

Should it be in accord with the wishes of the Government and people of Australia, it would be highly acceptable to him and pleasing to the American people for the Australian Government to nominate General MacArthur as Supreme Commander of all Allied Forces in the South–West Pacific.[31]

Roosevelt's offer was one that Curtin could not refuse — nor did he want to. In Australians' darkest hour a warrior had arrived to save them.

'Just where is General MacArthur now?' asked a bemused Curtin. He was travelling south in his private train, getting some sleep or gazing from the window at the vast size of the country he would have to defend.

Curtin wasted no time in cabling Washington and London that he admired the way General MacArthur had defended the Philippines, declaring his leadership of the Allied Forces in the new area would be an inspiration to the Australian people and all the forces privileged to serve under his command.[32]

Meanwhile, some of MacArthur's staff had flown ahead to collate information about the resources and men MacArthur would have at his disposal to immediately launch an offensive to regain the Philippines. Colonel Marshall rejoined the train a few miles from Adelaide. 'Including Australians, there are about 32 000 troops, mostly non-combatants. There are also a few hundred aircraft, most of them obsolete,' he told MacArthur, and there was more: 'many ships had recently been lost to the Japanese in the Java Sea and there were rumours in Melbourne that the top half of Australia would have to be abandoned in the event of invasion.' MacArthur sat stunned and murmured, 'God have mercy on us'. Later he recalled that this was 'the greatest shock and surprise of the whole war'.[33]

The arrival in Adelaide was the curtain-raiser to MacArthur's main entrance in Melbourne, but in the City of Churches he delivered a speech that concluded with three words that would make history:

The President of the United States ordered me to break through the Japanese lines... for the purpose, as I understand it, of organising the American offensive against Japan, a primary object of which is the relief of the Philippines. I came through and I shall return.[34]

I shall return — one of the great quotes of the century, right up there with, *We met the enemy and he is ourselves.* It was a Shakespearian, *My kingdom for a horse*, a domestic, *Kilroy was here* and a theatrical, *You ain't heard nothin' yet.* Even LeGrande Diller, who by this time had become Macarthur's press officer, suggested that, 'We shall return' might be more prudent in as much as the General was here in Australia massing forces for a return. MacArthur would have none of it. 'I shall return' shot around the globe, and MacArthur would use it time and time again. It thrilled the world, that is except for the garrison at Bataan. A sergeant at Corregidor heard the three little words and immediately jumped to his feet. 'I am going to the latrine,' he announced, 'but I shall return.'

On 21 March the MacArthur entourage arrived in Melbourne. When the train crawled into Spencer Street Station, 50 policemen were attempting to contain a crowd estimated at 5000. There were plenty of bureaucrats there to greet the Americans, including the deputy Prime Minister and Minister for the Army, Francis Forde. General Brett was prominent; 360 American soldiers formed an honour guard.

MacArthur's entrance was worthy of a prima donna. Dressed

in a bush jacket, worn khaki pants and checked socks, wearing his gold-braid cap and carrying a cane, the General was drawn to an ABC microphone like a magnet: 'I am glad indeed to be in immediate cooperation with the Australian soldier,' he said. 'I know him well from World War days, and I admire him greatly. I have every confidence in the ultimate success of our joint cause.'[35]

MacArthur proceeded to state that much material and resources would be needed to meet the strength of the enemy. He also expressed his faith in the two governments and ended with yet another personal epitaph: 'In any event, I shall do my best. I shall keep the soldier faith'.[36]

The weary MacArthur family moved to the Menzies Hotel, which became their home for the next four months. MacArthur's staff settled down to business, moving into headquarters at 408 Collins Street and preparing press releases for the insatiable Australian media. The following was not amongst them:

Who had the right to say that 20,000 Americans should be sentenced without their consent and for no fault of their own to an enterprise that would involve for them endless suffering, cruel handicap, death or a hopeless future that could end only in a Japanese prisoner of war camp. A foul trick of deception has been played on a large group of Americans by a Commander in Chief and small staff who are now eating steak and eggs in Australia. God damn them![37]

This was written by a senior American officer who, like thousands of others, was preparing for the last Japanese onslaught against Bataan. It was then handed to General Wainwright.

The final offensive against Wainwright's ragged but valiant soldiers started on 3 April. Six days later Bataan fell, and 78 000 troops fell into captivity. It was the beginning of a horrendous ordeal that started with a death march of 105 kilometres to prisoner of war camps. After Bataan there was still the belligerent fortress of Corregidor to be overcome, where Wainwright and 15 000 others were preparing for the final battle.[38]

Sergeant Bill Bentson had been in Melbourne for only a few

days when he and 35 other specialists were interviewed at Camp Pell by an American colonel. The Trustees Executive Building at 408 Collins Street had been chosen as General Headquarters South-West Pacific Area. An elevator, stairway and empty offices greeted Bentson and twelve other officers who had been chosen to establish the new HQ for MacArthur. Bentson recalls:

There was nothing there. We had a priority clearance to requisition all the equipment we needed. Typewriters, cabinets, desks, paper, a mimeograph machine, the list was endless. We took equipment from offices, schools, businesses and wherever else we had to.

The General did not bring any staff with him, only his senior staff. We hired some Australian girls to do typing and shorthand. Americans would be assigned later. It was a big operation and it had to be done by the clock.[39]

Before he moved in to his new offices, MacArthur met with the Australian government. The harmony of this relationship would be crucial to the forthcoming crusade.

MacArthur saw a lot more of the country as he was driven to Canberra in a black Packard, supplied by the Australian government, that became his preferred mode of travel. On 26 March MacArthur walked up the steps of Parliament House and met, for the first time, the Prime Minister of Australia, the Right Honourable John Curtin.

Despite his pacifist background, Curtin was in control of the country's war effort. He had defiantly argued with both Churchill and Roosevelt to return Australian troops from the Middle East to defend Australia against the Japanese menace. Curtin was 56 years of age when he led his Labor party to victory in October 1941. Judged to be one of the most eloquent and effective parliamentary speakers since Federation, he had used these skills trying to influence the great powers for more defence emphasis on the Pacific theatre, in direct contrast to the Europe-first policy. Curtin had not met Churchill or Roosevelt. He had not left the country since the election. However, his Minister for External Affairs, Dr H.V. Evatt, was in Washington at that time, conveying Australia's policies and requests.

Curtin and MacArthur had diverse backgrounds and different dispositions — the politician and the soldier; the pacifist and the warrior. Curtin was obsessed with taking defence actions in Australia, MacArthur with launching offensives. But seldom have two such contrasting personalities produced such a quick, effective rapport.

At a dinner in his honour in Canberra, MacArthur delivered a masterly address:

I have come as a soldier in a great crusade of personal liberty as opposed to perpetual slavery. My faith in our ultimate victory is invincible, and I bring you tonight the unbreakable spirit of the free man's military code in support of our joint cause.

The speech was delivered with forceful sincerity, and its conclusion inspired cheers and spontaneous applause. 'There can be no compromise. We shall win or we shall die, and to this end I pledge the full resources of all the mighty power of my country and all the blood of my countrymen.'[40]

The directives for MacArthur in his role as Supreme Commander were lengthy and explicit. The first duty listed was the one that appealed most to Curtin: 'Hold the key military regions of Australia as bases for future offensive action against Japan, and strike to check Japanese aggression in the South-West Pacific area'.

The last directive was doubtless the first priority for MacArthur: 'Prepare to take the offensive'.

Curtin was told that there would be two allocated theatres in the Pacific. The South-West Pacific area under MacArthur and a South Pacific area under Admiral King.[41] On 17 April, Curtin sent a letter to MacArthur assigning all combat sections of the Australian armed forces of the South-West Pacific area under his command. Curtin instructed his commanders that as from midnight on Saturday, 18 April: 'All orders and instructions issued by the

Supreme Commander in conformity with this directive would be considered by such commanders as emanating from the Australian Commonwealth'.

The same day, MacArthur as Commander in Chief issued General Order No.1, creating subordinate commands and selecting commanders. It seemed prudent to select at least one senior Australian officer, and MacArthur nominated General Sir Thomas Blamey as Commander of Allied Land Forces. The American officers, Lieutenant General George Brett and Vice Admiral Herbert Leary, were assigned authority over Allied air and Allied naval forces.[42]

Despite requests from Marshall and Eisenhower in Washington, MacArthur refused to appoint any Australian officers to his headquarters staff. 'There is no prospect of obtaining senior staff officers from the Australians,' replied MacArthur. This was untrue; there was no shortage of competent officers available, including some splendid Australian and Dutch officers who were not only competent but had battle experience. The war, to MacArthur, was an intensely personal issue. Where possible, he would conduct it under his own terms. The 'Bataan Gang' moved into 408 Collins Street.[43]

Both MacArthur and Curtin, for obvious reasons, believed that the Pacific war should have the priority of men and supplies. It was soon apparent that, as he had done with Quezon in the Philippines, MacArthur would exert a powerful influence on John Curtin and his government.

However, MacArthur soon became frustrated with the lack of resources allocated to him from the American Chiefs of Staff. If Washington could not cater for his requirements, then the General had to go elsewhere.

On 29 April 1942 Roosevelt received a cable from Churchill. Acting on MacArthur's behalf, Curtin had supplied Churchill with a shopping list: one British infantry and one armoured division should be diverted to Australia for a temporary period. Churchill further elaborated in his cable C-82:

General MacArthur also asks for a British aircraft carrier, pointing out that it is wasteful to operate an unbalanced naval force. He further requests an additional allocation of shipping on the Australian—American run, stating that the present amount of 250 000 tons is quite inadequate to complete requisite strength apart from offensive action.

I should be glad to know whether these requirements have been approved by you and whether General MacArthur has any authority from the United States for taking such a line.

We are quite unable to meet these new demands which are none the less a cause of concern when put forward on General MacArthur's authority.

Churchill's cable drew an immediate response from Washington. Chief of Staff George Marshall gently suggested to MacArthur that he use normal channels when requesting additional forces and supplies. In a defensive response, MacArthur suggested that Curtin had used his own initiative; he told Marshall he had passed on his views only for Curtin's personal information. The President told MacArthur to ensure that Curtin understood that confidential talks were not to be used for publicity or as a basis for appeals to Churchill or Roosevelt.

On 30 April, Roosevelt responded to Churchill:

It seems probable to me that the request made upon you by Mr Curtin for two divisions and for additional marine assistance was made upon his own responsibility although undoubtedly probably based upon conversations with General MacArthur.

The lack of disciplinary action against MacArthur for deliberately defying superior authority reflected once again the extent and strength of his influence over Congress during the early years of the war. To completely exonerate MacArthur, Roosevelt told Churchill, 'you will know that any request reaching you from Mr. Curtin is made on his own responsibility'.[44]

MacArthur was soon immersed in his war odyssey. In his map room he pondered the enormous size of country and length of shoreline he had to defend. He had also learnt one or two lessons thus far in the war. He told his staff: 'The Japanese are the greatest exploiters of inefficient and incompetent troops the world has ever seen'.[45]

MacArthur could well have added 'commanders' to his categories of those being exploited. The Americans and Filipinos were about to be taken off the Pacific map in MacArthur's room. Bill Bentson was in Collins Street when the final dispatch came from Corregidor: 'Surrender is imminent,' said the dispatcher, 'but please tell my mother that I'm okay.'[46]

On 6 May 1942, two days after a Japanese offensive, General Wainwright, in a hopeless position, surrendered his American garrison in Corregidor. Three days later, General William Sharp, commander of the Central Philippines Army, ordered the surrender of all remaining forces. The Philippines were lost.[47]

MacArthur fumed in Melbourne: 'How could he surrender? Americans don't surrender. Why couldn't he hold out?'

In fact the Philippines had held out for five months, which was a remarkable achievement considering the early blunders committed, the lack of supplies, poor morale and a catalogue of adversity.[48]

This did not alter MacArthur's historic pledge; it just meant that he could not return so soon. He had plans for an offensive in New Guinea. An Australian unit was already at a place called Kokoda and was to arrive at Buna on 31 July to protect the proposed airfield there. On 21 July a Japanese force of 2000 men under the command of Colonel Yosuke Yokoyama landed at Gona, a few miles north of Buna. Their mission was to prepare the Kokoda Trail for a crossing by the main South Seas Detachment under General Tomitaro Horii, which was to land in the Buna–Gona area in mid-August.

On the same day that the Japanese landed at Gona, MacArthur left Melbourne for Brisbane. He was travelling in a maroon rail carriage that had been built for a visit by the Prince of Wales. Two flat-bed carriages were behind. MacArthur's Packard was on one and Sutherland's Cadillac on the other. The Bataan Gang would follow soon.

The great soldier was fulfilling his destiny, moving ever closer to the sound of cannons and the smell of gunpowder.[49]

CHAPTER SEVEN

STORMY WEATHER

(PLEASE DON'T TALK ABOUT ME WHEN I'M GONE)

By early 1942, the forces from the great arsenal of democracy were becoming firmly established in Australia. It seemed that all the Americans had to worry about was the prosecution of the war. Then came the events of May 1942.

On 3 May, the discovery of a woman's body in Victoria Avenue, Albert Park, Melbourne, started a chain of events that resulted in the first challenge to the alliance. The unfortunate woman was 40-year-old Ivy Violet McLeod. She had been badly beaten and strangled; her clothing had been torn and her body was semi-naked. Robbery did not appear to have been a motive as her purse still contained over a pound's worth of change, but during the autopsy it became apparent that whoever killed the woman possessed considerable strength. What soon alarmed the American military was the information that, shortly before the discovery of the body, an American soldier was seen loitering in the area. This incident may well have faded into oblivion had it not been for the discovery of a second body six days later.

Pauline Thompson was a pretty 31-year-old woman actively involved in the war effort. She had enjoyed charity work and singing in concert parties for the troops. Pauline was extremely busy, being a stenographer by day and a switchboard operator and receptionist for a radio station by night. Her husband was a police constable based in Bendigo, about 150 kilometres from the city. The two met on weekends when they spent time with their children, an adopted seven-year-old son and an infant daughter.

On the last day of her life, Pauline told her husband and son that she was going to a dance with a group of girls from work and an American soldier. She played down her husband's concern about strangers by telling him that the American was only a boy of 20 and that she would be with a large group of people. Proceeds from the dance were to help purchase an ambulance and to pay for more troop entertainment. The dance was held at the Music Lovers' Club; however, Pauline had arranged to meet Private Justin Jones at the American Hospitality Club prior to the dance at 7 pm. They had met casually the week before and agreed to attend the dance the following Friday evening.

The fact that the young private was 30 minutes late inadvertently sealed the fate of the young woman. Jones had eventually arrived to find the woman gone. He waited, ate some sandwiches and then returned to Camp Pell.

Tired of waiting, Pauline Thompson had left the club before Jones arrived and was next seen in the company of a soldier at the Astoria Hotel. The couple had left shortly before midnight on that dark, rainy and miserable night.

Four hours later, Henry McGowan, a nightwatchman, found the body of a woman on the steps of Morningside House in Spring Street. She had been throttled; there was bruising on her neck that was attributed to large fingers; her clothing was torn and in disarray. It was later revealed that she had recently broken her arm and would have been virtually defenceless in the attack.

Police reconstructed the woman's movements for the previous evening and concluded that the last person to see her alive had been an American soldier. The Melbourne newspapers told their readers that a maniac was at large and that he was probably wearing an American uniform. One thousand miles away the Brisbane *Courier-Mail* suggested that a Jack the Ripper-type killer was on the loose. The media were already calling him 'the brownout strangler'.

The panic reached the streets and bars. Women walked in groups; Americans with girls were bailed up by police and questioned; taxis did brisk business; many a Yank would be stood up; relationships were terminated and parents told rebellious daughters that this was the consequence of dating a Yank. The clergy called it God's will, a punishment for the sexual and alcoholic debauchery brought about by the occupation.

Gladys Hosking was a 40-year-old, single woman who worked at Melbourne University as a secretary and librarian. She was also an accomplished musician and was involved in opera and ballet. 'I am terribly afraid to go out at night,' she wrote to her father in Perth. 'It is a great disappointment having to stay in, as it interferes with my war work.' She saw Americans every day, for Camp Pell was only a short distance from her home in Parkville, and she had even visited the camp on one occasion. But she was not the type of woman who enjoyed the company of men in bars — whatever their nationality.

The rain that had frustrated Pauline Thompson was still set in over Melbourne as Gladys Hosking and her friend Dorothy Pettigrew left the university for their short walk home on 18 May. The two women said goodnight and went in different directions.

Only Gladys Hosking would know why she decided to walk a shorter route home and why she allowed an American soldier to share her umbrella and escort her. Several witnesses saw the couple walking in the rain, apparently quite relaxed. A short time later, a young Australian soldier, Private Noel Seymour, saw the figure of an American soldier appear out of the dark, covered in mud. The Australian had been guarding army vehicles outside Camp Pell. 'Where do I catch a tram to Camp Pell?' the American asked Seymour, who replied, 'Where the hell have you been?'

'I fell over in the mud going across the park ... My girl is nice. I've been out with her all day'.

'Do you live in Camp Pell?' Seymour asked.

'Yes, over in the street near the zoo, in Area One.'

Seymour pointed out the direction to the American and watched him disappear. A few hours later, at 7 am, in Royal Park, another

Australian soldier, named McLeod, discovered an umbrella, then a hat, and finally, in a slit trench close to Camp Pell, the body of a woman. The woman was subsequently identified as Gladys Lilian Hosking.

Melbourne was gripped by fear. Police were concerned that the ever-rotating shift in United States personnel might result in the suspect being posted elsewhere. After the news of the third murder, all American soldiers were confined to base. Camp Pell was closed and placed under armed guard. It was a testing time for the police and for the American military.

The massive publicity regarding the case led to some developments. Several women contacted police to tell of earlier attacks involving an American soldier. In one instance, a woman told police that a GI had attempted to force his way into her house, but her uncle had been there and had told the intruder to 'Get to buggery out of here!'. He had complied, but not before the uncle had a good look at him.

Another woman told an astonishing story of being almost strangled by an American soldier. He had forced his way into her flat and had assaulted her. It was only the chance sound of a person in the corridor outside the flat that saved her life. She had screamed and the intruder quickly fled with his clothes in his hands, leaving behind his GI singlet which was stamped with the initials EJL.

This incident had taken place before the first murder, but had not been reported. It was desperation time for police and provosts. The 15 000 men at Camp Pell were lined up as police escorted potential witnesses to the camp in an attempt to identify a suspect. It looked like being another futile exercise until attention was drawn to a group of men waiting to enter the PX canteen. 'That's him!' said the uncle of one of the victims, 'That's him. That's the bloke who followed my niece home.'

The suspect was paraded in front of Private Seymour, who agreed that he was the soldier he had seen with the muddy clothes. Soon the soldier was handcuffed to a bed rail and placed under armed guard in the Camp Pell stockade. He was 24-year-old Private Edward Joseph Leonski, no. 32 007 434, from the 52nd Signal Battalion. Soon his tent-mates were telling police about suspicious behaviour by Leonski and chance remarks he had made about the murders. A full confession by Leonski ended the investigation.

The impact of the Leonski offences would soon be felt in other aspects of the Australian-American alliance. However, the first contentious problem with the case was a legal one. Ever since the arrival of the Americans, the subject of legal jurisdiction had been a sensitive issue. Before they arrived, the Australian government had required that the Americans comply with civil law. It had been agreed that they would supervise their servicemen's discipline, but that the laws of their host land were non-negotiable.

It was not until the arrival of MacArthur that America responded to the situation. There was a suggestion that to conform to these requirements would be impractical. MacArthur's predecessor, General Brett, had written to Curtin suggesting that any absences of American personnel from duty while they faced Australian authorities or courts would impair the efficiency of American units and the successful accomplishment of their common mission. Brett believed it was imperative that decisions regarding Americans being taken from duty would have to be made by the American military. Brett concluded his letter to Curtin by stating that appropriate justice would be delivered for major and minor offences.

What the Americans wanted was to deal with their own servicemen for any offence either military or civil. There were many in Canberra who were firmly against such an arrangement. It challenged the Constitution, and surely the Americans had enough control and influence in the country without them circumventing Australia's legal system and procedures. How would the states react? What would be England's view? A decision would need to be made soon as there were several Americans under provost and police arrest in most states awaiting justice.

Seven days after Leonski's arrest, a response was made to the

Americans that the Australian government would rely on their assurances that sufficient justice and appropriate penalties would be dispensed in a prompt, efficient manner. In short, the Americans were given the right to deal with any of their servicemen who were charged with any civil or military offence. Police were instructed to hand offenders over to the American military to be dealt with. This major concession to the visitors compromised many legal and moral issues. However, the Australian government had little choice. To many it was another, small price to pay for the war effort, but to others it was yet another humiliating capitulation to American will.

Always an effective diplomat, MacArthur was gracious. He responded to Curtin and allowed him to maintain his dignity by personally thanking him very much for his cooperation. The Australian government was doubtless relieved when Uncle Sam later obtained similar concessions from New Zealand, India, Canada and, most notably, the Mother Country herself. 'This was a very considerable departure from the traditional system and practice in the United Kingdom,' stated Anthony Eden, Britain's Foreign Secretary, and the government informed the Americans that the arrangement was temporary and exceptional, dictated by the conditions of war and tolerable only because of the mutual feelings of comradeship.

Leonski knew nothing of the significance of these developments as he stood before an American military court, charged with the murder of three Australian women.

To the American military, Eddie Leonski was the soldier from hell. He had a history of violence back in the States and his home life had been disastrous. A brother had been committed to a mental institution and another was well known to police. Leonski had joined the army in February 1941 and three months later had almost strangled a girl in San Antonio, Texas. The case was processed as an assault and Leonski was not prosecuted. It was a warning that was not heeded.

Leonski had arrived in Melbourne in February 1942 and for his first three months there seemed to have embarked on an alcoholic binge, amusing buddies and bar patrons by consuming three dozen beers in one session and walking on bars on his hands. Evidently while in Melbourne, Leonski had seen the MGM screen version of *Dr Jekyll and Mr Hyde*. He even suggested that he had a darker self — a 'Mr Hyde' — and, like the Spencer Tracy character, Leonski became obsessed with women's voices. While Dr Jekyll concocted a potion for the transformation into Hyde, Leonski transformed himself with alcohol.

Leonski was a social misfit who could express bravado and then revert to weeping like a baby. He should never have been accepted into the army as his emotional state had always been in serious question. Now he was in front of a court martial, pleading for his life. This well-publicised trial was held in a hall in Russell Street. From the beginning, there was never any doubt that Leonski would pay the ultimate penalty. The American military virtually had no choice and clearly felt the need to demonstrate that it was prepared to deal with such matters without mercy.

Eddie Leonski was sentenced to be hanged. Commander-in-Chief Douglas MacArthur confirmed the sentence on 4 November; the execution was to be carried out five days later. However, for a country which had demonstrated such methodical effectiveness and almost instant mobilisation, the United States military had not thought to bring a hangman to Australia and certainly did not have a scaffold ready. In the utmost secrecy, an arrangement was reached whereby the sentence would be carried out in Melbourne's Pentridge Prison, where the necessary implements were in place.

Eddie Leonski did not command any sympathy and, until the end, stated that death would be wonderful and that he would exercise so as to be in peak condition for the event. He also read incessantly — particularly about Australia's favourite rogue, Ned Kelly. The Americans ultimately employed the services of a local hangman and Leonski met his maker with little fuss and without knowing that Ned Kelly had fallen from the same scaffold 62 years earlier.[1]

The Leonski affair had caused the Americans much embarrassment, and had made it particularly difficult for the servicemen and women who were enjoying the hospitality of so many Australians. Although the affair soon lost its immediacy, many would not forget. For all the wrong reasons, Eddie Leonski, Australia and World War II, are united in infamous memory.

The American military executed over a 100 servicemen during the war and there were several, other than Leonski, who met their end in Australia. Private Avelino Fernandez was executed for the savage murder of a part-Aboriginal girl, Doris Roberts, in Brisbane in 1944. Rather than attract negative public opinion, the authorities executed the unrepentant soldier in Oro Bay, New Guinea, on 15 November 1944.[2]

A little known but tragic event occurred late on the evening of 19 August 1942 when Leon Begay, a military provost, walked into the Lyceum Theatre in George Street, Brisbane, and accosted a young woman called Gwendoline Lloyd in her dressing-room. Ordering her to her knees, Begay shot her with his revolver and then turned the weapon on himself.[3] There was also a mass execution of six black American soldiers in New Guinea for the rape and assault of a white nurse at Milne Bay.[4] There were, of course, many more serious crimes attributed to the Americans, but considering the size of the garrison force and their immersion into Australian society, it was to be expected that there would be some unfortunate incidents.

There were also many cases of violence against the Americans. Perhaps the most tragic were the deeds of the so-called 'Man in Grey', who conducted a violent campaign against American soldiers late in the war. He believed that the Yanks 'were out to get him'.

Frederick William Everest was a 34-year-old Australian who had been discharged from the army in 1944. In January 1945, he

shot dead a popular American officer, Lieutenant Allen
C. Middleton, as he left a public convenience. Thirteen days later
Everest also shot dead Petty Officer John D. McCollum as he was
standing on the front porch of his rented home in Alderley, Brisbane.
Everest was diagnosed as suffering from incurable paranoia and
spent the rest of his life committed to a mental institution.[5]

For every unfortunate murder, shooting and assault, military or
civilian, committed by either side during the war years, numerous
fantasies and myths have evolved and become entrenched in
national folklore.

Queensland Railways and the town of Rockhampton have
become interwoven in one of the great stories of the war. The so-
called 'Battle of the Trains' incident purported to be a confrontation
between American and Australian soldiers shooting at each other
from trains, resulting in many deaths. The story has been recounted
so often that many believe such an incident really happened.
Evidently, the motive for the incident came from one of the Yanks
telling the Aussies as they were being transported to the front,
'Don't worry, Digger, we'll take care of the girls while you're gone'.
This is supposed to have provoked a fierce firefight between the
two sides, resulting in over 20 dead. It was, of course, covered up,
according to the storytellers.

This episode has been given credence by some mischievous
writings and an irresponsible account perpetuated in the 1986 film,
Death of a Soldier. Despite the fact that veterans and historians
have found little or no evidence and have concluded that the episode
is a myth, or an elaboration, the legend lives on, with many still
claiming that it was an authentic incident and that the cover-up
remains in place. In some aspects, the story is true. There was
shooting from trains and some soldiers were killed, but the 'Battle
of the Trains' appears to be the amalgamation of two separate
incidents that might have given some credibility to the legend.

In November 1942, the Queensland Commissioner of Police sent
a letter to Major General J.M.A. Durrant, the Australian

commander in Victoria Barracks in Brisbane, and a copy to Colonel Donaldson at United States Headquarters Base Section 3, relating to an incident that had been reported by the district Inspector of Police at Rockhampton. A few days previously, the stationmaster at Gladstone had telephoned police to say that a troop train carrying American and Australian troops had just left the station and that troops were discharging firearms. The firing continued at a siding called Rodd's Bay and bullets entered the officers' quarters. Soldiers in two carriages had discharged about 100 rounds, mostly from .303 rifles and revolvers. An Australian Officer — Major Stanford — was approached by a guard and walked towards the carriages where the gunfire was evident. Stanford was on his way back to New Guinea after a rest period and promised to make a full report to the authorities when the train arrived in Townsville. Only a carbon copy of half of this strictly confidential letter survives in State Archives. Although the event appears sinister, it may have been nothing more than some bored, reckless soldiers shooting at targets from the windows of the train.[6]

However, there is no doubt that an extraordinary incident occurred less than a week later. It reads like a work of fiction, but has been validated by detailed police reports. The story of this tragic encounter began when the stationmaster at Bowen approached Corporal Peter Jamieson, 12th Australian Ordnance Ammunition Company, who with Provosts Irwin, Vincent and Hill, was rostered for security duties on the ammunition train, *65 Down*, travelling from Brisbane to Townsville. The stationmaster was with an American serviceman who appeared tired and desultory. 'Corporal, can you take this fellow to Townsville?' said the Stationmaster. 'He is based at Reid River and has to be back by morning.'

The American was Corporal Frederick Theodore Simons, who was attached to the 408th Bomb Squadron, 22nd Bomb Group, at Reid River, 55 kilometres from Townsville. Twenty-eight-year-old Fred Simons had arrived with his squadron six months earlier. He was arrested at Mackay after a disturbance and had spent the night in the local lockup. The following day, after telling police he had no money, he was transported to the Bowen railway station with the intention of getting a ride to Townsville.

Australian provosts seldom carried side-arms, but on this occasion Jamieson and the others wore hand guns for their guard duty. The Australians welcomed Simons aboard and he rode with them in their carriage, even sharing sandwiches and refreshments with them. All was well until the train stopped at Inkerman, a siding ten kilometres south of Home Hill and 170 kilometres from Townsville.

Jamieson had carelessly taken off his holster in order to lie down for a rest. Simons was noticed to be prowling around some of the ammunition carriages and was told to move away by one of the provosts. It was 10.30 pm. Inexplicably, Simons took Jamieson's handgun and shot Corporal Cecil Irwin dead with a round through the head. The American then ran away from the train, shooting randomly.

Simultaneously, another train pulled into Inkerman. It was the *290 Up*, a troop train in transit to Brisbane with Australian troops aboard. There was also another train following. This was the *266 Up* which was carrying, along with cargo, 35 wounded American soldiers who had been evacuated from New Guinea. Lieutenant Mark M. Temkin, 12 Station Hospital Townsville, was in charge of the wounded who were being transported to Brisbane.

The Australians on *290 Up* were aware that something was wrong. They could hear anxious voices and see torch lights. An Australian provost then boarded the first carriage — it was Jamieson. 'A Yank has gone amok!' he shouted. 'One of our chaps has been shot. Are you armed?' The carriage contained men of the 2/1st Australian Army Survey Corp, AIF. One soldier said that he knew where some weapons were stored. Jamieson then ordered a detachment of Australians to arm themselves and to follow him, but to 'be careful: look out for the Yank. He's mad! He's got a gun!'

One of the men who took a rifle was Private Richard George Carr. Another soldier, M.J. Murnane, armed himself with a .45 revolver. Soon there were at least six Australian soldiers, armed and in pursuit of the American. They moved quickly towards the ammunition train and some climbed aboard the guard's van. There were others between the two trains with flashlights, while railway staff used lanterns. Simons evidently fired towards the train and Carr, seeing the American illuminated by the lights, fired a number of rounds at him. Murnane also fired. The man was blown off his feet, virtually doing a pirouette before falling to the ground.

More lights were directed at the figure on the ground as the men walked cautiously toward the prostrate figure, jabbing and poking him with feet and weapons. Temkin, the American officer from 266 Up, arrived on the scene and inspected Irwin and then Simons, pronouncing them both dead. 'Where are your officers?' Temkin asked the rapidly growing group of Australians. 'Go and get somebody in charge.' An Australian officer, Lieutenant Ronald Playford, quickly arrived at the scene and ordered the men to stand fast. Soon there was a semblance of order as American and Australian soldiers, and railway staff, congregated on the scene, scarcely comprehending what had happened or what to do about it.

An autopsy revealed that Simons had been shot twice; once in the chest by a round from a .303 rifle; the other wound was in the leg, thought to be a round from a .45 revolver. The full details of the tragedy have been confined to the coroner's files. No inquiry was undertaken and the matter seems to have faded, a sensitive episode that was overwhelmed by the black cloak of censorship and the grievous casualty lists from the battles in New Guinea.

Shortly after the incident, there was profound confusion. The 290 Up train, with Carr, Murnane and the other Australians, was allowed to proceed to its destination without any official action. Only a few hours after the incident, Sub-Inspector Osborne, from Mackay, telegraphed Constable Clifford in Rockhampton. Lacking specific details, Osborne made some provocative and erroneous claims:

Two American soldiers were shot at Inkerman late last night, or early this morning.

There were two train loads of soldiers at Inkerman when the shooting took place. One was loaded with American soldiers and the other with Australian soldiers.

An American soldier named Fred Theodore Simons got a revolver and shot Corporal Irwin, another American soldier.

Another American soldier named Jamison heard the shot and saw Corporal Irwin fall. He called out for a rifle and shooting took place... Other American soldiers are also believed to have taken part.[7]

Coupled with the impact of censorship and some fertile imaginations, these two train incidents may well have been conflated into the mythical full-blown encounter story that has been retold so often for the past 58 years, usually with variations and usually with a drink. The same adage holds true now in peace as it did during the war — never let the truth stand in the way of a good story.

The massive influx of servicemen in cities with brownout conditions resulted in many minor crimes and misdemeanours. The large number of surviving state and national files relating to petty arrests indicate that to their credit, neither military nor civil police took any nonsense from servicemen, regardless of nationality.

Disorderly conduct seems to have been a popular pastime. Usually induced by alcohol, these matters, according to the arrest sheets, demonstrated the formidable command and scope of profanities the Yanks possessed. Aussies knew all the words as well, but the Yanks had more variations. It should be recognised as a triumph, both socially and culturally, that some much loved verbal expletives did not linger in the Australian vocabulary after the American vocalists left the shores. The term describing parental copulation and another relating to a form of activity with the male genitalia were extremely popular with Yanks, but somehow did not become major entries in the dictionary of Australian profanities.

Assault was also common. Most confrontations were over in moments, but some required the intervention of authorities and arrests were made. Punishments through the military courts could be severe, especially when delivered by provosts keeping the peace.

Theft was rampant and perpetrated by both servicemen and citizens. Money was not always the prize. In wartime, alcohol, tobacco and petrol were equally valued and there was a flourishing black market. Those convicted of petty theft did not avoid retribution. Archives reveal arrests for stolen objects of a bewildering variety. One Australian was arrested for breaking a plate-glass window, another for stealing one. There were not really enough domestic motor vehicles around to represent sufficient appeal to thieves. Bicycles were popular, however, and there were many arrests for their theft. Stern sentences handed out suggest a parallel to stealing a horse in the American West. The names and details on yellowed arrest sheets indicate that authorities were not able to eliminate wartime crimes, but there certainly was a concerted attempt to minimise them.[8]

Driving on the roads of Australian cities was precarious, military vehicles seeming to be everywhere. The main problem the Americans had with Australian road conditions concerned driving on the left-hand side. A week after the Americans arrived in Australia with the *Pensacola* convoy in December 1941 an American officer, Lieutenant Milton Kaslow, was involved in an accident when the vehicle in which he was a passenger turned over due to the driver's confusion over local road rules. The 21-year-old officer died two days later.

The volume of traffic on city and country roads during the war was unprecedented. An observer in Townsville counted 300 military vehicles on a main road in a fifteen minute period. The presence of trams in Brisbane, Melbourne and elsewhere also led to a number of traffic calamities. By August 1943, the number of accidents between trams and military vehicles was so great that the General Manager of the Tramways Department of the Brisbane City Council wrote to the Commissioner of Police requesting assistance to minimise these incidents. And on 9 September the Queensland Commissioner of Police wrote to both the Australian and American military authorities asking for more care and caution and also quoting some alarming statistics. In the period from January 1942 to August 1943, Australian Defence Department vehicles had been involved in 645 collisions and US Army vehicles were responsible for 794. A grand total of 1439 collisions was obviously of sufficient concern for the commissioner to write to the authorities; however, there seems little doubt that the prime motive was a horrifying accident that had occurred two days earlier involving an American military vehicle and a Brisbane tram.[9]

Early in the evening of 6 September, a southbound tram, filled to capacity and carrying mostly young women munition workers, was about to enter the suburb of Moorooka when the driver noticed an American truck approaching on the wrong side of the road. The tram had virtually stopped and was sounding its bell in warning when the truck struck the tram on the right-hand front section. The vehicle was driven by Private Hugh James Copeland, 126th Infantry, 32nd Division, from Camp Cable. There was a 44-gallon drum of petrol on the back of the truck which rolled loose and ignited, producing a fireball which raced through the tram. Four women between the ages of 20 and 29 died, either at the scene or soon afterwards. Thirty-eight more were injured — most of them seriously. Six weeks later, 26-year-old Heather O'Brien died in hospital bringing the death toll to five.[10]

Private Copeland admitted to having a few beers earlier in the day. He was immediately arrested and delivered to the American authorities. Commissioner Carroll wrote to the United States Army asking for Copeland to be surrendered, in the first instance, to Queensland police. Brigadier General L.S. Ostrander replied, quoting National Security Regulation No. 6:

Where any member of the United States Forces in Australia is arrested or detained on a charge of having committed, or is summoned, charged or otherwise proceeded against for having committed an offence against the law of any State, the appropriate officer of the United States shall be notified and, if he so requests, the member shall be handed over to him.[11]

In such an appalling case, it must have been frustrating for the Queensland police. The incident was well-publicised and, in light of the circumstances, there was an outcry for justice. Ostrander concluded his letter:

Private Copeland has since been tried by Court Martial on the charges and sentenced to dishonourable discharge, forfeiture of all pay and allowances due or become due and is now confined at hard labor for a period of three years. It is to be hoped that the information contained herein will enable your department to close its case insofar as it concerns charges against Private Copeland.[12]

One of most perennial of military offences, as old as warfare itself, was the act of being AWOL — absent without leave. The motives usually involved females, futility, frustration or fear. This offence was very much a military concern and usually handled with a closed-door confidentiality, but with Uncle Sam in a strange country the assistance of the Australian authorities was regularly sought. Surviving in the Australian archives is a complete set of previously confidential documents that convey the resolve and vigour of the authorities in apprehending such offenders. It is also an explicit example of how effectively the two nations could function together.

In August 1941, only four months before America entered the war, two American heavy cruisers, *Northampton* and *Salt Lake City*, paid a surprise visit to Brisbane. They docked long enough to take on stores and for 2000 men to enjoy some brief liberty. Seven seamen enjoyed the short stay so much that they declined to continue with the cruise. On 10 August, as the *Northampton* pulled anchor, Captain W.D. Chandler was writing a communique to the American Consulate in Brisbane.

The following named men were absentees from this vessel at the time of her departure from Brisbane.

Culbertson, James Alexander, Seaman 1st Class USN

Edwards, Alfred Jr, Machinist 2nd Class USN

Prosser, Robert LeDroit, Seaman 1st Class USN

Vacchiano, Felix Joseph, Seaman 2nd Class USN

Wrobleski, Edward Joseph, Seaman 2nd Class USN

It is requested that should any of the above men be apprehended or report to your office, or to the authorities at Brisbane, after the departure of this vessel that this vessel and the Navy Department, Washington, DC be advised by dispatch.

The *Salt Lake City* was also short two sailors, William F. Crobe and Minden Ferrall.

The next day, Joseph P. Ragland, from the American Consulate, sent a letter to the officer in charge, Commonwealth Investigation Branch in Brisbane.

I would enclose a copy of a communication received by pilot from the USS *Northampton* furnishing descriptions of five members of the crew of that vessel who were absent when the vessel sailed. It would be greatly appreciated if you would have a look-out for these men and let me know should they be found. It is believed that they should be kept in detention pending authorisation to make necessary expenditure for their transportation.

In an admirable display of efficiency, Queensland police began apprehending the offenders. It appears that Culbertson, Edwards and Prosser literally missed the boat and duly reported to the Brisbane Water Police. Wrobleski and Vacchiano were in police custody and being held in the city watch house. William Crobe was more elusive, but was eventually apprehended in the New South Wales town of Murwillumbah, 150 kilometres from Brisbane. Crobe was in the town jail and under the jurisdiction of New South Wales police. Ferrall was still on the run.

The American Consul quickly displayed its appreciation to the Queensland police, but there were legal complications.

I am told that Queensland Police are reluctant to hold the men in detention for more than ten days. It would therefore be appreciated if you would be good enough to consider holding the men under the new Section 14A of the Alien Control Regulations until transportation can be provided. It may also be desirable when transportation can be provided to have an escort for Vacchiano and Wrobleski with surveillance over Culbertson, Edwards, and Prosser to a vessel at Sydney.

Bureaucracy now begins to complicate matters. Inspector Foote from the Commonwealth Investigation Branch in Brisbane conveyed the request and a copy of the letter to his superiors in Canberra.

As Vacchiano and Wrobleski were to be released after ten days detention if no charge is preferred against them, and this period expires on 21st August, a telegram that the Ministerial Order has been issued for the information of the State Police is necessary, as these men would, it is thought, if released, seize the opportunity to again abscond.

Canberra suggested that, in the interim, the absconders should be confined to a military detention complex. The American Consul was in agreement:

With reference to the United States naval absentees now detained at the City Watch House I would inform you that the Consulate has no objection to their removal to a military camp for continued detention prior to their repatriation. It might be preferable for them to be in the camp than at the Watch House because of greater facilities for exercise. Such a transfer in your discretion would meet my approval.

It was also preferable to the former watch-house guests. The camp at Grovely was indeed more suitable. It had more facilities but, alas, less security. Shortly after being admitted to the camp, Wrobleski and Vacchiano were gone — through the wire and over a fence. An embarrassed commander of the Grovely military camp informed the police, who ultimately informed the American Consulate.

Fortunately for the Australian authorities, the two sailors were once again apprehended. In a letter dated 4 September 1941, the Consulate asked for details of the escape and the recapture. Wrobleski and Vacchiano had escaped on 31 August by forcing staples out of the posts, then parting the barbwire and climbing through the fence. Vacchiano had been picked up by a police car at the Woolloongabba Fiveways at 3 am on 1 September. He was in the company of a woman and wearing civilian clothes. Wrobleski was captured an hour later at Breakfast Creek, still wearing his uniform. As if the duo were not in enough trouble, the commander of the Grovely camp quickly informed the American Consul: 'These men broke out of camp after being confined for only one day. They are now subjected to the full severity of Detention Camp rules.'

The next response came from the American Consul to the Commonwealth Investigation Branch in Brisbane:

It would be greatly appreciated if your Department would be good enough to arrange for an escort of three officers to take the men from Brisbane to the SS *Monterey* leaving Sunday 18 September 1941 for Honolulu. The men will be turned over to the United States Naval Authorities at Honolulu.

The Consulate has been authorised to take care of all necessary expenses and I shall be glad to turn over to you eight railway tickets from Brisbane to Sydney as well as ten pounds in cash, for the meals, taxi fares, etc. for themselves and for the men.

Quite prudently and appropriately, three first-class and sleeping-car tickets for the escorts return journey were also supplied. There was also a further request: 'For my own accounts it is important that each of the men sign a receipt for the expenditure and service in his behalf'.

What followed was a proliferation of letters and documents for the legalities, such as income tax clearances for the men to leave the country. On 5 September 1941, the Queensland Police Department issued a request to the General Staff, Northern Command, Victoria Barracks, Brisbane:

I have to advise that the American Consul, Brisbane, has applied to this Office for three officers to be made available in escorting the absentees to Sydney.

In this matter, the assistance of your department is requested. The arrangements are at present that the absentees and escorts leave on the Wednesday morning, the 17th September, so as to arrive in Sydney on the day of the departure of the ship, in order to obviate the necessity of the surveillance of the men in Sydney.

On 15 September, the American Consul once again contacted the Queensland Police:

It is respectfully requested that your escorts be good enough to pick up the steamship tickets from the Matson Line Office and also return to me a receipt from the Master of the SS *Monterey* for the delivery of the five absentees.

Once again it was stated: 'Please return to this office full receipts for the expenditure of the ten pounds, with your signature and that of the escorts'.

It was now the turn of Major H.A. Cummins, Australian Military Forces — Northern Command to become involved:

I have to report that the American absentees left for Sydney this morning, with escorts, Corporals Adams, Swallow and Kilgour. The absentees will be taken straight from the train to the *Monterey*, which is expected to sail within a few hours of their arrival.

At 1.30 pm on 18 September, a telegram was received by Roy Retallack at the Commonwealth Investigation Branch in Brisbane: 'Escort delivered Everything satisfactory Tom Adams'.

There was more communication to the American Consulate, and upon the return of the Australian escorts a letter was supplied from G.C. Streng, for the Master of the SS *Monterey*, 18 September 1941, Sydney, Australia:

I, the undersigned, certify that the officers of the Government of the Commonwealth of Australia acting as escorts have duly placed the United States Absentees on board this vessel this day. Their respective Liberty Cards have also been delivered and received.

Joseph Raglan, the American Consul, also received attached cash receipts, detailing the fate of the £10. Corporal Adams had meticulously accounted for the funds. There were meals in Casino and Coffs Harbour, refreshments in Taree and breakfast in Sydney. All personnel on the journey, including the American absentees, had signed the receipts.

The American Consulate might have regretted that the £10 had been fully spent, but was doubtless impressed that, in a stunning example of Allied frugality, Corporal Adams had insisted that the group of eight use only one taxi for commuting from the railway station to the wharf.[13]

The Americans were on their way to their fate in Honolulu and few officials in Australia mourned their departure. The absentees might have avoided being crew members of the *Northampton* and *Salt Lake City*, but their adventures were only beginning as they arrived in Hawaii just in time for the Japanese attack on Pearl Harbor.

The American military would always take a dim view of AWOL offenders, and later in the war Uncle Sam spared no expense or effort in apprehending various absconders and runners. Most were caught and dealt with by American authorities, under an agreement that had not been in place when the *Northampton* and *Salt Lake City* were in port.

Surviving archives reveal an extraordinary resolve by the Americans to hunt down their deserters. State police were constantly informed and briefed about the latest batch, and bulletins were sent to police in country and outback areas. The absentee Americans could be quite conspicuous by their speech, mannerisms and, in most cases, their uniforms. What is more their offences were never forgotten. Deserters were still being sought long after the war and Queensland police were arresting offenders well into the 1950s. Many of the men had created new lives, a number of them marrying and raising families in blissful domesticity. The past may well have been forgotten and the future be looking bright until, one day, a uniformed figure knocked on the front door.

CHAPTER EIGHT

THAT'S ENTERTAINMENT

One of the most remarkable features of the American 'occupation' was the speed with which it was undertaken. In December 1941, the *Pensacola* convoy disembarked 4600 servicemen in Brisbane. Hundreds of specialists arrived soon afterwards to organise and prepare for the main influx of personnel then in transit or loading in ports of embarkation.

By June 1942, there were 88 000 Americans on the continent. Divisions swarmed ashore and by early 1943 a quarter of a million were stationed in large camps and bases around the cities of Brisbane, Sydney and Melbourne. Thousands more arrived in rural and outback locations.[1]

The whole endeavour was a supreme feat of organisation. Once the billeting, housing, feeding and clothing of the Americans was accomplished, other priorities became obvious — notable amongst them, how to occupy the occupiers. Thousands of miles from home in a foreign land with confusing customs, the GI felt alone. The more he thought about home, the more he missed it. Conversing, drinking, reading, writing home, playing ball and other socially limited activities, combined with ever-increasing periods of liberty, soon bred idleness, which resulted in boredom — which affected morale.

Entertainment was the answer. The Yanks took stock of the situation. Sightseeing was widespread. Newsreels of Americans patting kangaroos, cuddling koalas and chasing emus were novelties that soon evaporated. Singles, duos and larger groups paced and reconnoitred cities large and small. All you could do was hang out. It was all very interesting for a while but it did not last — so now what?

'Like South Dakota by the sea,' remarked one Yank upon seeing Townsville. Three thousand kilometres to the south, another observed that Melbourne was 'half as big as New York City's largest cemetery — and twice as dead'.[2] The average American knew little about his new allies or their customs. Melbourne might have been half as big as New York's biggest cemetery, but the entire population of Australia was less than that of the Big Apple.

The continent had only been settled by Europeans 150 years earlier, and it was only 40 years since Federation had combined the colonies as a nation. The tradition was still colonial, the mood conservative, and there was an aura of naivety.

What did Australians do for amusement? Very few had cars and public transport was also limited. Visiting was popular — as was sport. The two major football codes totally perplexed the Americans — but not as much as cricket, which a few Yanks had seen shortly after their arrival. The races were a popular pastime, but this decreased as the American hordes constructed camps on several of the hallowed tracks. Radio was popular, but not everyone had a set.

Aussies certainly seemed to enjoy gambling and drinking. The pubs were usually full, but their opening hours were limited and they were closed on Sundays. Much of this changed through the war. The semi-darkness lighting restriction called the 'brownout' was implemented in major areas, thousands of miles from any potential enemy.

With the massive influx of US servicemen, there were never enough facilities. In Townsville, one cinema had catered for the civilian population. Now there were an extra 60 000 servicemen. Sunday was the commercial as well as the religious Sabbath — everything closed. A *Newsweek* reporter called John Lardner wrote:

Australia's night out, her Saturday-Night-American-Plan, comes on Friday night. By Saturday evening her basically pious population of English-Scottish-

Irish stock is beginning to taper off to a grave and immaculate Sunday that falls with an almost mortuary hush upon the ears of American soldiers stationed near towns and cities there.[3]

In Australia, Sunday had always been sacred: nobody traded; nobody entertained. On the Easter break, there were four Sundays. In Brisbane, after a Sunday service, Major John Kinney, an army chaplain, walked for seven miles before finding a shop where he could buy a sandwich.[4] Others who wanted to purchase items such as tobacco walked just as far only to find shops with closed signs hanging in the window — or empty shelves. Men stayed on bases or ships, boredom and melancholia festering. It would be a long war.

The quest to open facilities and amenities on Sundays for American servicemen led to some of the earliest disputes between the visitors and their hosts. A molehill that would soon become a mountain.

The *Sydney Morning Herald* suggested that initiatives had been taken in Great Britain for Australians and Canadians to find entertainment on Sundays. The *Truth* saw potential for social adjustment and encouraged the Americans: 'if you crash the wall of wowserism that's been built up over the years you'll be doing a great service to the pleasure-cramped people of Melbourne'.[5] General MacArthur was conservative: 'It is your land and it is for you of Australia to determine your own laws and methods of life,' he said. 'The American Forces will accommodate themselves to the results.'[6]

In Sydney on 16 April 1942, a meeting including delegates from Australian and American military forces, union officials, government and civic bodies, clergymen, Actor's Equity, the press, broadcasting and theatrical representatives, social welfare and cultural organisations was convened to discuss potential Sunday amusements and entertainment requirements. The offensive commenced:

We should hesitate before we force large numbers of people to work for other people's pleasure. It has taken the unions years to have these rights. They are hard earned. This is the beginning of an insidious campaign to weaken the labour movement.

This will result in internal paganism. What if Sunday in our cities becomes secularised?

A member from the Baptist Union suggested: 'Instead of opening cinemas and restaurants, is it not better to organise community singing of an appropriate character and addresses to strengthen faith and morale? Let us not forget the significance of this day.'

Bishop Hilliard: 'Australia has its convictions as to how the Sabbath should be observed'.

The flak was heavy: 'What if the cinema times clash with church services?' 'Who will clean up after the Americans?' 'This is a conspiracy to overturn religion simply to please the Americans.' 'They will become continental Sundays. This will destroy our way of life.'

With the much needed support of his military allies, Major Lynn Cowan from the Morale Branch of the American forces was energised and eloquent. Jumping to his feet he retorted that servicemen were

forced to wander around darkened streets where thoughts that were never in their minds creep in. If you have groped your way around the darkened city, you will realise it is no place for a young man to be. We believe that you are big enough and fair enough to change your laws and open two motion pictures shows, a theatre, and a dance hall on Sundays.

We do not want to have to build our own cinemas and dance halls. Why should essential war work be interrupted by the time and effort this would take? Surely it is stupid to open a separate amusement network.

Major Cowan told the gathered clergy.

There are 125 million Americans and we are not heathens. We go to Church and have the forms of amusement we want.

We are not asking you to give up anything religious in this country. We are going to have entertainment for our boys.[7]

On 20 April 1942, the *Sun News-Pictorial* told its readers:

Three thousand sailors, soldiers, airmen and women friends packed the Town Hall last night for a concert held as the first Sunday night entertainment for troops on leave.

So great was the crowd in Swanston Street before the show that the doors had to be opened at 6.40 pm — 20 minutes before the scheduled time.[8]

The first pastime that the Allies had in common was visiting the cinema. Americans called them the movies; Australians called them the pictures. Australians' love for the medium was insatiable. In 1921 there were 68 million paid admissions to 'the pictures' — four times the number of visits to the races and theatre combined. The average suggested that every man, woman and child in the country went to the pictures ten times a year.[9] Not surprisingly, the visitors soon found the cinema a popular choice of amusement. Once inside it was like being home, virtually everything on the silver screen was American in content.

The cinema was the ideal medium for both sides. Cost-effective and secluded, it offered another world. The war could be forgotten for a couple of hours. It was the inevitable choice for the first date. Starting in the front stalls, the couples would move further to the rear of the theatre with each visit. It was the best non-medicinal relief for the pressures of the times.

In contrast to the passé appearance of most Australian cities and the obvious lack of modern facilities, the picture theatres were state of the art in every aspect.

There were beautiful cinemas in Australia during the war — genuine picture palaces. The big cities had about six main cinemas: the Hoyts, the Regents and the Metros. Some could seat as many as 2000 patrons and at the weekend very few displayed an empty seat. In Melbourne there was the Capitol theatre, Perth was proud of the Ambassadors, and the Wintergarden in Brisbane was palatial, regal and resplendent.[10] The Regent in Melbourne was fantastic with staircases, Gothic foyers, porcelain ceilings, domes and chandeliers. There was a cloakroom, and bowls with fresh flowers everywhere.[11] Most of the Americans had never seen anything like it. You would have to check your atlas to make sure that this was still Australia. Once inside, the Yank could see a microcosm of Australian culture. The confectionery counter provided Fantales, Jaffas and Minties, while the affluent might share a box of Old Gold chocolates. Flavoured cold water drinks washed down the popcorn. A grand piano played in the foyer and a large photograph of the King was always prominent.[12]

Now that the men were off to war, the ushers were replaced by usherettes. Some big city cinemas had a dozen of them.[13] Before the screening, an organ would rise from the depths of the grander cinemas and entertain the audience with music from the feature. The program always commenced with a salute to the King — and later, to Uncle Sam. Then came heroic, sanitised war news in newsreels from Movietone and Cinesound.

The features were predominantly American productions. Although Australia was an early motion picture pioneer, the Depression and then the war had crippled the industry. The screening of an Australian feature-length film was rare by 1942. Popcorn fodder during the early war years included: *Northwest Passage, Mrs Miniver, Fantasia* and *Bambi*. It seemed that *Gone with the Wind* was always showing somewhere. Abbott and Costello and Andy Hardy knew no cultural division. *Bambi* was the big Walt Disney film during the war. At the Brisbane Wintergarden, the patrons were deadly silent as the baby deer cried for it's mother. 'Where's my mommy! I want my mommy! During the poignant silence that followed, a booming voice of a Digger came from the back of the stalls: 'She's gone out with a bloody Yank!'[14]

Other, less salubrious options for cinema showings could include a shed with a projector, or something quickly improvised in an outdoor camp. There was no shortage of audiences for these impromptu premieres. On many occasions there would be far too many men wanting to see the film, so rather than miss out it was only a minor inconvenience to watch the film from behind the screen. It may have been back-to-front — so what — it was better than nothing.

The middle option was the suburban cinema. Most cities had dozens of them and virtually every country town, large or small, had at least one picture theatre. Conditions varied, but most earned the title of flea pits.

In Queensland, most of the seats were canvas strapped to wooden beams. The curtains creaked; the aged screens often had stitched portions. Once inside you could gaze around and see the bare rafters. Holes in the roof were noticeable — even more so when it rained. The corrugated-iron roofs were a popular target for delinquents throwing objects that sent shock waves through the acoustically unfriendly interior. The uncovered sloping floors were ideal for the cacophony of empty pop bottles or candy Jaffas rolling toward the screen — invariably at a quiet emotional moment during the feature. Commotions were common and torches would flash in the isles and behind the stalls as attendants kept the peace.

The old picture theatres may have been basic, but they had character. Two features were shown and there were serials, cartoons, shorts, trailers — plenty of entertainment. Yanks soon adapted to the atmosphere. The informality, dimly lit areas and the canvas seats soon became their domain, and it was easy to take booze in. The movies were never first release; many of the guys had seen them back in the States — *Mutiny on the Bounty, San Francisco, Angels with Dirty Faces* and *Broadway Melody* or something or other. The supporting fare was pretty bad, with any amount of low budget programmes: westerns, *Blondie*, the Pete Smith one-reelers, *Our Gang*; some of the theatres were still showing Laurel and Hardy silent shorts. Later in the war, Yanks would watch Frank Capra's 'Why We Fight' series — perhaps in an attempt to understand why they were sitting in an Australian picture theatre watching an American propaganda film.

Australian films were on the way out as the Yanks came in. *Dad Rudd M.P.*, the latest Dad and Dave feature, amused the Yanks. The Rudds reminded the boys of Ma and Pa Kettle. Those who saw Charles Chauvel's *Forty Thousand Horsemen* not only got to see a superior film, but were also given an excellent insight into the unique character and qualities of the Australian soldier.

Transport was a major problem when seeking entertainment in the suburban areas and many a night was rounded off with a long walk back to base — longer still if you went in the wrong direction. So what? At least it was something to do.[15]

With the relaxed restrictions on entertainment and the hospitality industry, commerce started to cash in on the affluent visitors. Sodas, malts, hamburgers and of course the fuel for the American war machine, Coca-Cola, were quickly added to the menus. Facilities cashed in as well: The Dugout, in Collins Street, Melbourne, offered something for everyone: 'Good Eats! Good Band! Good Entertainment! Hot & Cold Showers, Barber's Shop! Writing & Reading Room.'[16] Dancing partners were provided and there was a shoe-shine facility, obviously designed for the only Allied soldier who could afford such a luxury, or who had shoe leather worthy of the treatment.

There were dozens of such establishments during the war often open daily — from 9.30 am to 11 pm, including Sundays. Most enjoyed regular patronage and most were quick to promote the appropriate activity for the Yanks. In Townsville they had the Americans covered. In March–April 1942 three dance venues offered the following: 'A District Waltz Contest', 'Jazz and Old Time' and 'A Complete Evening of Jazz'.[17]

The dance hall was an excellent entertainment and introduction option. Many new venues opened and many existing ones were rejuvenated. The Coconut Grove, Palm Court, Cabarita, Tivoli and others were familiar haunts. There was a Trocadero in Brisbane, Sydney and Melbourne. Each had an orchestra, a dance floor and the appropriate ambience. The Brisbane Troc could hold 2000 dancers.

The Australian dance bands were first-rate. Raised on a generation of seminal American jazz and pop records, the musos assimilated the influence while adding local touches.

Abe Romain had a top notch orchestra at the Sydney Trocadero. Frank Coughlan had the baton at the Melbourne Troc, while Billo Smith was the leader for the Brisbane Trocadero. Smith had been in Brisbane since 1925. He had served in the First AIF, having part of his face shot off in the process. He played excellent reeds — albeit out of the corner of his mouth.[18]

The Swing Era was in full swing. The influence of predominantly black music on local musicians and their followers had always been frowned upon by moralists and reactionaries. Now with the halls and clubs jumpin' and the jukebox increasingly prominent, the devil's music was everywhere. Some moral guardians recognised the dangers. According to Professor B.B. de Looze, 'The barbarous nature of their music only dragged the white race down to their level', while the Communist Party decreed, 'This music is a protest against industrialisation and the Bourgeois morality'.[19] Such varied concerns were compounded when the Yanks accelerated the activity. Fear set in when the flower of Australia's youth indulged in the erotic and vulgar dancing the music inspired. The fear turned to panic when the devil's messengers — the black American GIs — arrived on Australian docks.

The dancing was considered as dangerous to youth as the music. The Lindy-hop, Suzy Q, truckin', shaggin' and other jive variations horrified the senior generation raised on waltzes, quiksteps, foxtrots and other sedate forms. The 'No Jitterbugging' signs were as ubiquitous as the 'House Full' signs but no-one took any notice. The pop music of the early '40s was jazz-influenced quality material. Popular music was good and good music was popular.

Artie Shaw's recording of 'Frenesi' was a gigantic hit, with copies in every one of the 400 000 jukeboxes in the United States.[20] The most troubled time in modern history inspired the most romantic music. Also in the jukeboxes were romantic laments. Tommy Dorsey's 'I'll Never Smile Again' featured the Pied Pipers and a razor-thin Italian with a fat voice called Frank Sinatra. Jimmy Dorsey played 'Maria Elena' while his baritone crooner Bob Eberly swooned the lyric and Harry James and Helen Forrest told everyone that 'I Don't Want to Walk Without You'. Glenn Miller catered for the sweet and swing fans with 'Adios', 'Stardust', 'Tuxedo Junction', 'Elmer's Tune' and every band was playing 'In the Mood' — the anthem of the Swing Era. Then there were the geographical hits like 'Chattanooga Choo Choo', 'Kalamazoo', 'Deep in the Heart of Texas', 'Just a Little Bit South of North Carolina', 'Georgia on My Mind', 'Manhattan Serenade' and 'San Antonio Rose'.

The Yanks might never have seen a white Christmas down-under, but they had the Crosby record, which was breaking everybody's heart. There were the sleep songs: 'I Can Dream Can't I?', 'I Couldn't Sleep a Wink Last Night', 'I Had the Craziest Dream', 'A Million Dreams Ago' and 'Dream'. Woody Herman's 'Woodchoppers Ball', Benny Goodman's 'Why Don't You Do Right?' and Charlie Barnet's 'Cherokee' were musical folklore. Everybody was beating, daddy, eight to the bar and not sitting under the apple tree with anybody else but him or her.[21] Even some of the old songs were coming back, ancient ones like 'For Me and My Gal', 'Oh Johnny, Oh Johnny, Oh!' and 'Put Your Arms Around Me, Honey'.

There was also plenty of junk. The popularity of Orrin Tucker, Kay Kyser, Horace Heidt, Bob Wills, Sammy Kaye, Dick Todd and Kenny Baker never survived the war. Squares listened to Larry Clinton and Sammy Kaye while the mainstream followed Glenn Miller, Benny Goodman, the Dorsey Brothers, Artie Shaw and Bob Crosby. Swingers and hipsters were listening to Duke Ellington's 'Cottontail', Count Basie's 'Tickle Toe' and Lionel Hampton's

'Flying Home'. Bing Crosby's popularity was indestructible and the Andrews Sisters were everybody's relatives.[22]

As they had been with the cinema, Australians were bred on American music. The local product had yet to find an identity and, like the film industry, it was in hibernation. Record companies and subsidiaries were pressing the American releases. Deccas, Columbias and HMVs cost four bob — almost an average day's pay. The Regal Zonophone cost a more palatable 2s 6d.[23]

Orchestras at dances, restaurants and nightclubs played what stock arrangements were available of big-band standards. Arrangers with good ears earned a small fortune transcribing charts from the original records. Most Yanks, like the Aussies, knew the music only through the medium of the recordings, but many of the guys from the big cities of New York, Chicago, San Francisco and Los Angeles had seen and heard the bands live. In addition to the inevitable homesickness, many of them also heard of their social and musical scene back home slipping away. The story was that the Glenn Miller band has broken up in the States and that Miller had joined the army. The word came through that Bunny Berigan had died in New York.

The Trocaderos might not be the Pennsylvania Hotel, the Paramount Theatre or the Glen Island Casino, but they could have been worse. Ask the men who were stationed in New Guinea, New Caledonia, Esperitu Santo or the Solomons.

Things were changing. The Armed Forces Radio Service bought the major networks to the Yanks. V-mail brought letters and V-discs the record industry. There was to be more. The United States always had a big heart for its servicemen and resources to boot. Shortly after Pearl Harbor, an organisation was formed that would supply celebrity entertainment for troops in the war zones. The United Services Organisation (USO) was inaugurated in January 1942. Two weeks later, Al Jolson was touring camps in the southern states. In June, he was in the Aleutians. Others were to follow.[24]

The USO also provided personalities for the South-West Pacific area and Australia. In November 1943 Gary Cooper was smiling, waving, singing 'Pistol Packin' Mama' and shaking hands at camps, bases and Red Cross centres. Cooper also indulged in public relations, appearing in posh hotels. Australians saw him too. They had heard of him of course; he was the Westerner who was winning World War I in *Sergeant York*, which was still in release. The Brisbane *Courier-Mail* sent an awe-struck staffer to talk to Cooper at Lennons — the hotel that also housed the MacArthur family. 'He is much more handsome off screen,' exhorted Nancy Maxwell. 'He has so much style, even drinking a cup of coffee.' In regard to Cooper's travelling companions, minor starlets Phyllis Brooks and Una Merkel, Ms Maxwell was more reserved: 'they wore simple dresses and no jewellery'.[25]

A month later another celluloid hero arrived. John Wayne arrived in uniform. Had he enlisted? No way. The closest the Duke ever got to a uniform was from the rack of the studio wardrobe department. Still, he was here and he could shake hands with the best of them. Australians knew him as the man who was winning World War II with *Flying Tigers*.

Wayne was accompanied by the usual duo of Hollywood glamour girls one of whom was Carole Landis. Wayne and his entourage toured New Guinea, talking to guys in hospitals while wearing a Colt .45 automatic on his hip. During the long nights he would sit with them, telling stories and ribald jokes and savouring their potent jungle juice brews. But he was soon to return home. The 'reel' world needed him to for his next celluloid battle called *Back to Bataan*.[26]

Joe E. Brown also came to Australia. His son, Don, was due to be posted to Australia but was killed in an air crash shortly before his departure. Don's father came instead and all of the boys became his sons. Jack Benny arrived with a star troupe which included harmonica virtuoso Larry Adler, the ubiquitous Carole Landis and Martha Tilton — a girl who had sung with Benny Goodman back in the States.

With his patter and violin playing, Benny was popular with the guys but he didn't have to follow Carole Landis, who walked on stage with a flimsy brassiere. At the sight of her formidable chest assets, the guys yelled and clapped approval, even more when she bowed. Adler had to follow her with his harmonica. 'Hey you guys!' he yelled. 'Wait a minute. What's the matter? Haven't you guys seen a mouth organ player before?'[27] Bob Hope started his road to war with a trip to the South-West theatre. Francis Langford was the vocal and visual asset. Jerry Colonna was there to taunt Hope — just like he did back home on Hope's radio programs.

The least glamorous but most talented femme celebrity to visit was Eleanor Roosevelt. Touring the continent in late 1943, she inspired audiences with her stirring oratory and pledges. Mrs Roosevelt sent copy back to the States for her popular syndicated newspaper column. The First Lady, like many others, had come under the spell of MacArthur and she concluded one of her columns: 'The Australians are proud to have their men serve under him and they feel happy in their cooperation'.

There were also detailed accounts of the First Lady doing battle with the country's mosquitoes, as Australian as the kangaroo:

This is the first place where we have met with any mosquitoes, but here I was introduced to a bomb used to drive them away. My net was carefully let down around my bed, so I would be sure not to take any mosquitoes with me.[28]

There were Aussie show troupes as well. The many groups of 1st Australian Entertainment Unit gave more than 12 000 performances to millions of servicemen and nationals of all countries. There was something for everybody: musicians, dancers, comedians, singers, jugglers, acrobats and specialty acts of all types. There was another splendid unit which toured as the All in Fun (AIF) Army Revue. The organisation consisted of a large orchestra led by Wally Portingale, comedy by Rex 'Wacka' Dawe and a variety of acts including vocalists, acrobats, jugglers and female impersonators. All in Fun travelled over 50 000 miles during the war, from the Middle East to New Guinea.[29] There were other units like the Sons o' Guns, Waratahs, Kookaroos and the Tasmaniacs, which played first-class big-band jazz.[30]

The war produced the greatest mobilisation of Australian show business in history. Soon performers became soldiers in greasepaint. Amongst them were Gladys Moncrieff, Bebe Scott, George Wallace, Michael Pate, Jenny Howard and Colin Croft. Americans enjoyed the Australian talent as well. There was even a joint Australian and American entertainment unit called the 50–50 Show.[31]

The Trocadero in Sydney, as in the other states, was a busy and favourite haunt for men in uniform. Abe Romain, who led the band, knew the music as well as any of the Yanks. A gifted reed player, he was a pioneer in Australian jazz, making his recording debut on tenor sax with Al Hammett's Ambassadors Orchestra in Sydney in 1926. This was well before most of the current American swing stars had made their first recordings. Romain had also played with Louis Armstrong in Europe before the war.[32] He enjoyed the Yank audiences and was happy for the odd one to sit in and play — but no more. If there was anything that frustrated Abe, it was the Yanks who'd tell tales of playing with Dorsey, Miller or Goodman back in the States. Or the ones who claimed to have written 'Jersey Bounce' or 'A String of Pearls'. One even insisted that his Father had discovered jazz. Another thing that got to the Australians was the number of Americans who asked to sit in but could not cut the charts or solo. Abe had been embarrassed more than once.

But Abe was soon wise to them. In front of the band, with his clarinet under his arm, he was a purposeful, dominating figure. He barely noticed the American sailor who waited between sets and walked up to him one night. 'Abe, do you mind if I sit in with the band?' asked the sailor, who held an instrument case in his right hand. This is another one, thought Abe.

'What instrument do you play, mate?' he asked. 'It looks like you play a horn.'

'Yeah, I play trumpet'.

'Have you played with a band before?'

'Back in the States, I played with some'.

'Anyone we know?' said Abe, turning and smiling to the band.

'Let's see,' said the American. 'I've worked with Les Brown, Glenn Miller and Bob Crosby.'

'You left out Benny Goodman,' said Abe mockingly.

'I haven't played with Benny, but I was with Artie Shaw for two years.'

'Yeah? You, mate, and half of the other bloody Yanks in this country,' said the band leader. 'Look, we're sorta booked up at the moment- sorry mate.'

Abe would have been totally embarrassed had someone from the band not recognised the American as John Best — one of the finest and most reliable section trumpet players in the business. Abe called him back, apologised and shook his hand before introducing him to the members in the band. Later, Best was the centre of attention as the musicians asked him numerous questions about his associations and records he had made. Best told the musicians that was currently assigned to the United States Navy Band 501, but was in Australia on leave. The band was at present in New Zealand, working its way to Australia. It included a lot of great jazz musicians and the leader was Chief Petty Officer Artie Shaw.[33]

It did not take long for the news to get around the Australian musical scene. The brilliant, feisty enigmatic Shaw had enlisted and put his band on two weeks notice the minute he heard the news about Pearl Harbor.

A virtuoso clarinet player, Shaw had developed an incomparable style of playing and his various orchestras were amongst the most musical and creative of the era. In 1940, at Oglethorpe College in Atlanta, a vault called *The Crypt of Civilisation* was sealed under the college campus. Scheduled to be opened in 8113 AD, the crypt contained essential artefacts of America, circa 1940, including newsreels, photographs, literature, a device to teach English, a set of Lincoln Logs, a quart of beer and a selection of Artie Shaw recordings.[34]

While at boot camp in Rhode Island, Shaw believed that his services could be utilised in a more creative capacity. He requested a meeting with Admiral Forrestal. 'If I was leading a band for the amount of time that I have been in the Navy,' Shaw told the admiral, 'I would have earned enough money to build the navy a battleship.' Soon Shaw was forming a special navy orchestra of hand picked musicians who were being drafted into the service, amongst them Claude Thornhill, Sam Donahue, Dave Tough, Max Kaminsky and John Best. The band was designated Navy Band 501. Enlisted men called it the Rangers. The Rangers were billeted at Pearl Harbor for six months before Shaw sought permission to visit American personnel in the Pacific war zones.

Leaving the comparative comfort of the Halekulani Hotel and the Breakers Ballroom, the Rangers endured the stench and filth of Guadalcanal island where the 1st Marine Division and army units had driven the Japanese from the island. They played in a clearing in the jungle. A few planks and drums comprised the stage. There was seldom any PA or amplification for such concerts; jungle rot was a constant problem with the guitar and bass violin; woodwinds swelled with the heat; pads often dropped out of the reed instruments; sweat dropped on to the sheet music and many instruments were held together by rubber bands. Harold Wax played a piano accordion in the band, genuine pianos being at a premium in the Pacific.

No musicians played under worse conditions, but there was solace in the genuine appreciation of the uniformed men who heard the band, be they a division, a ship's company, or just a handful of men in an isolated posting.

After a stay in New Zealand, the Rangers arrived in Brisbane on 3 September 1943. The men — like their instruments — were in poor condition, but at least in Australia there were facilities and the opportunity to rest. The Artie Shaw Navy Band 501 performed in concert at the Brisbane City Hall on 9 September and then travelled to Sydney where Shaw played a concert mainly for American service personnel at the Trocadero. The Troc could hold 2000, but by the time the concert started there were 5000 lined up in streets around the city waiting to get in. The band started to play 'Nightmare' as the crowd was allowed to enter — two or three at a time. 'Jungle Drums' was next and then 'Everything is Jumpin', which aptly described the Troc. The crowd cheered as they recognised the introduction to 'Begin the Beguine', which had been Shaw's first hit record.

Stories of how non-combatant personnel managed to get in to hear the band are legion. Especially the local musicians. Duke Farrell begged an American WAAC to escort him in. Arthur Christian put on his navy cadet uniform and walked in. Fifteen-year-old Don Burrows gave up trying and listened from an alleyway, but nothing was going to stop Wally Norman. No sooner had the band started to play than he went to work on the lock at the tradesman's entrance of the Troc with a pair of bolt cutters.

Inside, nobody danced — they just listened. The band in navy attire was sitting under the double-eagle banner and draped American ensigns. Artie Shaw was on the music stands; he was also out front playing clarinet, resplendent in his petty officer's uniform. Outside, the crowd became impatient, but there was no more room. Some walked away; others sat on the footpath, smoking and listening. Shaw's mellow clarinet on 'Stardust' contrasted with the austere, bleak, brownout atmosphere outside. Men forgot for a moment where they were and why. 'It Had to Be You', 'Non Stop Flight', 'Moonglow' and, before long, 'Nightmare' — this time in closing.

The band toured north Queensland, playing in Cairns, Townsville and Rockhampton. Fifty years later Shaw had vivid recollections of his Australian visit: 'Cairns and Mackay were only little villages then. In Brisbane I saw dirt roads and horses and carts. We stayed there a few days. I remember walking and sitting on the sidewalk — there was nothing to do.'

This was the first major international musical attraction to perform in Australia and Shaw has the distinction of being the first pop music star to tour the country. On 26 October 1943 the Shaw band left Brisbane for San Francisco, arriving there on 11 November.[35]

There were many service bands active in Australia during the war, but Navy Band 501 was the one best remembered and most revered. In fact it was one of Shaw's greatest triumphs, both patriotically and musically. It is now confined to the history books, however, for it was never recorded; no V-discs, no transcriptions — nothing. Said Shaw: 'I led that band and I tell you those guys were something else. By the time we got to Australia we were at the end of our tether. Dave Tough did not live long after the war, nor did some of the others.'[36]

Jazz and dance music were not the only art forms to be conveyed by American performers. The world of classical music was buoyed by a special appearance by American conductor, Eugene Ormandy, in 1944. The former Hungarian prodigy was a professor of music at seventeen and in the early '20s emigrated to the United States. At the time of his Australian visit Ormandy was the conductor of the Philadelphia Orchestra.[37]

Ten days before the concert the *Sun News-Pictorial* reported a recently formed organisation called the Encouragement of Art Movement. The Lord Mayor of Melbourne, Mr Nettlefold, was in attendance as the objectives of the movement were highlighted: 'To promote and encourage all creative cultural activities in factories, offices, homes, and camps'. Mr A.R. McClintock told the audience in Kelvin Hall: 'There is a definite need to raise the cultural level of Australians, who are generally backward in the arts'.[38]

The new organisation would have been comforted by the support given to Eugene Ormandy's concert with the Melbourne Symphony

Orchestra at the Melbourne Town Hall on 23 July. Only 2000 of an estimated 4000 thousand music lovers managed to be admitted for the once only performance.[39]

American and Australian military units had a considerable number of creative artists active in all fields. The literary journal *Meanjin*, edited by Clem Christesen, was an excellent medium for poetic and literate Americans.[40] Leon Black produced many American flavoured dramas at the Brisbane Repertory Theatre.

There were American theatre attractions in most states during the war, amongst them *The Man Who Came to Dinner* and *My Sister Eileen*. Those who enjoyed less formal musical culture could see American vaudevillian Will Mahoney, who enjoyed the modest billing 'The Greatest Comedian Of All'. His wife, the attractive Evie Hayes, was billed as 'The Californian Songbird'. The eccentric and talented Mahoney knew the tastes of the American visitors well. The American-style revues *Ridin' High, All in Favour* and *Good News Ahead* and regular vaudeville shows resulted in Mahoney, Hayes and comedian Bob Geraghty becoming resident talent at Brisbane's Cremorne Theatre for most of the war.[41]

Another excellent Allied cooperative was the Unique Radio Show, which was produced by the members of the US Army. The program was extremely popular and was billed as: 'A fast moving full hour program — the first of its kind broadcast in Australia — provided entirely by artists drawn from the American fighting forces in Australia'.[42] Although acetates of this program appear to be lost, scripts held in the Australian Archives suggest that this excellent program was commendable for its variety and scope, and was almost totally devoid of propaganda. The emphasis was on reflecting the culture and attitude of the typical American, rather than the typical American fighting man.

The fuel for wartime entertainment was booze. Obtaining liquor during the war was a war within a war. Beer was relatively common, but there was never enough, and hard liquor was tough to get. Bourbon was the Holy Grail brew. Most GIs were given a ration.

Officers always got the best of it and glamour warriors like submariners and air crews received extra rations. Isolated units like the 32nd Division, whose base was in the bush, 60 kilometres south of Brisbane, were rationed three bottles of beer a week. Logistics and excessive usage always affected rationing. Sometimes the Dogface (soldier) would miss out. Before long, anything was a bonus.[43]

Queues would form before the pubs opened. Stocks would soon vanish. Licensing laws and trading hours were tested. In July 1942, the *Herald* in Melbourne told of liquor abuses:

Some of the revelations of flagrant and open violation of the Licensing Act have been astonishing and disgusting. The public will want to know why such conditions have been tolerated if those in authority were aware of them; or, alternatively, why they were unknown to the authorities whose business it is to police the licensing laws.[44]

Nine days later the *Herald* was more specific, claiming that hotel liquor conditions in Melbourne were worse than in any of the capital cities. The major problems were:

Excessive sales of bottle beer and spirits. After-hours trading. Sale of whisky in bottles over the counter by barmen to American soldiers at grotesquely inflated prices. Peddling of liquor by taxi drivers among Australian and US soldiers and civilians.[45]

There was also alarm concerning 'mixed drinking in hotel lounges and consumption of liquor in doorways, back lanes and park lands'. The paper noted that a trainload of troops returning to base had 200 bottles of whisky ready to combat the boredom. A publican was known to sell bottled beer at the outrageous price of two bob a bottle, but the purchaser then retailed the grog at a sly groggery at 2s 6d per. Welfare workers who dispensed coffee to Allied soldiers at night spoke of witnessing shocking behaviour. Spencer Street was: 'full of soldiers and girls kissing in a wrestling hold in the middle of the pavement, prolonged and unashamed'.

Lord Mayor, Sir Frank Beaurepaire: 'What I saw in the city during Saturday and Sunday nights presents a very definite problem and it gave me and the Lady Mayoress who was with me on Sunday night, much food for thought'.[46]

In addition, the legacy of Eddie Leonski was still being felt. It was revealed that the 'Brownout Strangler' had been seen drinking up to 30 beers a night and was a good customer in many hotels. It was also revealed that one of his unfortunate victims, Mrs Pauline Thompson, was seen drinking in mixed company in a bar — and on a Sunday night.[47] The Women's Employment Board reluctantly sanctioned the use of female bar attendants in hotels. There was little choice with the manpower shortages. However the board did receive the concession that barmaids should not be under thirty.[48] Church representatives and the temperance organisations massed forces and 90 000 Victorian citizens signed a petition to tighten the liquor laws. Premier Dunstan was forced into action. Soon there were new restrictions:

Effective: July 30 1942.
The consumption of liquor will be limited to private homes and hotel premises. It will be an offence for liquor to be drunk in a hotel after 8 pm.

It will be unlawful to serve liquor on any licensed premises, to any female under 21, and no liquor may be sold for drinking on premises, or for removal, to any male under 18 or to any female under 21.[49]

Other states followed suit. The restrictions had an immediate effect: the prices went up and the quality went down.

In the boom years, 25 percent of all booze sold came from the black market or grog shops. Scotch whisky sold for £6. Australian whisky sold for £2 10s. Beer peaked at four bob a bottle. Not to be outdone, home-brew merchants competed for market share. Crude concoctions were everywhere. Most whisky was watered down. Whisky mixed with milk was called Moose Milk. Submariners sometimes drank a watered-down brew made from liquid alcohol. Mixed, this was potent enough, but drinking it straight was to risk an internal Armageddon. Medical staff at the Royal Brisbane Hospital admitted two Americans suffering the effects of drinking embalming fluid.[50]

Prostitution was rampant during the war. The media and authorities generally ignored the practice, thereby giving tacit approval both to the service and to subsequent growth in the industry. In early 1942, the *Herald* suggested that the percentage of sexual offences in relation to other crimes was the highest for over 30 years. The factors suggested were war strain, lack of parental control and diminishing moral values. The reality was that the sex industry at that time had yet to cater for the dynamic influx of servicemen of all nationalities. Like so many industries and commodities during the early war years, prostitution was overwhelmed by the increased demand.[51]

All the cities had many brothels — whorehouses, cathouses, or whatever the vernacular. It was easy to find them in rural and isolated areas. Easy access and proximity to camps and bases were the geographical keys. Brisbane was the garrison fort of the country, with tens of thousands of men stationed there at the peak of the occupation. Twenty houses of sin were situated near or in the city centre.

A three-minute encounter was a quid. Outside the Polynesian Playground, Golden Hands or the Mandalay, lines formed. Impatient or busy clients fretted at the end of long queues.

Propositions were common:

'Say, buddy, I'll give you two quid for your spot.'

'Get lost!'

'Three quid.'

'Shove off!'

'Look, I'll make it four quid.'

'Let's see the dough.'

Some Yanks and Diggers soon profited by such a routine, waiting in line, selling their spot and quickly retiring to the nearest pub.

Officers took advantage of prostitutes also, but generally with more discretion. An attractive woman in a hotel foyer displaying a red handbag was usually signalling her availability.

Units arriving or departing saw the need for a first or last fling with a sheila or broad. Many did not bother to join queues. Extravagant offers often had prostitutes performing night and day, indoors or out. The war was a sexual rush hour, 24 hours a day.[52]

The working girls came from all backgrounds. Most were young. Some had men overseas, some were married, most were single. Others had children to support. Many saw the opportunity to make money. A few were doing it for nothing before, but now it was worth something. A few girls were already in the industry, but during the war most of the girls were new to the oldest profession. The financial rewards were considerable. Hard working girls could earn as much as a £100 a week. One girl earned almost £4000 in a year, enough for a new home and a new life.

The dangers were soon obvious, for once 'V' did not stand for victory. Venereal diseases were common. The Americans set up prophylactic clinics. Enlisted men also had prophylaxis kits, consisting of a condom and anti-VD ointments.

Inspection for the clap was called a 'shortarm parade' and confirmation after the inspection was as feared as being 'flak happy'. The VD infection rate for the first three months of 1943 was 41 per cent higher than in 1942. The federal government supplied £25 000 to the Australian Society for Eradication of Venereal Disease. Culpability in transmitting this disease caused much furore between women's organisations and the American military. Mr Fitzpatrick, from the New South Wales Community Hospital, was candid and explicit: American authorities asserted that every US soldier who landed in Australia was free from infection, and it was foolish to pretend that the men who were now suffering from VD were not infected by Australian women.[53]

However, it was naive to believe that the American military had infection-free servicemen. Early in the selective service period, inductees were rejected if they tested positive to venereal disease. But from March 1942 some infected men were allowed to serve their country. From December 1942, VD carriers were also inducted. These men were called 'venereals' and were usually cured by doses of sulfa and penicillin. As a preventative measure, graphic motion pictures were shown to trainees warning of the perils of indiscreet and unprotected sex. A young actor called Ronald Reagan was employed to convey the dangers of fraternisation.

Neither Mr Fitzpatrick nor anyone else in Australia knew that while the prevalence of syphilis with white American draftees was 17 per 1000; the rate for blacks was 252 per 1000.[54]

The President of the Feminists' Club, Mrs Cameron, responded to Fitzpatrick's remarks by observing that:

The responsibility for the spread of VD rested on both parties. It is objectionable to infer that there was not a moral woman left in Australia.

We must inculcate into the minds of all men in uniform that Australian women are the wives, sweethearts and sisters of Australians, and they should be treated as they would like their womenfolk back home treated.[55]

A survey of 400 men by the Director-General of Social Hygiene concluded that 77 per cent of men infected with gonorrhoea were single. Only 16 per cent of them had been infected by prostitutes. The figures suggest how great was the shortage of professional women. Of the married men surveyed, a disturbing statistic suggested that 36 per cent were infected by their wives.[56] Where the spouse received the dose was doubtless a volatile domestic issue.

Emotional and physical scars were common. Contraception was still regarded as something not quite respectable, as a result of which there were few preventative measures. Australia was an ultra-conservative society. There was only two birth control clinics in the entire country. Pregnancies were unavoidable. Abortions were so common that botched operations were second only to road accidents as a cause of death amongst young women.

Brisbane was not the only centre in need of womanpower. The call also went out from Mount Isa but the response was poor. No working girl in her right mind would leave the trade in the big cities. Initially, black brothels were also created. However segregation vanished as women became indifferent to the race of their clients. In fact many women liked the black visitors. They paid more, were courteous and many were majestic in physical stature.[57]

Military high command tolerated prostitution, regarding it as a regrettably essential service. Admiral Lockwood, a submariner, commented: 'The "flesh pots" were great for morale and it is that, not morals, that I am interested in'. Writing about a Townsville brothel, a unit historian stated: 'The place did such a tremendous volume of business and proved so satisfactory that such an arrangement might contribute to the efficiency of the fighting forces, if made available to all'.

The innumerable scuffles, fist fights, bashings, brawls and other problems stemming from the ancillary aspects of the profession were overshadowed by what was indisputably an invaluable contribution to the war effort.

Although sordid activities and intemperate behaviour involved many Americans, there were of course many thousands of Yanks who never went near a cathouse, seldom drank, rarely went to the movies, did not venture far from base, saw no movie stars and never went to an Artie Shaw concert. In September 1942, when the United States Army conducted a survey detailing off-duty activity for servicemen posted overseas, half of the men stated that writing home was their preferred activity. It was clear that home life was the thing that most men missed, and the most difficult thing to replace.[58]

Inviting a Yank home became a popular pastime, and for the visitors it was a welcome relief from military and emotional pressures. A boy from Birmingham, Alabama, visited a family in Mount Isa Queensland. Another from Denver, Colorado, stayed with someone in Fremantle, Western Australia. Chicago and Brisbane, New York and Cloncurry, Norfolk and Rockhampton. The motives for the peaceful home invasion prompted a cautionary statement from the Rev. H.L. Hawkins, the officer in charge of the Hospitality Bureau:

> Many people want to get more out of the hospitality than they are prepared to put in to it. A woman telephoned me the other day and asked me to send out two Americans for the night to entertain her small children. Another asked if I could send out two handsome young Americans for the evening. They should not be engaged or married, as the woman had two pretty, eligible daughters ... troops must not be taken for granted or regarded as objects for charity.[59]

Usually, however, Hosts and visitors alike relished the congeniality and genuine warmth of the meetings. Yanks, immaculate in their uniforms, brought flowers and wine on their visits, tobacco, sometimes even nylons, and chocolate for the children. The grass would be cut. After enjoying cold beer from an ice-box and home-cooked meals served with the best china, the visitor would pass around photographs of his family and the girl back home. Framed mantelpiece photographs of a son overseas would be shown, along with portraits of relatives, or of Dad in the First AIF. Sometimes men cried and many visited again — next time with a buddy.

Norm and Edith Brown lived in Ipswich, Queensland. Their eldest daughter, Val, used to go by train to a weekly dance at the Redbank School of Arts. An American base was nearby and Val became good friends with Gerald Horne from New York City. Norm went to Redbank with Val one week and asked Gerald and two of his friends to come over for tea on Sunday night. Gerald and his buddies from Camp Freeman, at Inala, were not accustomed to visiting the homes of families like the Browns, but before long they got together regularly. Photographs of Gerald and Norm and others taken in the backyard show the water tank, fibro panels, house stilts and the outdoor dunny. Gerald and his buddies always enjoyed the visits. They were the only social occasions where their being black appeared to be of no consequence.

Gerald wrote home after the visits and his mother, Estella, wrote to the Browns to thank them. The Browns also visited Camp Freeman and enjoyed the iced coffee and spare ribs. On visits like these, tall tales were often told, impossible to verify and sometimes impossible to believe. But Gerald Horne was different. He often spoke about his kid sister back in the States. She was talented, she had sung with some name bands, and she had just written him to say that she had signed a motion picture contract with MGM. Her name was Lena, and Gerald was proud of her. Only the war could have provided the circumstances that drew the Browns and Gerald Horne together.[60]

In essence, it was not the big USO tours, pretty girls, movies, dances, alcohol or casual sex that made the war tolerable for the Americans. More rewarding was the contacts they made with the Australian people. It was here that the Yanks realised that they were not that different from them.

Entering the Aussies' world and bringing them a little of theirs, pointed to the irrelevance of so many cultural and social differences. Whether they spoke of a 'mate' or 'buddy', a 'sheila' or a 'dame', the two nations shared the same beliefs, had the same purpose, and were united against the same enemy. For thousands of Americans, contact with the Australian people gave them solace and comfort to help them through what lay ahead.

CHAPTER NINE

TAKING A CHANCE ON LOVE

Leslie Cottman had been in the navy for a year before the war started and he was 21 years old when he saw the Japanese devastate Pearl Harbor. He was no big city boy. He was born in a place called Ink in Polk County, west Arkansas, which few other than the 51 people who lived there had heard of. Les had to repeat the name often when people asked him where he was from, and he was always ready for the 'Do you write home often?' jokes.

Les was based at Pearl Harbor when the submarine tender *Fulton* berthed. He had always wanted to be a submariner and had passed his medical and physical examinations to become one. So when a chief from the *Fulton* asked if anyone on the base had any mechanical aptitude, Les quickly put his hand up. He was transferred to the *Fulton*, but this was the closest he ever got to the submarine service. He finished up working with coding equipment, which ultimately became one of the most valuable weapons of the war.

From Pearl Harbor, the *Fulton* arrived at Midway a little too late for the battle but in time to ferry survivors from the crippled aircraft carrier *Yorktown*. Midway became the home for the *Fulton* and her crew for four months until they received orders to proceed to the South-West Pacific. Nobody knew where they were going but the scuttlebutt was New Zealand or Australia. Their destination was confirmed when the paymaster announced the next pay would be in pounds, shillings and pence.

Les did not know much about Australia, but he had met some Aussies in Pearl when the boat they were on — 'The Empress of something or other' — came to transport non-combatants back to the States. He had gone to a bar with them where they exchanged rounds money, and addresses. Les remembered one saying, 'See ya later, mate. And if you're ever in Perth, give us a call.' The *Fulton* was a new ship, less than twelve months old and one of its roles was to look after the submarines from the more glamorous service. Tenders were vital to the submarine service, and other ships in the fleet also needed servicing. The tender was so versatile that it became known as the 'USS Can Do'. Wherever submarines went, the *Fulton* followed.

★　　★　　★

All off-duty ranks on the *Fulton* were topside in November 1942 as the pilot boat escorted them towards Brisbane, passing by Redcliffe, Scarborough, Woody Point and then into the mouth of the Brisbane River. They saw some houses built on stumps, with red roofs that looked like tin. 'It must be an institution or something,' somebody said.

Clusters of people on the river banks waved and cheered. The *Fulton* was a big ship and at 9700 tons and 520 feet overall, it was a difficult task to dock her in the narrows of the Brisbane River. The sailors on the *Fulton* found that they were based at a place called New Farm where there were two large buildings that looked like factories but were actually wool stores. Nobody on the base would ever get lost as the buildings loomed so large.

★　　★　　★

Like thousands of other young girls, for Yvonne Verrall the war meant boys in uniforms. Like her friends, her introduction to American men had been through Hollywood. In her eyes, America was Hollywood and Hollywood was America. Clark Gable was delicious and dazzling and Errol Flynn was daring and dashing.

In March 1941, Yvonne had been one of the quarter of a million Queenslanders who welcomed the American naval squadron to Brisbane. She was also one of the Wrens, a volunteer service whose main contribution to the war effort was in keeping its members busy. She wore the Wrens' uniform of blue tunic and white blouse on that day. There were thousands of other people in various uniforms, too, mostly American sailors, Marines and Aussies.

The welcome had been a spectacle that Yvonne would never forget — hundreds of Americans, all so young and handsome, tanned, all with perfect teeth and with uniforms that looked tailor-made. She had thrown streamers at them and cheered like everybody else. It was a thrilling time. The war still seemed far away.

Later, Yvonne actually met some of the Americans and giggled when they called her 'Ma'am'. She even asked some of them to autograph the sleeves of her blouse. But, like thousands of other girls, she hadn't had the opportunity to go to the City Hall for the big dance to welcome them. It was an 'invitation-only' affair and, anyway, her parents would not have allowed her to go. The Americans might have been dashing, but to many they were also dangerous — especially if you had a 17-year-old daughter who was your only child.

The squadron left the following day and nobody saw the Americans again for a while. But then, one day in August, there were two more American ships at the Hamilton wharf — cruisers, the *Northampton* and the *Salt Lake City*. There was no fanfare this time, and no marches, but there were plenty of sailors on liberty. Yvonne was a bit cheekier by now, and having said a few words to Yanks on their last visit she felt confident. Besides, she had recently turned eighteen.

'Hey, Mum, do you mind if four American sailors come over for tea tonight?' she asked. The question was academic, as she had already asked them.

Charles W. Dodge, Jr. was from Wisconsin, Chris Carveth from Connecticut, Rupert and Harold Kent from West Virginia, and all were from the *Salt Lake City*. They took the tram from New Farm to 134 Boundary Road, Rainworth.

Yvonne's dad, Frank, admired and respected servicemen, no

matter where they were from. He had been a soldier himself with
the First AIF and had fought at the Somme so it was no wonder
that the four American enjoyed their visit and were overwhelmed
by the Verralls' warmth — and their home cooking. The boys hired
a car and drove Yvonne and the family around. They went to a
zoo called 'Lone Pine' and saw Australian animals and reptiles.
Frank told the boys that there was a place called Lone Pine in the
Dardanelles and told them all about Gallipoli.

The *Salt Lake City* returned to Brisbane once or twice during
the next year. The Verralls always knew when she was about to
dock as one of the ship's four Kingfisher observation aircraft would
fly over the city beforehand, and this was the signal to dust the
house, put beer in the fridge and chop wood for the stove.

The ship's final visit was as melancholy as it was joyous. 'Things
are a little tense at the moment, what with the war in Europe and
things going on with the Japanese,' said Charles Dodge. 'We don't
know whether the ship will be back this way for a while.' They all
waited for the last tram and, with the Verralls in their front yard
to farewell them, the sailors boarded. As the tram grunted and
gonged into motion the four sailors, standing on the running board,
gave their Australian hosts three cheers and raised their caps in
the air. Nothing would be the same again. The sailors never
returned, but for the next 50 years, mail with a Wisconsin postmark
was often delivered to 134 Boundary Road Rainworth.

★　★　★

Yvonne enjoyed being in the Wrens as she was able to meet people
at the training and recreation room in Charlotte Street where naval
personnel of all nationalities visited. There was a dance floor, a
piano and kitchen facilities. The commandant of the Wrens, Mrs
J.L. Selwood, had great plans for the venue. She envisioned Wrens
teaching the visitors to dance and to play bridge, and an ambitious
long-term plan was the acquisition of a ping-pong table. It mightn't
have been the first place that someone with a 24-hour-pass would
seek, but it was always popular.

There were other interesting routines for the Wrens. Yvonne was in the motorboat squadron, and river cruises were used for teaching navigation skills and signalling. She learned semaphore and was very competent with the flags.

One morning in November 1942, Yvonne was on the *Marion*, a tiny craft carrying the Wrens on the river. They enjoyed cruising past New Farm because it was possible to get close to the subs. On this day there was a huge ship there as well — as big as anyone had ever seen on the river. As the *Marion* went past, there were the usual waves and whistles from the sailors.

June Henderson, Josie Hodgson and Iris Rankin waved back, but Yvonne took a flag in each hand and conveyed by semaphore: 'What is the name of your ship? What do you represent?'

Men on the ship waved and pointed and a sailor on the bridge replied in semaphore. Yvonne could see him and the flags clearly. 'We are the *Fulton,* a submarine tender. What is your phone number?'

The girls on the *Marion* giggled and then shrieked as Yvonne semaphored: 'My number is FM 4363'.

A few moments later came the reply: 'Thanks. I will give you a call tonight.'

★　★　★

Two hours later, Yvonne asked her mother, 'Mum, can I go and meet a sailor tonight?'

'What, a sailor? Who is it?'

'He's an American from a ship called the *Fulton*.'

'No, I don't think so, dear. You don't know anything about him.'

'But I've already arranged a place and time,' protested Yvonne.

Her father intervened. 'Look, dear, she'll have to go. You can't leave an American boy standing on the street by himself. It's not good manners. We can go along with her.'

Yvonne had arranged to meet at a carnival conducted by the Catholic Church in Fortitude Valley, only a few minutes from her home. As the meeting time approached she became very nervous.

She didn't even know the sailor's name, or what he looked like. This is probably not a very good idea, she thought.

When Yvonne arrived at the meeting place, there were plenty of people wandering around, but there was one sailor who looked like he was waiting for somebody. Their eyes met.

'Excuse me, Ma'am, are you Yvonne? My name is Charlie Payne.'

Yvonne was surprised. The man was at least in his mid-thirties and was a little short. But, wondering what she had got herself into, she held out her hand and took his.

The man spoke again. 'Let me introduce you to your signaller.'

Another man came out of the shadows and introduced himself. 'Hi, Ma'am, my name is Leslie Cottman and I am from Arkansas.'

This was a much younger man, taller, very well dressed and very handsome. Yvonne introduced herself, then turned to a group of people behind her. 'I would like you to meet my father. This is my mother and this is my cousin Vera.'

There followed a perfunctory chat, and then an invitation which would be mirrored by thousands of others as the war went on.

'How would you blokes like to come over for tea tomorrow?' asked Frank Verrall.

Les was on watch that day but agreed to go to tea a day later. Then he realised that he did not know when 'tea time' was, but he assumed that the afternoon was a likely time for Aussies to have a cuppa. If it was at night, he reasoned that they would call it supper, so he caught a tram and arrived a little before 2 pm.

The family was unprepared for him and Les was embarrassed, but it did not matter.

Meanwhile, Yvonne had gone to the city. However, she was anxious to be back in time for Leslie because she found herself interested in him. He was charming, attractive. Mum and Dad also liked the look of him, but when Yvonne arrived home at 5.30 there was no-one there. Wondering where everyone was, she heard laughter and singing coming from her cousin Vera's place next door. She hurried around and found her parents and crowds of other people holding hands and singing. She also saw Leslie playing Chinese checkers with Vera and jealously wondered what was going on. 'I saw him first, and, anyway, Vera is engaged!'

The Verralls were a tight-knit family and many of them, including Vera and her family, lived near Yvonne. Nobody was ever alone and this became a problem for Yvonne as she started wondering whether Leslie was coming to her home just for something to do and somewhere to go. Yvonne's questions were answered when, at Christmas 1942, and having known her for only six weeks, Les gave her a heart-shaped locket and kissed her for the first time.

Les Cottman now virtually became a member of the Verrall family. The New Farm submarine base was next to the tram terminus so it was easy for him to board the Riverview tram to travel to their home. Frank even told him that they'd leave a key for him in the front door.

On one early visit to the Verrall's, Les and a buddy decided to take some meat with them. It wasn't necessary but it made them feel better if they contributed something. They went to the convenience store next to the base, which sold just about everything but meat. The store had made a meagre profit before the Americans arrived, but it had become a thriving business, particularly as it stocked chocolate, ice-cream and preferred brands of tobacco. The owner told Les where he could find a butcher and on arriving at the shop Les asked for ten bob's worth of meat. 'Sort of mix it up,' he said when asked what cuts.

Les Cottman had learned a lot about Australia during the war, not the least being the value of the pound, so it was a good thing that he had brought a buddy along to help with the meat. The 'ten bob's worth' looked like it was a whole Texas steer and both men struggled to deliver it to the Verralls.

The ship's food was always edible, but the meals at the Verralls were something else. Les Cottman weighed twelve stone when the

Fulton berthed, but when it weighed anchor eleven months later he needed to have a new kit fitted to accommodate his fifteen stone frame.

The Verralls discovered Les was not just good company. He was also useful. Frank found him a pair of shorts and no job was too small or too large for him to tackle — the refrigerator, the radio, the roof awning...

Nor was Les the only serviceman who caught the New Farm tram to Boundary Road at Rainworth. Vera's house had a surrounding verandah which was used for sleeping during the hot Brisbane summers. It was not uncommon for someone to come home and find the verandah laden with American sailors or soldiers, sometimes even Australians. Some would be dressed in casual clothes, pyjamas, shorts and shirt, others in overalls. A glance at the clothes line revealed white, navy blue and khaki garments, and there were usually piles of clothes in the laundry waiting to be ironed.

The men brought gifts, usually flowers, to show their appreciation. Many brought letters and photographs to read and to show to the Verralls. The house became like a submarine rest house. It was not luxury, but Uncle Sam could never have bought the warmth and heart it offered. Before long Les was calling Yvonne's parents, Dad and Mum. His letters home were full of accounts of Brisbane and the people who were so kind and hospitable to him.

One night after an evening at the pictures, Les asked Yvonne to marry him and she said yes. Frank Verrall's only concern was that his daughter was so young, but it seemed that nothing would deter her or Les.

Frank relaxed somewhat when he realised that the couple were not rushing to the altar. The marriage process for an Australian citizen and an American serviceman was complicated and time-consuming. There were forms, discussions and requests, but Les coped with everything, including the comments from his ship-mates who told him that he was crazy, reminded him that there was a war on and suggested he should wait because he might forget about Yvonne after a while. The letters from home were anything but encouraging, but Les was not too worried about them as his family had not yet met Yvonne.

Applications for permission to marry were filled out. There was a multitude of counselling sessions, including a private audience for Les and Yvonne with the chaplain of the United States Seventh Fleet. The most crucial and difficult condition imposed on them was a compulsory waiting period of six months. It was thought that many a star-gazing romance would fail to survive this cooling-off period. Yvonne was asked a bewildering number of questions. Was she pregnant? Was she prepared to live in America? Did she know what it was like to be married to a sailor?

But then circumstances conspired to make sure that everything had to wait even longer. In October 1943, after eleven months at New Farm wharf, the USS *Fulton* with Les Cottman aboard left Brisbane for Milne Bay. This was the place where, in the previous year, Australian units had defeated Japanese land troops for the first time in the war. It was also a place of Spartan living conditions, remote, and very different from the settled conservatism of Brisbane.

The *Fulton* was needed to support the submarine fleet that had recently arrived in the area, and she stayed there for several months. The men had liberty but found that the amenities were limited. However, there was baseball and other sports, and there was much contact, usually friendly, with Aussies. Les enjoyed both the fishing and the friendly company of the native people. One of the other sailors from the *Fulton* collected butterflies and ended up with a magnificent collection. Another pastime was writing letters. It took a while for return mail to get through, but receiving a new letter made the long wait worthwhile.

On 17 March 1944, the *Fulton* left Milne Bay and headed to the submarine base at Fremantle, where Les was transferred to another tender, the USS *Griffin*. It stayed in Fremantle for some time, but as the submarine war against Japan began its push north it seemed likely that the *Griffin* would follow, even as far as the Philippines.

Meanwhile, nothing had changed between Les and Yvonne. If anything, their bond was stronger. Their letters proved that. A decision had to be made. They had not seen each other for nearly a year. Would Yvonne go to Fremantle to get married? She decided she would and her parents would go too. A decision was made to leave in September. The Verralls would fly to Melbourne and then complete the journey across the continent by train.

Almost from the start, things began to go wrong. Yvonne's parents were not allowed to travel with her as their daughter's marriage wasn't sufficient reason to give them a priority rating to travel. For the first time in her life, Yvonne left Brisbane — alone.

Her flight to Melbourne was interesting and a thrill. However, on arrival she discovered that the railway trip had been postponed for a week. What a disaster! She was faced with spending a week by herself in Melbourne and was also worried about her family and Leslie. Luckily, fortune sometimes favours the romantic and Yvonne met a fellow traveller from the plane who invited her to stay for the week. It was an invitation that she gratefully accepted.

Finally on the train, Yvonne found the trip was an adventure to remember. It was a troop train laden with Australian soldiers. The four-day trip seemed to take four years. The boys all wanted to talk to Yvonne, but there was plenty of 'Yank bashing' as well, so much so that, rather than tell the truth, Yvonne said she was going to Perth to visit family. During the journey westward she had her twentieth birthday.

Les was there to meet Yvonne at the station and was disappointed by the absence of her parents. He had a best man for the wedding from the ship's crew but there was no-one to stand at Yvonne's side. Les didn't know any women in Fremantle to ask to attend, but then remembered the Aussies from the *Empress* he met at that saloon in Pearl. He searched through his memory for the name and address of the sailor from Perth. The name was a funny one like Aussie, he remembered, similar to a band leader back in the States — Ossie Nelson. Finally, he remembered it was Ossie Smith and that he lived in Hatfield Street in Perth.

Les phoned, only to discover that Ossie was at sea, but his sister Doris who answered the phone accepted Les's invitation. So, everything was all set. Les was ready. All on the ship wished him well. One of the black kitchen staff gave him a present wrapped in cloth with instructions to open it only on the day of the wedding. On opening it, Les found a beautiful set of silverware which looked just like a set he had seen in the officers' mess.

Leslie Cottman and Yvonne Verrall were married in Fremantle on 4 September 1944. Representing the United States of America was Gideon Van Winkill Stivers from the *Griffin*; representing the Commonwealth of Australia was Doris Goodchild of Fremantle.

Les and Yvonne settled into married life in Fremantle for a time until, ironically, the *Griffin* was sent back to Brisbane and then to the Philippines.

For Yvonne, San Francisco became her destination. When the war ended she was one of 1200 wives who left on the *Mariposa* for the USA. The ship had brought American divisions to Australia in the early months of the war and now it was returning with their legacy. The *Mariposa* docked in San Francisco in March 1946 and Les was there to welcome Yvonne. She quickly met his folks and they welcomed her into their family just as the Verralls had accepted Les.

Les and Yvonne Cottman settled in San Diego and had one daughter. It was the end of the beginning of their life together.

★ ★ ★

LeGrande A. Diller was born to be an army career man. In 1923, at the age of 22, he graduated from Syracuse University majoring in chemical engineering, and then entered the army as a second lieutenant of infantry. He married a pretty lady called Harriette, who was the daughter of a general.

Diller was posted to Hawaii from 1931 to 1934. In 1941 he joined the Philippine Division as assistant to the assistant chief of staff for intelligence. In July 1941, after a fortuitous meeting with General Sutherland, Diller joined the MacArthur entourage and was appointed chief press officer. Diller was cultured, intelligent, trustworthy and loyal — all qualities which endeared him to the general.

When MacArthur was besieged at Corregidor, Diller's importance to the general became evident when he was one of the chosen few to get a seat in one of the PT boats that provided MacArthur and his staff with a means of escape prior to the fall of the Rock. Four boats were needed for the task and Diller was in the third, PT 35, under the command of Ensign A.B.Akers.

MacArthur was always a high-profile public figure so the need for an effective public relations and media liaison officer was paramount. From the moment that MacArthur and the Bataan Gang arrived at Melbourne's Spencer Street railway station in March 1942, the PR machine moved into overdrive. The Australian media and public were desperate for stories about the celebrity general, his wife Jean and their son Arthur. The odd piece about the war was welcome too, but anything to do with MacArthur was considered news.

So this was 'Pick' Diller's war, a war that he always won by having full control of all publicity emanating from MacArthur's headquarters. He censored all despatches and news stories, 'sanitised' press releases, and became expert in vetting and creating palatable public and military communiques, usually with the personal approval of MacArthur with whom he met daily.

One of the first communications from the headquarters of the United States Army in Australia was a list of accredited correspondents which was circulated to commanding officers and unit commanders in all base sections. Authorised by Lieutenant General Brett, it was a list of 43 journalists, photographers and broadcasters, most of whom were associated with international magazines such as *Time, Life, Colliers* and with major newspapers or agencies.

Credentials for the chosen few who would be supplied with the carefully prepared statements and heavily censored war news were issued from MacArthur's headquarters in a statement dated 30 March 1942. Even after being approved, any copy prepared by these war correspondents had to be submitted to headquarters for a signature of approval so that MacArthur's office could exercise media control which was amongst the most controlled, stringent and biased of any democratic society.

This was Diller's environment. He was responsible for press and public relations policies and their enforcement and, like all other senior MacArthur officers, he stayed at the Menzies Hotel in Melbourne.

The challenges necessary to immerse the high-profile Supreme Commander into the Australian lifestyle, both domestically and politically, were many and the pressures they brought were immense. Diller had never been so busy, so whenever it was possible he would walk for relaxation or have a drink in the bar of the Alexander Hotel, which was a little more comfortable and elegant than most of the saloons in the city. Enlisted men generally did not patronise it, so it was a quiet place to drink and relax. However, Diller was seldom alone. Media people were always seeking a scoop or an exclusive from him, wanting to know the whereabouts of the General and his wife and when he was going to give a press conference.

One Friday evening, late in March 1942, Diller was with Colonel Harry Williams, a British officer, when he noticed three women sitting on the opposite side of the room. Diller was a strict follower of protocol so he asked the head waiter to approach the women to see if they would allow him and the colonel to join them for a drink.

★ ★ ★

Joy Foord was an independent young woman with maturity and poise beyond her years. Born and raised in Ballarat, she was the only child of John and Marie Foord, both of whom were successful in commerce and in sport. They had had strict but fair rules for Joy's education and social life. She had been taught the virtue of dignity and independence and to her there were only two classes of people — first class and no class.

Marie Foord was in charge of a workroom in a clothing factory. She was an expert designer and cutter and, as a result, Joy was always dressed well and seldom looked less than elegant, which added to her air of learning, maturity and confidence. When the Americans arrived, she was living with a girlfriend's family in Melbourne and was working in the staff office of the Myer Emporium, one of the city's largest department stores.

Although she saw plenty of Americans on the streets and in the store, Joy had no real interest in them although she acknowledged that they had a 'look' about them and were certainly well dressed. She was one of several girls from the store who had a Friday night ritual of going for an after-work drink. The Australia Hotel was a popular choice. It might have been noisy, but it was never dull.

One Friday evening, however, Joy suggested a change of venue. She proposed they go to the Alexander Hotel, where it may have been dull, but it was never noisy. When the head waiter approached her group with the request to join two senior officers for drinks, they consented. The American introduced himself as LeGrande Diller, lieutenant-colonel in the United States Army.

Joy saw a man in his early forties; short, thin, and not especially attractive. But he turned out to be an excellent conversationalist, and was charming and gracious. Joy was not surprised to learn that he was involved with the press and public relations.

For Diller, it was a rare moment to be in the company of someone with whom he did not have to conciliate. He guessed Joy to be in her mid-twenties. She was well-dressed, confident and interesting, and he assumed she was involved in some service capacity. Their conversation was congenial and she agreed to join him for dinner.

A week after their first meeting, Joy left the Myer store and hurried to the Menzies Hotel where MacArthur and his staff were billeted and where she was to meet Diller for dinner. Once past the security measures, Joy greeted Diller who thanked her for coming and led her into the dining room. Once seated, he asked her to call him 'Pick'.

In contrast to the role he played in the war effort, in this situation Diller was candid and honest. He told her about his wife and son back in the States, how much he liked Australia, and that the General was a great man. Whatever fears of incompatibility existed between the couple soon evaporated and they agreed to meet more often. Before long the Colonel's room became their venue for dinner.

When arriving at work each day Joy could not help but notice the large photo of MacArthur in the Myer's window. It was considered good for the store's image, representing a sort of photographic allegiance. It was no collector's item. Photos like this were all over the city. One day, when no-one was looking, Joy rolled up the photo and took it with her when she went to meet Diller. The store's management assumed that the photo had been souvenired and were making plans to replace it with another when it suddenly reappeared bearing the message: 'My best wishes to the customers and staff of the Myer Emporium. From Douglas MacArthur.' This made it a collector's item and Joy was happy to claim both the responsibility for it and the gratitude of the store's management.

Her relationship with Diller was not covert. This was the way Diller wanted it and Joy admired him for it. One night, while waiting for him in the foyer of the Menzies Hotel, Joy noticed activity near the door of the elevator. People had formed into a group and there was much whispering. Suddenly Pick emerged from the group, smiled at Joy, and gestured for her to come to him. She walked towards the group, wondering what it was all about.

'Joy, I would like you to meet somebody,' said Diller. The group seemed to stand back for an instant and Joy saw a uniformed man of average height and build wearing a cap and a leather jacket.

'This is General MacArthur. General, this is Joy Foord, the girl I told you about.' MacArthur reached out and took her hand. 'How do you do, Joy. Are you having dinner with Colonel Diller tonight?'

Joy had met many important people in her life, including others introduced to her by Diller, but she immediately sensed that this man was someone special. MacArthur radiated charm and she felt he had an aura about him.

In July, Pick informed her that the headquarters were being moved to Brisbane, as it was closer to the combat areas. Preparations were under way to shift the entire staff and facilities to Queensland. As their relationship had progressed, he asked her if she would relocate to Brisbane to be near him. He offered to organise everything, including a job and accommodation. This was a big decision for Joy. She knew her parents would not be pleased with the move. They did not approve of the relationship and had no desire even to meet Diller. But Joy told him she would go anywhere to be with the man she loved.

There were no comforts for Joy Foord on her flight to Brisbane. She was the only woman on board the C-47 Dakota which was full of officials and war correspondents. It wasn't just the hard aluminium seats that made the journey uncomfortable, but also the incessant questions directed at her by some of the correspondents. She did not know any of them, but most of them knew her by sight and hoped she might give them some inside information on why GHQ was moving to Brisbane, who was this general called Blamey, and more personally, whether she was Pick Diller's girl. Most of the questions she could not answer because Diller never spoke about work when he was with her. The answers to the other questions were none of their business.

Once in Brisbane, the MacArthur headquarters were established in the AMP Building on the corner of Queen and Edward Streets and the General and his staff were accommodated at the new Lennons Hotel, where they had requisitioned the entire top floor. Joy was billeted at the Yale Apartments on the outskirts of the city centre. She reported for work to Somerville House where she was assigned to the postal department.

The Yale Apartments were only a few blocks from Lennons and Joy walked the route often. The city was inundated with servicemen, mostly Americans, and felt like a big fort. Brownout restrictions gave it an eerie, sinister look. Joy sometimes felt uncomfortable moving around, as there were often disturbances, and Diller sometimes sent a car or an escort for her. However, they also often walked together on the streets of the strange and gloomy city. On these occasions, Joy felt secure and also proud to be with such a high-ranking officer.

One night they were walking when three Australians approached. They seemed to be intoxicated and began insulting the couple. One of them pushed Joy aside and abused her. At this, the diminutive Diller removed his coat and challenged the trio to a fight. Fortunately the incident was defused by the arrival of two Australian provosts. Diller ordered them not to charge the Australians and the couple walked on.

The General Headquarters of the South-West Pacific area might have experienced many military privations during the early months of the war, but now creature comforts were considered a necessity and a relationship such as that between Colonel LeGrande Diller and Joy Foord was not unusual.

Mrs MacArthur's aide, Lieutenant Colonel S.L. Huff, a favourite of Joy's, was seeing a young girl, Keira Tuson, also from the Myer Store, and they married after the war. Diller had a young officer aide, Frank C. Kunz, who met an Egyptian girl in Brisbane whom he married in July 1944. General Sutherland had a relationship with a young lady whose perfume often emanated from the elevator well. Even the management of the hotel became involved with members of MacArthur's staff. The hotel manager, Mrs Margaret Byrne, fell instantly in love with First Lieutenant Richard S. Fuld, who was responsible for the 24-hour security watch over the MacArthurs, and young enough to be her son.

So, one of the accommodation items most prized by all was a double bed. Joy and Diller often lamented the fact that in Diller's cot, two was a crowd. Having a bed for two was regarded as a symbol of distinction and prominence within the Bataan Gang. The General, of course, was provided with one, as was Sutherland, whose roomy queen-sized bed gave faithful service during his stay at Lennons.

After spending a night with Diller in the hotel, Joy would leave via a private elevator. On the ground floor she was usually greeted by the one-armed doorman, Harry, who was accustomed to seeing her leave the hotel alone. However, one morning, as she was in the private elevator her fear of being joined by someone else became a reality when MacArthur entered. They were alone. 'Good morning. Are you taking your constitutional?' asked the General.

At various times Joy met a number of the celebrities who always called in at Lennons Hotel. Gary Cooper was there one day in 1943 and Joy had drinks with him. She thought he looked older than his screen image but found him pleasant company. Their conversation was curtailed when a young officer approached and asked if Cooper would follow him to talk to another guest; General Blamey wanted to meet 'Sergeant York'. Ray Bolger was there one day. Joy knew him as the Scarecrow from *The Wizard of Oz*. Other entertainers, amongst them Jerry Colonna and Joe E. Brown, also dropped in to amuse the patrons.

Another American senior officer who was in charge of the Evaluations Board, Major-General W.E. Lind asked Joy if she would like to work in his department. It was situated in the *Courier-Mail* building in Queen Street. She accepted, and it was while she was working there that Diller informed her that he was to be transferred.

Diller had been away several times, including one special trip back to the United States where he had had an audience with President Roosevelt. On his return he reported on his trip to Frank Kunz before passing his observations on to MacArthur. The General aspired to the highest office and expected to be a nominee on the Republican ticket after the war. Diller's assignment had been to evaluate his chances of success. Diller informed MacArthur that although Roosevelt was ill and might not last another term in office, he was still enormously popular.

In April 1944, MacArthur decided to move his headquarters to Hollandia in Dutch New Guinea. The path to victory from there could only be north. Diller asked Joy to marry him and join him in the States after the war was over. She didn't feel sure and asked him for time to think about it as there were complications, not least the fact that he was already married and was also very much a career man. Joy was uncertain that their feelings were real and wondered if they had just been drawn together by the war. They agreed to write to one another and see if the situation became clearer.

In the months after his departure, Joy waited in vain for some word from Pick Diller, but there was nothing. It was impossible for her to contact him as she had no idea where he was. The passing months became a year and soon the war was over. Joy became bitter and resentful. She destroyed all the photographs of them together and threw away the gifts he had given her.

Joy Foord never married and always referred to the diminutive, modest soldier as 'the only one love of my life'.

In January 1945, LeGrande Diller was promoted to brigadier general. After the war he returned to his wife and son. He remained in the army, in which he served a total of 31 years during which time he commanded a division. His awards and honours included the Distinguished Service Medal, the Legion of Merit and the Silver Star. Diller retired from the United States Army in 1954.

Twenty-two years after she had last spoken to him, Joy finally heard from Diller. He had found her name in the phone book — the Foord spelling had made that easy. He was making a pilgrimage back to Brisbane and would like to meet her again. Joy had never been as nervous as when she once again walked into the foyer of the Lennons Hotel. There he was, Pick Diller. Now balding, paunchy and bespectacled. But it was him. And there was someone with him — a woman of about the same age.

'Hello, Joy, this is my wife, Harriette,' said Diller. 'Hat, this is Joy Foord, one of the many friends I made in Australia during the war.'

The three had coffee together and from then on, every year, Joy Foord received a Christmas card wishing her the compliments of the season. It was always signed Pick and Hat Diller.

CHAPTER TEN

ALLIED ALTERCATIONS — THE BATTLE OF BRISBANE

The confrontation between Australian and American servicemen which came to be known as the Battle of Brisbane shocked many, but surprised few.

Scarcely reported at the time and only sporadically since, the incident has largely faded into history. Most cannot remember — a few cannot forget. In hindsight, the significance of the battle is apparent. Not only was it the largest and most violent disturbance between allies during the war, but it was a significant factor in destroying Brisbane's innocence and an influential factor in the ever-changing relationship between the sides.

In 1942, Brisbane was the third largest city in the country. To many, however, it was more like a big country town than a city, its 340 000 inhabitants living in a quiet, conservative and isolated atmosphere. Not many people came to visit and even fewer stayed. Then came the Americans.

The geographical situation and the presence of MacArthur's headquarters drew American servicemen to the city centre in their thousands. Diggers were there too, their numbers increasing as the war effort grew and Brisbane swelled with the influx. By November 1942 it possessed sombre tenements, barbed-wire pickets and a deluge of khaki; it had become a garrison city. It was not even Brisbane any more. American High Command was calling it Base Section 3.

For servicemen based there, the enemy was not the Japanese — but boredom. Idleness was a companion. The pubs only opened three hours a day and the cinemas were closed on Sundays. You always knew when the few city cinemas were open, as the lines of people seeking admission extended several blocks. Hotel sessions were as limited as the available alcohol and any form of entertainment was hopelessly inadequate for the numbers seeking it. There was also deep resentment from many of the inhabitants, notably the Australian servicemen returning from the Middle East. They quickly concluded that the Americans had virtually taken over the town — both militarily and socially.

It seemed that most women, single and married, were in the arms of the well-groomed, prosperous Americans. The old grievances of pay, clothing, food and perceived preferential treatment festered in the mind of the Digger.

Overseas they had fought the common enemy, while the Yank was in the rear with the gear. Diggers called them 'Queen Street Commandos'. Conversely, the Americans could not understand why the conscripted Australian militia were not permitted to serve overseas or why the government sent Boy Scouts to war — who else would wear shorts? Tensions increased and violence escalated. From April to October 1942, 1032 American servicemen were charged with mischievous offences. The Australian equivalent was probably proportionally no less. Many incidents warranted the attention of the civil authorities, and some the Coroner's Court.[1]

On 9 October 1942, Private William Tatchell was stabbed to death in Wickham Street by Private Edward Balser, an American from the 9th Medical Supply Depot. The killing was the result of a fracas over attire and obscene language in front of a woman. Balser was charged and acquitted. On 14 October there was a fierce, violent encounter between a black and a white American. The following night an American soldier was murdered by a civilian. On 16 October, an American knifed a medical orderly in a fight at the Coronation Hotel. A week later another American soldier was arrested after knifing three fellow soldiers and a woman while under the influence of liquor.[2] Local newspapers condemned Americans carrying knives.[3]

The press was heavily censored at the time and very few details of serious offences reached the general public. The *Courier-Mail* conveyed homely, social aspects of the American presence by profiling each day a serviceman from one of the 48 States.

Private Emile Brown from Pennsylvania spoke of his state's steel industry, the fact that the Declaration of Independence was signed there — and how just the present cause was.[4] In addition the paper, editorially, told its 92 341 readers:

In the main the relationship between Australians and Americans in Brisbane and elsewhere continues to be excellent, but there have been a few instances recently where misunderstandings have been allowed to develop ... These ... small ... in themselves ... have been seized upon by some people as topics of idle and malicious gossip.[5]

The US Consul, Mason Turner, was not alone when he found the editorial of dubious validity. Turner advised the State Department that there was 'considerable dislike of Americans. Nurses complained of being harassed as they walked down the streets or travelled on trams.' He went as far as to suggest that, in many areas of Queensland, 'matters had reached such a pass that some Australians and Americans would rather kill each other than the Japanese'. In Brisbane, the Provost Marshall of the American forces, Lieutenant Colonel Harry H. Vaughan, reported that, in November, his MP units were breaking up 20 fights a night.[6]

The situation was similar in some southern centres. In Sydney, Colonel A.N. Kemsley confided to a colleague that letters 'intercepted from different areas' revealed that GIs had considerable ill-feeling towards Australian servicemen.[7]

Clearly, both sides had different views. The Americans detested the apparent casualness demonstrated by some Australians regarding the war. A subsequent War Department analysis of GI correspondence concluded:

The people, the Army, and the Government are apathetic towards the war and depend entirely on America to hold their continent. Plane production is slow, food supply adequate, but limited. No definite effort is made to conserve gasoline, transportation facilities and other vital necessities. Waste and general indifference to the war effort is prevalent. Strikes are particularly wide-spread among the coal miners and stevedores. Indecision by the Government is reflected in the Army. It gets its orders from a wrangling Parliament and is mediocre in efficiency and training.

The American Ambassador to Australia, Nelson T. Johnson, probably spoke for many when he wondered in a confidential dispatch whether the nation was 'worth saving from its fate'.

For the Australians, Major General J.M.A. Durrant, commander of Australian troops in Queensland, interpreted the ill-feeling as 'resentment at the first claim on accommodation, foodstuffs, and luxuries which, rightly or wrongly, they believe is accorded to US personnel because their spending power is so much greater than the Australians'. There was also further reference to the perennial problem of US troops and local women. Durrant made mention of 'the conduct of a large section of women folk who permit themselves to be literally, "mauled about" in public, irrespective of the time and place'.[8]

This was not an aberration. In Brisbane alone, divorce figures 1942–43 rose from 100 to almost 400. It was estimated that almost 200 of these involved adultery — with a third attributed to the Americans.[9] The cessation of engagements, fallouts with sweethearts and broken vows and hearts must have also been enormous in number.

There is no doubt that Brisbane was the Allied love nest during the war. Of the 15 000 marriages involving American service personnel and nationals, 5000 were at Base Section Three.

In November 1942 the favourite social haunts for both sides were two canteens located in the city centre. The Australian canteen was near the corner of Adelaide and Wharf Streets. Nearby at the corner of Adelaide and Creek Streets, was the American Post Exchange (PX) canteen. A United States Red Cross centre and cafe was opposite. The neutral Gresham Hotel, with its majestic balconies, overlooked the area. There was also an American barracks for headquarters staff situated nearby. MacArthur's offices were a block away on Queen and Edward Streets. The American PX had been relocated from Grey Street and had opened in July 1942. Compared to the Australian canteen, it was spacious, indeed palatial, and stocked with plenty of everything.

Both the Americans and the Australians had a resentment, indeed hatred, for most levels of authority. To many of them, the nemesis of authority were the military police, sometimes called provosts. With almost 100 000 servicemen in the city, the maintenance of law and order was hopelessly out of the reach of the civil authorities and military control was necessary. In Brisbane, in late 1942, the American Provost Corps had over 800 active personnel; the Australian provost staff in the area numbered 110. In November, US military law and order was the responsibility of the 814th and 738th MP Battalions based at Whinstanes, a few minutes from the city centre.

Duties varied. In addition to enforcing order, the provosts undertook sentry duties on docks and facilities. The suitability of the 738th Battalion personnel for their duties was suspect. According to the official history of the Provost Marshall's Section: 'At least half the members were unsuited for police work because of habits of insobriety, lack of dependability, physical weaknesses, physical build, and mental development'. The authors concluded that many of the provosts: 'had no experience in police work'.[10]

The typical provost was armed and aggressive, and one historian of the early war years has suggested: 'It is probably a fair generalisation to say that in the United States, the display of batons and firearms in the hands of police is an effective way of quelling a riot whereas in Australia it is an effective way of starting one'.[11]

If the military police were not to be treated with respect, then they were to be treated with caution. In early November, outside a US camp in Sydney, one of them had shot a taxi driver dead as he searched for his fare. There had also been a tragic encounter at Townsville in August, the recorded details of which are in parts so vague that many believe that the incident was only a myth.

George Hargrave was from Perth and in August 1942, aged 23, he was a stoker on the HMAS *Swan*. He and his ship had been in action almost from the beginning of the Pacific war. In January they had been attacked by Japanese aircraft near Ambon and a few weeks later the *Swan* was in Darwin when the Japanese attacked. The ship was damaged and three crewmen lost their lives.

Hargrave was a good bloke. On 28 August, with three of his shipmates, he enjoyed a night out in Townsville while the *Swan* was in harbour. The four sailors went to a cafe in Palmer Street late in the evening and ordered five bob's worth of fish and chips. Also in the cafe were two American military policemen — Ernest Helton and Way Hewitt. All who were involved in the incident recalled how quickly the altercation developed.

It seems that a dispute over the possession of a salt shaker led Helton to mount the counter and warn the Australians to desist and withdraw from the area. This directive encouraged a barrage of profanities and a well-aimed pop bottle. Ernest Helton then drew his .45 revolver from his holster and shot Hargrave in the stomach. After a brief melee, more military police arrived, Helton was relived of his firearm and Hargrave was taken to hospital, where he endured nine days of agony before dying on 6 September.

The frustrations experienced by civil police in attempting to pursue the matter with the American military become all too frequent for the remainder of the war. In a confidential report to the Minister for Health and Home Affairs, the Queensland Police Commissioner relayed an account from Detective Sergeant Currey of his discussing the possibility of Helton being available to file a statement with Major William T. Powers. The American replied that Helton would not be allowed to cooperate and that the US Army would take appropriate action. Currey then requested details of the orders issued to military policemen concerning the use of firearms while on duty. Major Powers declined to provide any more information on the matter. When the matter reached the attention of the Solicitor General, he at once reported to the Police Commissioner: 'I think that these kind of happenings should be brought to the notice of the Prime Minister'.

On 10 October, Ernest Helton faced an American Board of Inquiry on a charge of assault and causing bodily harm. In short order, it was ruled that the killing was in the act of self-defence and the matter was quickly shelved.[12]

However, there was a poignant postscript to the affair. Two days after Helton was exonerated, Mrs Eunice Hargrave wrote a letter to Townsville police:

Dear Sir,

My son, the late stoker George Hargrave F 3682 of H.M.A.S Swan passed away at Townsville Hospital on September 6.

He received a bullet wound in the stomach on August 28, while on shore leave.

We shall be very grateful if you will please give us some particulars on what happened as we have been informed it was in the hands of the civil police.

He was a fine boy in every way.

I remain his heartbroken mother,

Eunice Hargrave

Townsville police suggested that Mrs Hargrave contact the Naval Board in Melbourne. Mrs Hargrave had already done so, and had been informed that it was a civil police matter. An internal memorandum regarding this matter directed: 'Do not furnish any information to this woman, apart from the question of censorship, allied forces are involved'. The fate of George Hargrave is stated on his service record as death due to an accident.[13]

Able Seaman David James Wren was based at the shore establishment of HMAS *Moreton* in Brisbane when he met his death four months later. There is no glory for him; his death has been classified as misadventure. Misfortune would be more appropriate. On 19 January 1943, Wren was in the company of two Americans when a confrontation with another American, Fountain B. Williams, led to Wren being punched in the face. The sailor then pursued Williams down George Street until Williams stopped, knelt and with a handgun in a fixed-arm position fired two rounds into the chest of David Wren.[14]

These and other tragic episodes have a common denominator. In the heat of the moment a firearm resolved the situation. Without the presence of these weapons, these men would not have died. The numerically inferior Australian provosts carried only a baton, while the Americans, like lawmen from the old West, carried a holstered .45 calibre revolver — a weapon of devastating effectiveness. On many occasions, while keeping the peace with barfly soldiers — or fights in the streets — the weapons created more problems than they solved.

Not all servicemen were intimidated by heavily armed, combative provosts. A group of Diggers were once admiring a motorcycle outside MacArthur's headquarters when a passing MP intervened. A directive and a baton in the ribs of one Digger resulted in the provost being despatched to the sidewalk and his truncheon being despatched to the roof of the adjacent General Post Office building.[15]

Increasing tensions with provosts, servicemen, civilians and others in the depressing environment of a gloomy, dark and crowded Brisbane suggested that a day of reckoning was at hand. On 26 November 1942, fate was to place a company of the 738th MP Battalion in Base Section 3 with a few thousand servicemen, and with the lights out.

The day was a fine one in Brisbane — the start of the summer season. The Brisbane *Courier-Mail,* as always, carried more news about the war effort overseas than the war effort locally. The German 6th Army was facing destruction in Stalingrad. There was good news from Tunisia, with Rommel's army in retreat.

Americans and Australians in Brisbane could read only good news reports from the Solomons, where the 1st Marine Division and the United States Navy were engaging in desperate actions against the Japanese. A cautious editorial warned that the threat of Japanese invasion had still not abated and there was the usual, sombre Roll of Honour list. Local news focused on a downed Japanese bomber in Darwin and the tragic fate of a young girl in the north, taken by a crocodile. Americans were to celebrate Thanksgiving Day and page three featured a photograph of canteen staff enthusiastically carving up 250 turkeys for American troops in the Red Cross Services Club.[16]

Just before noon, there was an omen of things to come when an MP had tried to stop a fight in Albert Street. A baton struck the head of a Digger, which drew others to the scene. After a small but violent brawl, some peace was restored. Nonetheless, many observers believed that the authorities were losing control.

At 6.50 pm the pubs had closed for the second time that day and, as always, the darkening, unlit, streets were crowded with aimless servicemen and a few civilians. There was the clatter of the trams in the middle of the streets, with bells ringing, and they seemed to be the only objects with purpose.

Private James R. Stein, No 36504556, 404th Signal Company, United States Army, was about to inadvertently start one of the most notorious episodes of the war on the home front. Who Stein entered the Australian Army canteen with, and for what purpose, are now lost to history. When he left the canteen, Stein started to walk in the direction of the American PX canteen — 50 yards towards the MacArthur end of the city.

The Americans never really did get used to the local beer with the XXXX on the label, Private Stein included. On the short journey to the PX, the American walked into three Diggers who had also been drinking. If a serviceman bumped into another at that time, you would either talk or fight. Initially, on this occasion, there was talk.

Whether two American MPs or just one arrived on the scene is still in dispute. However, there is no doubt that Private Anthony E. O'Sullivan, 814th MP Company, challenged Stein for his leave pass.

'I've got it here somewhere.'

'Hurry up! I ain't got all night.'

'Provost bastards! Leave the bloke alone — he's with us.'

'Mind your business! Get outa the way.'

Nobody knows who struck the first blow. There was cursing; a baton was raised, once, twice; arms swung — then a boot. Soon the three Diggers became five — then ten — then twenty. Civilians came too. There were whistles from all quarters, then more MPs — most from the PX. There was a brief rally, thumps, curses, arms, feet, batons and webbing belts. The MPs were not used to being outnumbered and retreated to the PX. Stein stumbled in also, O'Sullivan was carried in and doors were quickly closed and bolted.

Immediately, there were frantic phone calls and alarms. Hundreds gathered outside and soon rocks, sticks, and bottles were being hurled at the canteen. Someone threw a parking sign through a window. This was not the kind of joint exercises that the Supreme Commander had in mind.

First Lieutenant Lester Duffin, from the 814th, arrived at 7.15 pm. 'There were about a hundred Australian soldiers struggling to break through a makeshift cordon around the PX door,' he later reported. 'They were shouting for the Yank bastards to come out — or they would come in.'

Inspector Charles Price was one of the first of the civil authorities on the scene. According to Price: 'The crowd was growing rapidly. They were hooting and shouting — Pull the bloody place down ... come out and fight, you bastards are yellow, you used the batons on our mates but you ran away at Milne Bay.'

The Red Cross Club was also menaced. Someone suggested that the Aussies were really after the turkeys. According to Captain Robert M. White, an American liaison officer who observed the action from the balcony of the Gresham Hotel: 'Civilian police were lined across the door, backed by US military policemen. Every so often green-clad soldiers milled in front of the door and rushed it, and I could see night sticks fly and there would be much fighting.'

On the balcony above, war correspondent John Hinde was also an observer. Hinde, who was later to witness battles in New Guinea and Bougainville, believed that 'The most furious battle I ever saw during the war was that night in Brisbane. It was like a civil war.'

The battle spread into other streets. For most of the soldiers this was their first time in battle — their first action against an unexpected foe. A GI had just left the Wintergarden Theatre after seeing *Lady in a Jam*. On the tram bound for New Farm, soldiers from both sides were engaged in a violent battle. He vacated the iron-clad quickly, by choice. The conductor left too; thrown off after trying to restrain the belligerents.

Women workers were evacuated and escorted clear of the area by soldiers with fixed bayonets. The MPs closed the Tivoli Theatre. The ticket lady was escorted to an anxious taxi driver by a group of Australians. Patrons, mostly servicemen, were ordered back to their barracks and ships.

In the PX, Private Stein attempted to retrieve his leave pass from the pocket of the prostrate Private O'Sullivan. Stein disappears from recorded history with a brief statement: 'I was told to forget about the pass. Someone gave me a club and I stood in line with the other fellows and helped them out.'

The area was cordoned off by military police of both sides, who formed pickets with the civil police. Many vehicles were turned back by armed men. Some were there through curiosity, some wanted to join in the fun. Others had more hostile intentions. A picket sentry that night, Duncan Caporn remembers detaining a small truck driven by an Australian officer and three men. The four were arrested after sentries found four Owen sub-machine guns, several boxes of ammunition and a quantity of hand grenades. By eight o'clock it was estimated the 2000 to 4000 people were involved in the melee, which showed no signs of easing.

The chance to stop the riot was lost when the local fire brigade appeared but could not — or would not — train the hoses on the crowd. The Americans would bitterly criticise this failure. 'We have no intention of using our services to quell military or civil riots,' said a bureaucratic fire chief, shortly after events. 'Our job is to put out fires.'

Some Australian MPs removed their armbands and joined the mob. Others tried to placate them.

Private Norbert Grant of C Company, 738th MP Battalion, was not even in the city when the battle started. He was in a park in South Brisbane reading a book. At 7 pm he left; it had become too dark to read and, besides, there was word that there was a fight in town. Not your everyday fight, but a real brawl — a big one. There was the cacophony of whistles, horns, alarms and some distant shouting. Grant thought it best to report for duty early. No sooner was he through the barracks door than he was handed a 12-gauge Stevens pump-action shotgun. It is a riot gun capable of firing a casing of 30 pellets, a genuine peacekeeper and devastating at close quarters. Grant was then ordered to join the others and proceed to the PX because: 'There is a hell of a riot — and our boys are getting hurt'.

The American and Australian MPs and civil police had shown considerable responsibility in not resorting to using firearms up to this stage of the running battle. O'Sullivan did not draw his revolver when being assaulted and beaten. The battle, however fierce and violent, had been fought with percussion instruments, broken bottles, swinging limbs and random objects.

It took only eight minutes for Norbert Grant and other members of C Company to reach the battle. Soon they were elbowing, pushing and swinging their way through the crowd to get to the PX where the Americans feared for their lives. Outside, they could see thousands of servicemen, civilians and Australian military and civil authorities.

'Why don't they try and break it up?'

'Where are the hoses?'

The least glamorous, most talented, star to visit Australia — Eleanor Roosevelt, Brisbane, 1943. *(John Oxley Library, Brisbane)*

The crossed flags on this occasion suggest a social alliance. Two well-fed Americans impress a local babe.

Beer shortage — only nine barrels for the American PX canteen, Brisbane, 1943.

Leslie Cottman, USN.

Yvonne Verrall.

Les and Yvonne Cottman with Doris Goodchild and Gideon Van Winkill Stivers, Fremantle, 4 September 1944.

Bill and Joan Bentson, September 1944.

Colonel LeGrande Diller, US Army. *(Courtesy of Mr Allan J. Campbell, AM, OBE, OMRI)*

Joy Foord at an art exhibition featuring war paintings. The officer is Major General W. E. Lynd.

Buddies, but not all Allied encounters were as congenial as this one. *(Courier-Mail)*

Witnesses to a stabbing leave the well-attended Office of the Provost Marshall — Base Section 3 (aka Brisbane). *(John Oxley Library, Brisbane)*

American provosts keeping the peace, Brisbane, 1942. *(John Oxley Library, Brisbane)*

'The object of our affection.' Six Yanks, six broads — no Diggers. *(John Oxley Library, Brisbane)*

The battlefield shortly before the war. A small, two-storey shopfront separates the Australian canteen and the American PX canteen (the two large buildings at the centre of the photograph). The Australian canteen is closest to camera.

Ian Gill's unfortunately inappropriate cartoon, published the day after round one of the riot.

Townsville, 1942. *(John Oxley Library, Brisbane)*

The remarkable Grady Gaston who survived almost five months in remote scrub of the Gulf Country.

'Christ, they're goin' to get in!'

There were armed sentries outside, manning the pickets and trying to pacify the crowd. Civil police were frantically attempting to protect civilians; some were also talking to the crowd. Police later stated that the armed picket guards were ineffective; some left, some joined the crowd, many remained passive.

'Shoot the Yank bastards, mate! Give me your gun and I'll do it.'

What Grant saw as he forced his way toward the PX was a sea of hostile humanity. Jesus Christ, he thought, I'm goin' to get killed tonight. Within an hour of reading a book in the tranquil setting of Musgrave Park, Norbert Grant was about to be immortalised in notoriety.

'Look!' someone shouted. 'One of the bastards has got a gun.'

'What are ya goin' to do with that bloody gun, Yank?'

'Get him!'

Grant told the subsequent court of inquiry:

Suddenly they all came for me and I had my back to the wall of the PX and I menaced them with gun and told them to break it up, and one of the Australian soldiers came close to me so I jabbed him with it. Then as I was standing against the wall they grabbed the front of the gun and this other soldier had a hold of me by the neck ... and this is when the first shot went off.

Three shots were fired. The first shattered the chest of Private Edward S. Webster from the 2/2nd Anti-Tank Regiment and his life ended before he hit the bitumen. Private Kenneth Henkel fell with wounds to the cheek and forearm. Private Ian Tieman fell with a wound to the chest, and Private Frank Corrie with a thigh wound. Private Walter Maidment was aged only eighteen when he was wounded in action on the streets of his own city. Private Richard Ledson, a comparatively old man at 35, suffered a compound fracture of the left ankle and gunshot wounds to the left thigh and left hand. Sapper De Vosso was shot in the thigh and a civilian, 38-year-old Joseph Hanlon, was shot in the leg.

There were shouts, screams, sudden movement and then a momentary silence. Grant scrambled from the footpath toward the PX, breaking the butt of the shotgun over an Australian's head in the process. Another American soldier, Private Joseph Hoffman, who was posted as guard on one of the PX's doors, was soon to bear the brunt of the Australians' fury. His skull was fractured.

From 7 until 10pm the Battle of the Canteens, as some called it, continued virtually unabated. Eventually it subsided. The crowd dwindled; the fire brigade left and the ambulances arrived. The lower section of the PX was destroyed and litter and broken glass became the mementos of the battle.

Considering the intensity of the riot, the casualty list was slight. One Australian was killed, eight had minor gunshot wounds, six had baton injuries. Hundreds more endured black eyes, split lips, swollen cheeks, broken noses and abrasions. Eight MPs were injured.

At 11 pm the Chief Censor's Office in Brisbane sent the following directive to all states: 'No cabling or broadcasting of details of to-night's Brisbane servicemen's riot. Background for censors only: one Australian killed, six wounded'.

The next day the *Courier-Mail* carried a brief, heavily censored account of a disturbance which left one dead and several wounded. No nationalities were mentioned and further details were sparse. The paper also printed a cartoon on page three by Ian Gill which showed a uniformed American shaking the hand of an Australian, with these words: 'THANKSGIVING — This, Dig, is our way of celebrating a good harvest — and we'll fight on together till we celebrate the greater harvest — VICTORY!'

The timing was ironic in the extreme. The cartoon was committed to print before the battle, although Gill could hear the sounds of the disturbance from his Queen Street office as he completed his caricatures.

In Brisbane and across Australia, the tight censorship had an adverse effect. With no official details, rumours were rife.

The Yanks were credited with it all. Ten Diggers — no, fifteen — had died when the Yanks shot — no — machine-gunned the crowd. Some were beaten to death by batons. One was run over and left to die. Nothing was being done to get the bastards who did it. Did you see that cartoon in the paper? They should have put a bloody baton and a gun in the hand of that Yank.

There was talk of vengeance and retribution — 'Tonight we'll go into town and fix the bastards!'

On Friday afternoon, groups of Diggers went into the city looking for Americans — and looking for trouble. One senior Australian officer called this element 'dingo packs'. However, trouble was expected and some precautions were taken. Both canteens were locked up and the pickets were manned by dozens of armed troops. The target for the Australian packs was not necessarily the PX, nor was it the American MPs. It was any American in uniform.

Further trouble might have been averted had servicemen of both sides been confined to their bases. Some were, but many still walked the streets. Round two of the Battle of Brisbane, started on Friday the 27th at brownout. Crowds had gathered outside the American Red Cross building — the area around the PX having been secured. NCOs in the crowd confiscated hand grenades and attempted to find their men. The situation was delicate. American MPs on the first floor were heavily armed.

The throng broke up and gathered again at the corner of Queen and Edward Streets, outside MacArthur's headquarters. They shouted abuse in the direction of the General's office, but it was in vain. MacArthur was in New Guinea on a rare visit to the front.

Warrant Officer Bill Bentson worked in MacArthur's HQ and has the distinction of being an eye-witness to both rounds of the battle. He recalled the Friday night disturbances:

I had left barracks and was walking to headquarters for my shift. When I got to Queen Street it seemed to be at a standstill. The trams and cars were stopped and people were everywhere. Then I saw a Yank thrown into the air — I could tell because of the uniform. It didn't look good so I ran down a lane and made a run for HQ. There was a crowd of 500 to 600 Australian soldiers blocking the intersection of Queen and Edward Streets. They were grabbing and looking for anybody in uniform.

Bentson watched further events from the window of the sixth floor office: 'There were three circles formed in the crowd and they were passing Americans in uniform over their heads and into the circles where they were punching and kicking them.'

A potential for disaster increased when a group of Diggers waving stolen MP batons faced a crowd of 20 US provosts in Queen Street. The Americans lined the tram track and drew their .45 handguns. An unknown Australian officer became the hero of the hour when he persuaded the American commander to get his men in a truck and to drive away. Two American MPs were caught in the open and bashed. There were more fights on the city trams. Any American uniform was a target, especially one escorting a woman. A 23-year-old Australian woman was with her husband, an American officer. They had been to an early evening session at the Metro to see *Mrs Miniver*.

The pacifist escapist fare on the screen had nothing to do with the real life outside. At 7.45 pm the couple decided to walk to a restaurant for a meal. The woman's account of what happened was conveyed in a letter to her mother. Somehow it ended up in the public archives:

John and I walked into Edward Street to find something to eat — John and I were then attacked by hordes of militia. They yelled, 'There's a bloody Yank — kill him' and rushed us. I got knocked over twice, but I couldn't see John except for about ten soldiers punching him. They kept yelling 'Kill him — kick him, kick his brains out.'

Fortune favoured the innocent. Somehow the couple escaped into a pharmacy where C.A. 'Big Bill' Edwards was just about to close his shop. Forty-five years later he told his story in a television documentary on the battle:

This young couple fell through the door, chased by hordes of Aussie soldiers. I closed the wire grille door after them. 'Give us the bastard, Bill, he killed our mate.' I told them that he didn't kill anyone, and if they found the one who did, I would kill him for them. After a while they broke up and left.

Casualties for the second and final night of the battle were 21 injured, of whom 11 were hospitalised. All were American. The figure included eight MPs and four officers.

Measures were implemented the next day to ensure that there would be no round three of the battle. Units prominent in the battle were moved, MP strength was increased, the Australian canteen was closed and the American PX was relocated. On 29 November, the Chief Censor's Office, Brisbane, decreed: 'Situation Brisbane — Quiet last night. Under no circumstances should censors permit reference to Americans and Australians being or having been involved in clashes.'

Before the damage was repaired and wounds healed, there was outrage from concerned citizens. The Rev. H.M. Wheeler, the President General of the Methodist Conference of Australia, went public: 'Disturbances which occurred in Brisbane streets last week called for a thorough, fearless public inquiry'.

An investigation began almost immediately. The Americans insisted that the incident was caused by Australians' involvement in an affair that had nothing to do with them. Australian authorities admitted that their troops were responsible for the incident. There was also the suggestion that the American provosts needed to learn the virtue of tact and restraint. There was much criticism of the ineffectual control shown by the civil authorities. Base commanders were taken to task for not confining non-essential personnel to base during the riot. There were calls for more effective communication between the sides. General Blamey believed a series of discussions and lectures could bond the fragile link between the Allies. MacArthur dismissed the idea as unnecessary: 'It would make the situation seem more serious than it is — and there are no staff or facilities to support such a venture'.

General MacArthur's priorities were winning the war and with personal glory. It should not be forgotten that the ultimate blame for inter-Allied harmony should rest with him as Supreme Commander. Events before, during and after the Battle of Brisbane occurred not only in MacArthur's resident city, but in the streets outside his office.

Positive developments to come out of the inquiries included an easing of the brownout restrictions and entertainment becoming more accessible. Soon the tensions eased. However, no authority had the power to resolve what was always the fundamental problem — the Australian soldier throughout the war remained the poorer relation to his American counterpart. The Battle of Brisbane might have started with a beer, a boot and a baton, but the festering frustration of the Australian servicemen was their battle with a foe they could never beat — the Yank down-under and his dominance of all things military, and otherwise. The Yanks may well have been, over-sexed, over-paid and over-here, but the Australians were under-sexed, under-paid and under MacArthur. The official history neatly sums up the main factors leading to the Brisbane battle and countless smaller affairs:

Liquor, GI pay and smarter uniforms, discrimination in shops and hotels in favour of Americans, 'the spectacle of American troops with Australian girls, particularly the wives of absent soldiers, and the American custom of caressing girls in public'.[17]

It all came to a head on the streets of Brisbane in November 1942. Many people involved in the battle and many since have played down the events of those two days as being a minor affair. Others have suggested that it was a major tragedy and that the death and injured toll was downplayed. Contemporary documents throw new light on the confusion and doubts.[18] Only hours after round one of the battle, the Queensland Commissioner of Police had composed a detailed report of the incident for the Premier, Mr Frank Cooper, who despatched a copy air-mail to Canberra. The confidential report, which also had a number of recommendations, was on the desk of Prime Minister Curtin late on the same day. Commissioner Carroll informed the politicians that:

One Australian soldier was killed and several were injured.

Apparently some members of the Australian Army, obviously with larrikin tendencies, and reinforced by having consumed a certain amount of drink, resented the action of the U.S. Provost men, and interfered, with the result that a fight on a miniature scale ensued. Like a proverbial snowball, the matter developed. Unfortunately our own Provost men are of little or no assistance in such circumstances, and during the course of the disturbance it was noticed that numerous members of the Australian Provost men removed their arm-bands and put them in their pockets, consequently, they could not be subsequently identified by the police who might want assistance of a member of the Provost Corps to deal with the soldiers.

Australian picquets were rushed to the scene, some were armed with rifles, some of them handed their rifles to Australian soldiers who were prominent in the disturbance. It was, however, learned subsequently that they were not supplied with ammunition.

Carroll interpreted Grant's action as being in self-defence. He also mentioned an emergency meeting on the morning of 27 November with participants, including Colonel Donaldson from US Army Headquarters, Colonel Vaughan and Captain Scallan from the US Provost Corps. The Australian provosts were represented by Captain Barnes. Major Cummins was present in his capacity as assistant adjutant-general of Victoria Barracks. There were also representations from the police, a press relations officer and the Censor's Office. After a lengthy discussion the group agreed on several priorities:

Preventing a repetition and dealing with a repetition should it occur.

Publicity:- Colonel Donaldson and Major Cummins, whilst not desiring to interfere with the press, consider that if there is no publicity in these matters, such matters will simply localise, and will die a natural death.

Adequate Australian Provost Staff:- The Premier of Queensland made immediate representations to the Prime Minister to have an extra 200 Provosts allotted to the Provost Staff in Brisbane and that these should wear special uniforms.

Question concerning firearms:- The Australian and U.S. Navy Provost Corps are armed with batons only. The U.S. Army carry batons and pistols, but they have strict instructions that the pistols are not to be used except in the case of self defence, and, generally this is observed. Picquets should be properly constituted and under no circumstance should they be armed.

The meeting also emphasised the urgent need to ease the brownout conditions. Commissioner Carroll elaborated:

Colonel Donaldson has returned from Port Moresby, and he sees no necessity whatever for the drastic lighting restrictions at present existing in the metropolitan area of Brisbane. He admits, of course, that there was a time when lighting restrictions appeared to be very necessary, but he considers that has passed, and he asks that the restrictions be lifted in the metropolitan area of Brisbane without further delay.[19]

While Curtin was digesting the report, the Chief Publicity Censor in Canberra sent a copy of revised instructions to all the Australian States:

All riot stories must be submitted to censorship. Censors will delete anything likely to prejudice training, discipline or administration of Australian or Allied Forces.

In reports of disturbances, the only reference should be to service personnel, without distinguishing the service or nationalities concerned.

Even carefully edited stories are harmful and censors therefore should keep statements down to the barest details.

Allow nothing provocative.

On 29 December 1942, Prime Minister Curtin replied at length to Premier Cooper's report of the Brisbane riot and his recommendations. It was obvious that Curtin had been further briefed on the incident. His comments included the following:

It will be appreciated that large numbers of troops are present in Brisbane as a result of the grant of recreation leave to units in Queensland, and because of the importance of that City as a staging area. When on leave, these troops, naturally, are not under any immediate disciplinary or other control except when an offence is committed.

It has been ascertained that some members of the Provost Corps were instructed to remove their arm bands and to mingle with the crowd in an attempt to apprehend certain ring leaders. Further, the allegation with regard to handing over rifles has not been substantiated. I have noted your remarks and agree that the less publicity given to the disturbance the better for everyone concerned.

It is considered that the increase in the Provost Corps which you have suggested is well beyond requirements, as it would result in Provost personnel in Brisbane, being in far greater proportion than in other capital cities.

It is considered that a special uniform for Provost personnel is undesirable. The question of supply would raise difficulties. Also, there are many occasions upon which it would be undesirable for Provost personnel to be made conspicuous by the wearing of a special uniform. Difficulty exists at present in securing suitable men for the Provost Service, and if a special uniform had to be worn, it would be very difficult to obtain any volunteers at all for the Corps.

With reference to the question of the lighting restrictions that have been in force in Brisbane, I desire to advise that, in December, 1941, the Defence Committee recommended certain lighting restrictions in A.R.P. (including Brisbane) and controlled lighting areas throughout Australia. These were that-

(1) Lighting should be reduced to bring about a so called 'brownout', by means of -

Extinguishing unnecessary external lights, such as advertisements. Subduing necessary external lights (such as street lights) by shading them or by painting all but the bottom of the globes.

(2) Arrangements should be made to enable a 'blackout' to be imposed at very short notice.

(3) 'Blackouts' should not be imposed at present.

Your letter refers to the, 'drastic lighting restrictions at present existing in the metropolitan area of Brisbane', and the Department of Home Security has advised that the restrictions which have been imposed go far beyond the recommendations of the Defence Committee. It would be in accordance with the policy of the Commonwealth Government if the streets of Brisbane were lighted in a manner recommended by the Defence Committee.

Curtin also sent a copy of the original directive relating to correct lighting restrictions. It seems that for over a year, and during its peak occupation, Brisbane endured misery, mischief and nuisance in an unnecessarily gloomy and dark environment. This appears to have been the result of an elementary misinterpretation of official requirements.[20]

On 27 February 1943 Private Norbert Grant, 738th MP Battalion, was court-martialled for manslaughter. He was found not guilty on the grounds of self-defence. As a result of the November riots, five Australians were convicted of various charges of assault, with one being sentenced to six months gaol.

Quarrels and fights were common until the war ended, but never on the scale of the Brisbane incident. The 'Battle of Brisbane' did more than show Brisbane the light; many have speculated that the relationship between the Allied troops improved as a result of the battle. It certainly provided the opportunity to give vent to inbuilt tension, resentment and even hatred, but it also defused them to some extent. Respect and unity, so desirable in the circumstances, were never nurtured completely successfully on the home front, but they were to be found on the battlefield, when the two nations fought together.

In the month of the battle, American and Australian forces fought side by side at the Buna and Gona beachheads in New Guinea. Shortly before, they had fought and died together in the sea off Guadalcanal. The 'Battle of Brisbane' has never been commemorated or effectively documented, but it is a matter of record that on two nights in November 1942, Allies became enemies and a city became a battleground.

CHAPTER ELEVEN

DON'T FENCE ME IN

The American presence in Australia during the war was chiefly in the major cities, with Brisbane, Sydney and Melbourne being host to the main concentration of the American forces. However, thousands of Americans and Australians, mostly air force personnel, served in outback areas not covered in any travel brochures.

Townsville, Rockhampton, Cairns and Mackay were almost idyllic compared with Alice Springs, Darwin, Cloncurry, Charters Towers and Longreach. Nobody sent postcards from Antil Plains, Batchelor, Reid River or Daly Waters, and even these areas were salubrious compared with Iron Range, Horn Island, Bohle River, Camooweal and Jacky Jacky. Ross River in north Queensland was so unpleasant that its name is synonymous with a mosquito-borne disease. Few servicemen or civilians from the big cities knew the extent of the difficulties and deprivations endured by the men who fought their war from these isolated areas.

Since 1920, the American air force had been under the jurisdiction of the United States Army. As the European war progressed there came a strong call for an independent air force. The new arrivals of men and machines for the war effort resulted in the Air Corps and the Air Force Combat Command being joined under the control of General Henry 'Hap' Arnold and in June 1941 the two forces became the United States Army Air Forces. Although still a unit of the Army group, the air forces operated with considerable freedom. Senior air staff assisted Arnold, who answered directly to the Army Chiefs of Staff.[1]

As the Japanese threat moved to the south-west Pacific, the Allies moved to north-east Queensland to counter it. The northern regions of Australia, particularly Darwin and Townsville, were of major interest to the American High Command, even before the war. The Commander of the United States Far East Air Force, Major-General Lewis H. Brereton, had visited many areas just prior to the Pacific war. The objective was to survey the aviation route across the Pacific, using facilities in northern Australia. Brereton found that only Townsville and Darwin could handle large aircraft.

One of the first American squadrons to use the still developing base at Garbutt in Townsville was the 435th Squadron of the 19th Bombardment Group. This squadron, soon to be called the Kangaroo Squadron, was formed in Australia in early 1942 from components of four different units. Some of the aircraft had been in action the day after Pearl Harbor, searching in vain for the retiring Japanese task force. Like many other American units, aircraft of the 19th Bombardment Group were ordered to proceed to Australia.[2]

John Lillback had volunteered to fly the Fortresses to Australia:

Sure, I put up my hand. Why not? I knew nothing about the land or the people. This was a new experience for me and for most of the other guys. We suffered from many shortages, most seriously a lack of spare parts. Also our maintenance crews were on the *Pensacola* convoy and they were diverted to Australia after Pearl Harbor. It took us a while to catch up with them.[3]

Lillback's group flew to Brisbane via Mindanao, Fiji and New Caledonia. Archerfield airfield in Brisbane was just that — a field. Landing small aircraft there was adventurous enough, but the wet grass runways were not designed for a 32-ton Flying Fortress. However, land they did. War makes many things possible. The airfield was a popular base for commercial aviation. In February 1937 a Stinson aircraft had taken off from Archerfield bound for Sydney. An hour later the plane vanished. A huge search was conducted without result until a bushman, Bernard O'Reilly, found the aircraft in the Great Dividing Range seven days later. Legend has it that the first thing the two badly injured survivors asked O'Reilly was the Test cricket score. It was a popular story in Australia during the war and many a Yank heard it over a beer.

On 5 January 1942, the Americans designated Townsville as Base Section 2, United States Armed Forces in Australia.[4] Personnel from the 435th Squadron were amongst the first of thousands of Americans to become a part of the north Queensland community, militarily, domestically, culturally and economically.

The Townsville airfield of Garbutt was already being used by the RAAF before the arrival of the twelve B-17s from Brisbane. However, Garbutt, like the rest of Australia, was unprepared for the huge influx of servicemen and equipment. It was a tent city for the Americans, with only a small wooden building used to house operations and headquarters. The cots were of sturdy steel with the ever-present mosquito nets suspended above them. John Lillback and the rest of the squadron knew that things could only get better:

When we got there the place was a hive of activity with the airstrip and accommodation facilities still being constructed. We lived in tents. It was a difficult time. The RAAF crews were fine but they were not familiar with our aircraft. There was not a lot of spare parts and we had to cannibalise other aircraft to get others airworthy.[5]

The 435th Squadron entered World War II history when General MacArthur, dissatisfied with the standard of aircraft available at Mindanao to fly his Corregidor evacuees to Australia, demanded replacements. It was three 435th Kangaroo Fortresses, under the command of Lieutenants Bostram, Lewis and Chaffin, that flew to the Philippines to bring the MacArthur entourage to Batchelor. This was only the first of a number of increasingly hazardous trips to the islands to rescue military and government officials. Shortly before the fall of the Philippines, the 435th flew to Mindanao for the last time to pick up essential personnel. This time it was Carlos Romulo, General Valdez and their staff.[6] John Lillback was the radio operator in a B-17 under the command of Lieutenant Fred Eaton:

It was getting downright dangerous to fly to the Philippines for any reason. It was at the utmost extremity of our range and the skies were full of Zeros. General Valdez was in our plane and you had to be there to believe it. With an army fighting for its life, they were bringing cabinets, chests and plants aboard.[7]

The main tasks of the air campaign from Townsville and other north Queensland airfields were a series of attacks on the Japanese base at Rabaul and air reconnaissance. In some of the earliest instances of Allied cooperation during the war, many of the 435th Fortresses flew with RAAF members who proved invaluable as navigators.

As the Japanese thrust in the Pacific extended south, the next logical offensive became New Guinea. On 4 May, a small task force with troop transports led by Major General Horii left Rabaul to join a much stronger naval force, including the carriers *Shokaku* and *Zuikaku*, which had left Truk some days before.

The Allies knew that an attack on Port Moresby was imminent but were unaware of the disposition and timing of the Japanese assault. An American task force under the command of Rear Admiral Frank J. Fletcher and including the carriers *Lexington* and *Yorktown* was primed to intercept. American and Australian aircraft flying from North Queensland airfields stalked the enemy and supplied invaluable reconnaissance for the American fleet. The ensuing battle was like no other in the history of warfare. The air reconnaissance of both sides led to the battle of the Coral Sea being fought without the surface fleets sighting each other. It was the first action to demonstrate that air power in the Pacific theatre would be crucial.

Japan won a tactical battle by sinking the *Lexington* and heavily damaging the *Yorktown*. The Americans sank the small carrier *Shoho* and damaged the larger *Shokaku* and *Zuikaku*. Both sides lost many aircraft and pilots but the loss of experienced pilots told against the Japanese. The battle was a strategic victory for the Allies as the Port Moresby invasion force of around 5000 men and their transports returned to Rabaul.[8]

The Australian people were aware that a great naval battle was being fought only a few hundred miles from the mainland, but knew little of the consequences. The Battle of the Coral Sea forced the Japanese to review their war objectives.

A decisive battle with the American Navy had yet to be fought. But as a result of the Coral Sea encounter, in late May the Japanese were led to a confrontation with the Americans near the island of Midway. Japan lost four carriers — *Akagi, Kaga, Hiryu* and *Soryu* — while the Americans lost only one, the *Yorktown*. This was one of the most crucial battles of the war. The crushing defeat meant that for the rest of the war the Japanese navy was capable of only limited offensives and holding actions.[9]

The second consequence of the Coral Sea encounter was that the Japanese now attempted an assault on Port Moresby by landing at Buna and Gona and trekking over the Owen Stanley Range. This strategy drew thousands of Australians and Americans to a cruel fate in New Guinea.

★   ★   ★

For the people of Townsville, with a population of 30 000, the war brought chaos. The once close-knit community was swamped by military forces. Townsville was a strategic base for the consignment of personnel and supplies to the northern combat areas. It also became the administrative centre for the Australian Army in north Queensland and the location of the United States Army Air Force, 4th Air Depot. There were numerous other units and supporting facilities, including barracks, stores, workshops, ammunition depots and several military hospitals.[10]

The locals endured shortages of foods, petrol, ice, water and most other things, except servicemen. In Townsville alone, Yanks, Aussies and others outnumbered the locals three to one. The khaki hordes, brownouts, rationing and noise pollution were bad enough, but in June 1942 the Japanese bombed the town. The damage was slight but did nothing to lessen north Queenslanders' realisation that they were in the most vulnerable area in Australia. Tensions were increased by routine brownouts and stringent regulations for hotels, which in Townsville could open for only an hour in the mornings. Milk, ice and most fresh vegetables became prized items. Public transport was irregular and operator assisted-telephone calls had a low priority.[11]

The roads were more hazardous than in the state capitals. The volume of military traffic was huge and the American drivers experienced adaptability problems. At the peak of the occupation, two people a day were being killed on north Queensland roads.[12] Any grievances by the civilian population were reciprocated by the troops. The Americans believed that Townsville was 'the hottest, lousiest, toughest and most overcrowded troop town this side of Alexandria, Louisiana'.[13]

Townsville became the strategic point of an Allied build-up in north Queensland which extended over the Charters Towers corridor and the Atherton Tableland. It was not until later in the war, when the Allied thrust moved further north and the number of servicemen decreased, that the pressure and the acrimony eased.

Meanwhile in August 1942 there was a new command reorganisation for the American air forces in the South-West Pacific Area. They were reformed as the 5th Air Force, with General George Kenney replacing General Brett.[14]

The USAAF 3rd Light Bomb Group was based in Charters Towers with B-25 Mitchell medium bombers. The 19th Bomb Group also had three squadrons, consisting of B-17 Fortresses, based at Cloncurry.[15] Charters Towers was a strange world unto itself. Allied servicemen overwhelmed the local population, with 15 000 Americans serving in this district during the war. There were shortages of everything, but for the locals it was the noise that was the worst of all. Aircraft coming and going at all hours and the din was constant.

There were several sincere attempts to explain American culture to the local population, particularly his leisure activities. 'Please paste a cutting of this article in your scrapbook for future reference,' suggested the *Northern Miner,* so Charters Towers residents could understand the finer points and skills of baseball. A drawing of a baseball diamond was included, along with a copious amount of information about the sport, why it is so popular and why, unlike cricket when you hit a 'four' — that is, if you hit a homer — *you have to run.*[16]

News of clothing and food shortages was relegated to the rear pages as the *Miner* attempted to satisfy insatiable local curiosity about the American and his equipment. 'It's called a Jeep,' revealed the *Northern Miner* in May 1942, commenting on the strange, ugly, sawn-off little car the Yanks had brought with them:

The US Army considers it the sturdiest vehicle ever made. It can travel at 60 miles an hour, carry six soldiers, tow an anti-tank gun, lay smoke screens, and believe it or not, for river crossings the jeep is driven on to a large tarpaulin, tied up like a pudding, and floated across.

Many bets must have been lost or won when the newspaper told its readers that 'The Jeep gets its name from the Army classification letters G.P., meaning general purpose'.[17]

There were also reports from people in the southern states, that the Yanks had a large vehicle that could carry 40 men, swim in water and then drive on roads. It was called a DUK-W, but everyone called it a Duck. The Australian people never lost their fascination for American innovation.

North Queensland airfield construction became a priority with the Main Roads Commission and American engineering and construction units. Existing airstrips like Bowen, Cairns and Mount Isa were upgraded and new strips were being laid in north and western Queensland. Areas were also cleared for support fields at places like Breddan, Torrens Creek, Fanning and Woodstock. There were also strips in the outback, usually hastily cleared for emergency requirements that few aviators would relish using, such as Balfes Creek, Southern Cross, Powlathanga and Prairie.

In Queensland alone, there were 190 airstrips available for permanent or temporary use. Constructing these and the associated roads was a tremendous feat of logistics, planning and deployment between civil and military organisations. The 8000 by 200 foot airfield at Mareeba was completed in only eight days.[18]

From June 1942, the Allies were located at an airfield called Iron Range, on Cape York, almost at the tip of Queensland. Nobody who served there would ever forget it. According to Ernest Rhodes, who was there from November 1942 to January 1943:

Iron Range was the pits! Right in the middle of the jungle ...We lived in six-man pyramidal tents and had one large tent for a mess hall ... The weather out of Iron Range to Jap targets in New Guinea and New Britain was horrible. We lost many planes and crews to bad weather.[19]

In late 1942, the US 321st Bomber Squadron of the 90th Bomb Group was posted to Iron Range with their B-24 Liberators. 'It seems that it was always raining,' remembers Bill Moran of the 90 BG:

Mildew seeped into everything ... The food was bully beef in every which way possible to cook. The coffee was something else, and what dehydrated foods we had was impossible to eat ... The Aboriginals on the beach with their fires generally got to retrieve and eat most of the fish.[20]

The conditions also made flying to and from Iron Range difficult, if not dangerous. Frank Allen remembers that on one night in November: 'a B-24 got a little off the strip on take-off at Iron Range. Result: three B-24s and one B-17, one gas dump and twelve men — all gone'.[21]

Flying missions to New Guinea was a dangerous business and not just because of the Japanese. On 2 December 1942, a squadron of B-24 Liberators left Iron Range to attack Japanese positions in the Buna area on the north-east coast of New Guinea. The Liberator with the name of *Little Eva* was under the command of Lieutenant

Norman R. Crosson. The weather was sometimes fierce over the mountain ranges of New Guinea, but few of the pilots were prepared for the hostility of the elements on this flight. Thunderstorms were so severe that *Little Eva* lost contact with the rest of the squadron. Flying on instruments in zero visibility, Crosson told the navigator to plot a course for Iron Range. It was a major feat for the B-24 simply to remain in the air and it was soon obvious that *Little Eva* was lost. Crosson ordered his crew to bale out just before the fuel expired.

The aircraft had a crew of ten, six of whom managed to parachute successfully from the aircraft. One other opened his chute too early and was entangled on the exit door. The three remaining crew members were unable to escape before their plane crashed.[22] The survivors landed in an isolated area in north-west Queensland. Crosson and Staff Sergeant Wilson managed to find the wreck and remain there until morning. They then followed some cattle trails in an easterly direction before arriving at the Escott cattle station, 15 kilometres from the township of Burketown. They had walked 110 kilometres in eleven days.

The search for the four remaining crewmen began as soon as Crosson and Wilson were found. Lieutenant Green and eight Australian soldiers from the AIF Station at Iluka, near Burketown, together with the three Walden brothers from Escott Station, Constable Marsh from Burketown police and three Aboriginal trackers, left to search for the wreck on 14 December.[23] Air searches were also coordinated and on 19 December aircraft from Cloncurry spotted the wreck. It was not until 15 January that Constables Marsh and Hagarty, with the Aboriginal trackers Norman and Archie, actually reached the location on horseback.

The charred bodies of Sergeants E.J McKeon, J.B. Hilton and Corporal J. Gurdos were found in the rear of the fuselage. A fourth body, believed to be Sergeant Charles B. Workman, was lying face-down beside the wreck strapped to a parachute that was still entangled on the rear door exit. Constable Hagarty noted the type of the aircraft — a B-24 Liberator, serial number 123762 — before wrapping the bodies in parachute silk and burying them in two graves with three empty oxygen tanks serving as temporary headstones.[24]

Six of the aviators had now been accounted for. But where were the other four — Lieutenant Dyer, Second Lieutenants Grimes and Speltz, and the radio operator Staff Sergeant Grady S. Gaston?

The subsequent search involved police, servicemen, citizen volunteers and Aboriginal trackers. Hopes were raised when four parachutes were found about 25 kilometres from the wreck. Incredibly, on Christmas Day, Aboriginal searchers from the Mornington Island Mission had found the tracks of four men in the vicinity of Rainbow Creek — but this was 65 kilometres north-west of the wreck.[25] The tracks were heading in the direction of the Gulf, even further away from civilisation, and soon faded. The combination of the wet season, worn-out horses and weary men led to the search being scaled down. It was officially called off on 5 February 1943. Even the indefatigable Constable Hagarty had serious doubts as to the prospects of the aviators. On 21 March 1943, he reported to the Police Commissioner in Brisbane:

Considering the time which had elapsed from the date of the crash ... It would be impossible in my opinion for the men to be still alive, as they have little knowledge of finding water or bush food. It is my opinion that the men have perished in the thick coastal scrub and their skeletons may possibly be chanced upon by musterers at a future date.[26]

At that time, three of the four Americans were still alive and for one, the ordeal was only beginning.

On the morning after the crash, Dyer, Speltz, Grimes and Gaston had gathered at a spot 25 kilometres from the wreck and pondered their supplies — little more than a few bars of chocolate, a jungle knife, a fishhook, some matches and two hand guns. They then made a fateful decision. They believed that they were near the east coast of Queensland, not far from Cairns, but were not sure whether

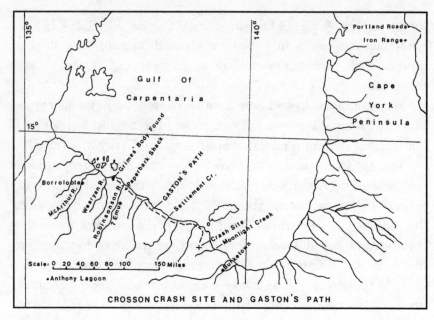

CROSSON CRASH SITE AND GASTON'S PATH

Cairns was to the north or south. In fact they were almost 600 kilometres west of Cairns, and the nearest coast was the Gulf of Carpentaria. Tragically, the four men walked away from civilisation.

They trekked for three weeks in some of the most wild and treacherous areas of Australia. Gaston was used to warm weather, having been raised in Alabama, but this heat was something else. The humidity was stifling. For the other three, who were all from North Dakota, it was even worse.

Before long, the crewmen started to succumb to the combination of the elements, exposure and starvation. Lieutenant Speltz was too sick to walk further than an old abandoned fishing shack near Seven Emus Station. Lieutenant Grimes was drowned in a futile attempt to swim across the crocodile-infested Robinson River. Lieutenant J. Dyer and Staff Sergeant Grady Gaston returned to the shack, frustrated, exhausted and ready for death. Dyer died on 10 February and Speltz two weeks later.[27]

This territory, however hostile to city dwellers, is not so to the Australian indigenous people who have lived in this land for thousands of years.

On 21 April 1943, Grady Gaston could just make out the image of a man on horseback approaching from the beach. It had been 141 days since the crash and his wasted body sported a long bush beard and hair which fell in his eyes and past his shoulders. He had remained at the old fisherman's shack and had somehow survived by eating the carcasses of dead animals and demonstrating a fierce survival instinct. The horseman was an Aborigine called Strike-a-Light. He worked as a stockman for Jack Keighran, the owner of the remote Seven Emus Station. Lieutenant Grimes' body had been found some weeks before and the search had recommenced, but hope had gradually evaporated. Gaston could not even stand or talk as the Aborigine knelt beside him.

'Are you the whitefella' from the plane?' Strike-a-Light asked him. 'Why did you not stay with the plane? What in hell are you doing here?' There was still no answer. 'Are you alright? Poor bugger, do you want a smoke?'

Gaston remembered the jubilation on seeing his rescuers:

We finally found a white man and several more black boys. They had been rounding up stray cattle. They fixed me something to eat. They called it 'Johnnie Cakes'. It tasted very good. After eating, they put me on a horse and we started to ride to his homestead. It was 27 miles away and the ride was very hard for me. He later killed a bullock, but I ate too much too soon and was very sick. Mr Keighran gave me some clothes and I stayed for two weeks and began to pick up weight. I was 168 pounds at the time of the crash and now I was down to less than a 100. He sent one of the black boys to the police station at a place called Borroloola, 75 miles away. It was the first case the police had handled for seven years. Later, fifteen Aussie soldiers came for me. They had blazed a trail through country that no vehicle had ever travelled. They went back to pick up the bodies of Lieutenant Dyer and Lieutenant Speltz. They then took me to Borroloola which had a population of one policeman and seven natives. I stayed with the policeman for a day or two. The Aussie soldiers then drove me 185 miles to a place called Anthony's Lagoon where a plane could land. We then flew to a place called Gamewell and then on to Cloncurry. I didn't have a thing, no money, no clothes, nothing. Folks took me into their homes. They wanted to give me money, food, automobiles anything. They were wonderful. I wanted to keep my hair and beard long, so the guys could see what I looked like, but the barber insisted that I cut it off. Some American officers then arrived and I had to give them a report. They then told me that Lieutenant Crosson and Sergeant Wilson had been rescued and this made me very happy.[28]

After a week in a Townsville hospital, Gaston was sent back to the States, as were Crosson and Wilson. Grady Gaston's report on the tragedy astonished officials, who instigated training in essential survival techniques.

The tragedy of *Little Eva* is a little-known, minor incident in a war which was dealing in death every day. Most Americans had seen the civilised Australia, but only a few like Gaston and his buddies witnessed the savagery and ruthlessness of a land that no great power, or great technology, could master.

It would have not occurred to Grady Gaston and certainly not to his buddies that the memory of the *Little Eva* incident would be immortalised by the Aboriginal people of northern Australia. While searching for the Americans, Karrijiji, an Aborigine known as Frank to the white population, was inspired to compose a chant commemorating the incident.

In the decades since the crash, generations of the Yanyuwa and Garrwa Aboriginal people perform the Ka-Wayawayma — the Aeroplane Dance. These indigenous people from north-east Queensland recreate the incident with intense enthusiasm and sincerity, effectively incorporating the wartime tragedy into an indigenous cultural celebration. *Little Eva* and the men from America are now firmly entrenched in Aboriginal folklore.[29]

Iron Range was a difficult posting. It was not, however, the most northerly airfield in Queensland. Horn Island, a few miles from the tip of Cape York, also boasted a landing strip. The island had been a civilian facility pre-war, used as a fuel and relief stop by the Sydney to New Guinea air service. In March 1942, there were about 300 men stationed there. It seems that the problem of fresh water and the poor wharf facilities were not the sum total of the deprivations. 'Present living conditions on Horn Island are disgusting,' a contemporary report noted, 'and the Air Officer Commanding will not move the 32nd squadron there unless better conditions are provided'.[30]

Another squadron based at Horn Island for a short period was the Australian 24th, which flew Wirraway aircraft. The island was the closest airfield to the New Guinea mainland, which meant that the Japanese were also close and the island became an attractive target. A young 19-year-old pilot with the 24th, Barney Davis, recalled that 'the biggest ablution and latrine shed I ever saw was at Horn Island — peppered with bullet holes. The Japs must have thought it was a workshop.'[31]

The Japanese first attacked on 14 March 1942 with eight Nell bombers escorted by nine Zeros. They were in for quite a surprise, as a squadron of Kittyhawks from the American No. 49 Fighter Group were temporarily based on Horn. Nine of the Kittyhawks took off to intercept the attackers. This was in contrast to the tragic fate of Major Pell's 33rd Pursuit Squadron, which had been surprised and decimated at the RAAF drome in Darwin three weeks earlier. On this day in March, the Americans shot down two Zeros and one bomber before beating off the attack for the loss of only one Kittyhawk.

Another Kittyhawk squadron, the Australian 75th, was also based on the island after its sterling service in New Guinea. If Horn Island was a terrible place, then it was also invaluable, being one of the few airfields that could accommodate large bombers like the B-17s and B-26 Marauders.[32]

The last time the Japanese attacked the airstrip was on 28 June 1943. It was a poor attempt by a lonely aircraft which created no damage and also reflected the changing fortunes of the Japanese war machine, which was by this time struggling to stem the Allied juggernaut. This raid was also the last time a Japanese aircraft flew over the territory of north-east Australia.[33]

The Queensland Main Roads Commission found more than its share of challenges during the war. These were not just in airfield construction but also in building or upgrading the numerous access roads, often in the outback. Very few roads in these areas were covered or weather resistant. The road between Mount Isa and Tennant Creek was upgraded in a project that began in March 1942 and was completed in late 1943. Over 600 kilometres of new all-weather road was built in some of the roughest and toughest areas in the country — through sand, desert and rock. The road was soon taking an average of 1000 trucks a day, from Mount Isa to Tennant Creek and then north to Darwin. Other priorities concerned an inland road from Ipswich to Charters Towers, which reduced pressure on the coast road from Brisbane to Townsville which was often cut by floodwaters. The route from Townsville to Charters Towers was also improved, with the road being widened with crossing strips where convoys of up to 500 vehicles could safely pass. There were also many conversions and other new work in the Atherton Tableland, Gordonvale, Mareeba and Cairns areas, with construction camps as familiar a sight as the military bases.[34]

Queensland Railways often worked beyond its normal capacity during the war. North Queensland had only a single line which resulted in chronic congestion and a build-up of rolling stock.

Munitions and troop trains had the priority. Civilian travel was limited and laborious, involving numerous diversions to any one of the many sidings constructed to divert low priority trains. Rolling stock was stressed and so were Queensland Railways personnel who were granted no recreation leave in the peak years of the war. In 1939–40, Queensland Railways registered 16 million miles of travel. In 1942–43, 24 million miles were logged.[35]

By early 1943, 80 per cent of all American servicemen in Australia were stationed in Queensland, either billeted there or in the process of being shipped out to the Pacific combat zones.

The town of Mackay is only a few hundred kilometres south of Townsville, yet the harmony between troops and civilians there was almost idyllic. Indeed, such was the appeal of Mackay that the *New York Times* told its readers:

A small town on Australia's northern coast is one of the most popular 'objectives' for men in our Fifth Air Force — and a model for Red Cross leave-areas outside of large cities. The small town is M'Kaye, pronounced to rhyme with 'high'. Chosen because it is the spot nearest to New Guinea that is malaria-free, M'Kaye offers a great variety of Red Cross sponsored recreational activities.[36]

The town was an obvious attraction to the Yanks, whether you spelt it correctly or not. It was relatively modern, it was clean, and there were very few of the male population still in the town. Mackay offered sun, sea and surf, with palm trees, no waiting at food lines, few Diggers, and always a seat at the cinema. The town was so popular that up to 1000 Yanks arrived a week, with a similar number reluctantly vacating the paradise. Mackay was a popular honeymoon destination — something of an Australian Niagara Falls.

By mid-1944, 75 couples had taken their wedding vows in Mackay. This included 22 local girls, with the remainder arriving from all over the country for the love of a Yank. They came from Brisbane, Townsville, Maryborough, Nambour, and one girl arrived from far-away Adelaide. The grooms were predominantly 5th Air Force members and a few navy personnel. It was also easier to get married now that the war was being won and the men were on the move. By 1944, in Mackay, all a consenting couple needed was a single document signed by the United States Adjutant General.[37]

The *New York Times* never made mention of the fact that the extremely popular town of Mackay also produced a postscript of tragedy. The Mackay airport was always a busy centre, with aircraft stopping for refuelling. Later in the war it was further inundated with air traffic from American forces enjoying rest and recreation leave. It may have been the fact that the Mackay airfield was not a priority facility that led to delays in upgrading and development. On 14 June 1943, an American officer placed a request to the RAAF Headquarters for some essential requirements:

Control tower at Mackay– Air traffic through Mackay now amounts to more than 100 aircraft arriving and departing each week. The field control people have been requesting a control tower ... and I believe one is urgently needed there.

Request that steps be taken to install one of your standard steel Control towers ... at Mackay. If this is not possible, then I request permission for the U.S. Army to construct some sort of control tower at the Airdrome.[38]

Only a few hours earlier the United States Army had suffered a grievous tragedy and Australia had experienced its worst air disaster.

It was 6.05 am when Sergeant Second Class D. Larkin answered the telephone at the Mackay District police station. The caller was Joan Harris, an 18-year-old local girl. 'An aeroplane has just crashed in our paddock,' she said. 'I think that it's a Yank plane — a big one. There's fire and smoke, please come quick.'

A B-17C transport aircraft, No. 40-2072 from the 46th Transport Carrier Squadron, containing 41 passengers and crew, had just taken off from Mackay Aerodrome when it suddenly crashed into trees near Bakers Creek, eight kilometres away. Most of the men had just enjoyed a ten-day period of rest and recreation and were returning to active duty in New Guinea. Forty of them died instantly, and only 21-year-old Foye Roberts survived.

Little consideration was given to passenger comforts for a flight such as this. The aircraft was a modified B-17C with many weapons and fixtures removed. Inside it was tight and uncomfortable. Men sat between each other's legs and back to back. It would have been a long, miserable flight to New Guinea. Nobody knew at the time how many men were on board, nor was there a passenger manifest. Most of the victims were in their early twenties.

The aircraft had been in continuous service since the early days of the war. It had survived being destroyed on the ground in the

Philippines and was flown to Australia. Like many others during the war, the accident was hidden under the dark cloak of censorship. Very few people knew then, or know now, the extent of the disaster. Relatives were told that their boys died in an air accident somewhere in the South-West Pacific Area.

When the Queensland Police Commissioner, Mr C.J. Carroll, sent a copy of the Mackay police report on the disaster to the American Base Section 3 Headquarters in Brisbane, he was compelled to compose a covering letter to be attached to the report. He completed the brief letter thus: 'I also desire to express to you the sympathy of this Department on this tragic occurrence'.[39]

A few weeks after the crash, a young Mackay girl, Mavis Doolan, found a ring in the mud near Bakers Creek. Much later it was revealed that it had been a school graduation gift to Alfred H. Frezza from Altoona, Pennsylvania. It was Technical Sergeant A. H. Frezza, 6949396, 27th Depot Repair Squadron, who was wearing it on the morning of 14 June 1943. For him and 39 of his buddies, the R and R leave would never end.[40]

The air disaster at Mackay was not an isolated incident. The crowded skies over the east coast of Australia during the peak years of the occupation were a dangerous place to be. Accidents and disappearing aircraft were virtually a daily occurrence. Telegrams from the War Department to families and spouses relating to a loved one 'killed in an aircraft accident in the South-West Pacific Theatre' were all too familiar — particularly in 1943.

A few weeks before the Mackay tragedy, on 27 March, an aircraft described as a Douglas RAAF transport crashed after taking off from a fog-bound Archerfield aerodrome, killing all 23 servicemen aboard. George Siebenhausen, who lived a mile from the drome, told authorities that he heard an aircraft engine backfire and then a loud crash. An inquiry held in late June proved to be an acrimonious affair, with the RAAF and police blaming each other for a lack of assistance. A failure to observe proper maintenance procedures was mentioned as a factor, but Air Commodore

J.H. Summers was more specific when he told the press that the cause of the accident was 'poor technique and an a error of judgement on the part of the pilot'. The Coroner, Mr J.J. Leahy, reminded the air commodore that the pilot, Flying Officer Alexander Arnold, was a sound pilot with over 1300 hours experience and 'was unfortunately not available to respond to any allegation'.[41]

No-one will ever know the cause of another disaster involving a Douglas C-47 which crashed west of Yaamba, near Rockhampton, on 19 December.

Henry Gale was in the kitchen of a property at Canal Creek when he heard an aircraft approaching. It sounded to him to be making a peculiar noise. 'I went on to the side verandah and looked in the direction of the sound,' he later told Rockhampton police. 'It was overcast and the plane came out of the clouds. It was spinning and smoke was coming from it. A few seconds later I heard an explosion and saw the plane burst into flames before it hit the ground.'

Telling his wife to ring the police, Gale jumped into his utility and drove to the scene. He would never forget the scale of the disaster that confronted him. 'I saw twenty to thirty bodies strewn among and around the wreckage of the plane which was still burning. I made sure that no-one was alive before returning to the station to wait for the police.' Gale was moved by the scene, especially when he realised some of the victims were women and that a member of the Salvation Army was also amongst the dead.[42]

A fire while in flight is a nightmare for any pilot and for Lieutenant Crecelius, the pilot of the C-47 VH-CHR on a flight from Townsville to Brisbane, it must have been a terrifying experience. It was cloudy and wet and the aircraft carried 31 passengers. All must have known of their imminent fate seconds, perhaps even minutes, before their death in a paddock near a town that none of them had heard of.

Few of the dead could be identified. Pay books provided the initial identification. There were 20 Americans, including three sailors who had somehow hustled a ride. They may have sat next to Lieutenants Williams, Smith and Korranda — all United States Army nurses. William Tibbs, in his Salvation Army chaplain's uniform, may have provided comfort as the aircraft entered its dive. Also on the flight was Lieutenant Nigel MacDonald, a YMCA welfare officer. Eight other Australians also lost their lives — a number of RAAF personnel and Harold Dick, a 26-year-old war correspondent. His father, a detective in the Criminal Investigation Branch in Brisbane, learnt of his son's death as he casually browsed a police report.[43]

Rockhampton, 600 kilometres north of Brisbane, was home to an entire American division — over 15 000 men. The town and the 41st Division enjoyed such a congenial relationship that it become a shining example of Allied harmony. Much of the credit must go to the popular and competent Major-General Robert L. Eichelberger, whose ability to communicate with his staff and with the Rockhampton City Council was a major factor in the success of the association. Mackay might have been as popular, but while that town was ostensibly a rest and recreation location, Rocky was a semi-permanent billet. The local Red Cross at the Penneys building was perhaps even more effective than the one in Mackay. It offered a wide range of services, including entertainment, laundry, grooming, correspondence, dancing lessons and invaluable tuition in boomerang throwing.

The American contribution to Rockhampton included a great deal of civil development which buoyed the commercial sector. By the end of 1943, most of the 41st had gone but few would forget Rockhampton as being the best thing about the war. The locals thought so too, especially the women. Three hundred of them carried their association into matrimony.[44]

Although many places in Australia had little or no appeal for the American visitors, the worst and the most feared posting was New Guinea. During and after the war, New Guinea was mandated territory under Australian administration. This permitted the

Australian militia to be deployed there. New Guinea was a sparsely populated, undeveloped and oppressive country. Jungles, mountains, heat, stench and disease awaited any visitors.

★ ★ ★

'The life of the MacArthurs at Lennons Hotel is one of simple dignity, almost monastic in its call to duty,' reported one of the reporters sanctioned by the Supreme Commander's headquarters. MacArthur's monastic existence was a top-floor billet in Brisbane's best hotel, that included four adjoining suites, each of which had a bedroom, living room, kitchen, office and library. In July 1942, the General had moved to Brisbane to be closer to the battlefields in New Guinea, where it seemed that at last something resembling an offensive was taking place.[45] From his office at the AMP building, two blocks from Lennons Hotel, MacArthur issued a statement to the press:

No nation is making a more supreme war effort than Australia. It is rapidly gearing to full capacity. Its effort is universal and embraces equally all classes and all parties. It has unanimously and completely supported me in my military command.[46]

MacArthur was eloquent and sincere as he concluded: 'The harmony and cooperation between Australians and Americans in this area is inspirational'.

Less than a month later, the only cooperation between the two sides was in damaging a block and a half of downtown Brisbane. The infamous Battle of Brisbane ended in a demonstration outside the AMP building. However, on the night of the rioting MacArthur was in New Guinea, attempting to resolve an apparent stalemate. The good news for MacArthur was that the Aussies and Yanks at the front were not fighting each other. If there was harmony and cooperation between the sides, then it was to be found in the jungles of New Guinea, where the Allies were meeting fanatical opposition from a powerful Japanese force.

The battlefields were at Buna and Gona, situated on the south-

Things to do in Townsville — booze and broads. *(Courier-Mail)*

Things to do in
Cloncurry — booze.
(Courier-Mail)

MacArthur inspires Eichelberger. 'Bob, take Buna or don't come back alive.'

Horn Island in the Torres Strait, 1943. 'Present living conditions are disgusting ...'

Jungle music — New Guinea. Digger, Gene Dolheguy, plays the blues. Note the empty bottles, gramophone and 'V' discs pinched from the Yanks. Don Reid tunes up in the background.

An unusual duo — the boy from Wisconsin and the local boy from Papua. The 32nd Division near Buna, November 1942.

The Brisbane submarine base, New Farm, late 1942. New S and T class boats and the tender *Fulton*.

The USS *Sturgeon*.

An old S class submarine
off the coast of Australia.

The shame of segregation. Two groups of American soldiers — one white, one black
— celebrate Independence Day in Cairns, 4 July 1942. A white officer fronts the
black unit. (*Courtesy of Mrs J. Harper,* Australia's Frontline: Remembering the 1939–
45 War, *University of Queensland Press*)

This may well be the first time this young Australian girl had seen a black man in uniform. It is doubtless the first time this mess steward had ever been asked for an autograph. (*Courier-Mail*)

The fair dinkum Australians in uniform. Aboriginal Privates S. Leonard and H. West pictured in Sydney before leaving for the Middle East, 1941. Both were killed in action before the end of the year. (*John Oxley Library, Brisbane*)

The vanishing Americans. Only one American sailor could be found to pose for this remarkable photograph. Brisbane, 1944.

The *Mariposa* bride ship departs, April 1946.

Les and Yvonne Cottman, 1997.   Bill and Joan Bentson, 1998.

The Bakers Creek Memorial, Mackay.

eastern coast of New Guinea. MacArthur wanted to eject the Japanese from Buna in order to construct airfields that would assist in his plans to advance along the New Guinea coast. By the time units of the 32nd Division had arrived in New Guinea in September 1942, the campaign had changed direction. The Japanese had been stopped on the Kokoda Trail and were now in full retreat to the beachhead of Buna, where they were to hold fast until they were relieved. The battles to dislodge the Japanese from Buna and Gona were fierce and bloody.

By November 1942, Australian and Japanese soldiers were battle-hardened veterans, but the Americans of the 32nd Division were not. Originally a National Guard Division, it consisted of volunteers who had joined in 1940. Apart from several large-scale peacetime exercises back in the States, the 32nd was untrained and inexperienced. They had been in Australia for six months before units were dispatched to Port Moresby. The bush camp back at Logan Village in Brisbane was the closest they had got to jungle conditions, with kangaroos in the bush rather than Japanese.[47]

The problems that the Australians experienced (and later the Americans) were compounded by the strategic ignorance demonstrated by MacArthur, Blamey and others who had little or no idea about the adversity of the conditions or the strength of the enemy. The Japanese had in fact been reinforced and in the Buna, Gona and Sanananda areas there were estimated to be over 8000 Japanese in fortified positions.

The American 32nd Division attacked the Japanese defences at Buna on 19 November 1942 with no artillery or tank support, and were slaughtered. They tried again and were repulsed with heavy casualties. The military objective was similar to many of the island campaigns that the United States Marines conducted throughout the Pacific war. The difference was that the Marines were highly trained and equipped. They had the benefit of ship-to-shore bombardment, artillery, amphibious and tracked vehicles, and as the encounters were usually swift and bloody they were spared the many rigorous jungle diseases that were crippling to the Australian and American forces in New Guinea.[48]

MacArthur arrived in Port Moresby in early November. He continued his 'monastic existence' at the royal and regal Government House. MacArthur wanted for nothing. General Kenney even flew a flush toilet from Australia for the General's use. It was the first water closet ever installed in New Guinea.[49]

It was at Government House that the General had his celebrated audience with Major General Robert Eichelberger, who he had summoned from Australia. Eichelberger was to relieve Major General Harding, the field commander of the 32nd Division. Other commanders were also to be replaced. MacArthur was at his most motivational: 'Bob, take Buna or don't come back alive.' There was more. 'If you capture Buna I'll award you the Distinguished Service Cross and, Bob, I'll release your name for newspaper publication.'

This last gesture was magnanimous, as usually there was only one name released to the press — MacArthur.[50]

When Eichelberger relieved General Harding he was appalled by the situation. The Allies were barely surviving against elite Japanese troops. In the front line, more than half the men were wounded or killed. According to Eichelberger, it could have been much worse 'if the malaria mosquito hadn't removed so many from the field of battle'.[51]

By January 1943, both sides were crippled by casualties and sickness but at last, after 60 days of intensive combat, Buna, Gona and Sanananda were captured. It had taken substantial Australian reinforcements and nearly 9000 casualties to destroy the Japanese. General Eichelberger received his medal and MacArthur the credit. The efficient, imaginative MacArthur public relations team, led by LeGrande Diller, made sure that any reports from the front line conveyed only favourable news, giving total credit to the infallible MacArthur. The General had his victory, but he would have no glory.

The Buna and Gona battles destroyed MacArthur's reputation for brilliantly conceived victories with low casualties. There was nothing brilliant about the battles. The courage and resolve of the men in the front line were the decisive factors and the casualties were appalling. In 1942–43, approximately 20 000 Australians served in New Guinea. Most contracted malaria, dysentery or dengue fever. There were 5698 battle casualties. The 126th, 127th and 128th Infantry Regiments of the American 32nd Division served in New Guinea. The 41st Division was represented by the 163rd Infantry Regiment making a total of 14 464 Americans. Of these there were 8659 casualties, mostly illness-related. When the 126th Infantry Regiment attacked Buna in November 1942 it had a strength of 3171. On 22 January 1943 there were only 611 on the active list.[52]

As the Allies tended their wounded and buried their dead, back at Government House in Port Moresby MacArthur enjoyed a victory celebration with his staff. Raising his glass as if to propose a toast, the General told his officers: 'I am reminded ... of the words of General Robert E. Lee — "It is a good thing that war is so terrible or we might learn to love it".'[53]

Survivors of the 32nd Division in New Guinea may have recalled eagerly joining the army in 1940, and the great adventure of sailing out of San Francisco and arriving in Australia to smiles and waves. Most had enjoyed their posting in Adelaide and then at Logan Village in Queensland. Many had hoped that the war would maybe pass them by and they could return home. Instead, they were amongst the first American divisions to experience combat, and in conditions that they could not have imagined. However, New Guinea was the turning point. They and the Australians won their battles, but they lost their youth and innocence. It was only the beginning for the 32nd Division. Their war was a long one, only ending with the Japanese surrender in Tokyo Bay.

CHAPTER TWELVE

GOODNIGHT, WHEREVER YOU ARE

On the evening of 6 September 1776, a peculiar barrel-shaped object bobbed up and down in New York harbour before submerging beside a British frigate, HMS *Eagle*. Inside, a volunteer sergeant of the American Revolutionary Army paddled and steered the craft attempting to place a special gunpowder charge attached to a crude corkscrew beneath the frigate's waterline. The attempt was a failure. The *Eagle*'s hull was sheathed in copper and the charge dropped to the bottom of the harbour. The submersible craft withdrew with its frustrated, gasping and coughing operator.

This manually operated machine, called the *Turtle* by its designer, David Bushnell, was one of the first in a series of craft that were to develop into the most potent naval weapon in history.[1] Other American prototypes included the *Nautilus* in 1801 and a number of submersibles used by the Confederate Navy during the Civil War.

One hundred and sixty-nine years after the *Turtle*, the defeat of Japan was not entirely caused by the apocalyptic weapon with the mushroom cloud. The atomic bomb ended the conflict with a knockout blow, but Japan had all but lost a three and a half year war of attrition.

Shortly after the war, General Hideki Tojo, the wartime prime minister of Japan, told General MacArthur that the main factors contributing to the Allied victory in the Pacific were the self-sufficiency of its naval task forces and their ability to stay at sea for indefinite periods; the leapfrogging and isolation of distant Japanese garrisons, and the effectiveness of the American submarines — especially the submarines.[2]

A large merchant marine was crucial to the economic and military requirements of the island nation of Japan. Vital imports included oil, iron ore, coal, rubber and food. Exports for wartime Japan were munitions, men and supplies that were constantly required by distant island garrisons. Iron ore and oil were particularly critical to Japan's war effort, and over 90 per cent of them were imported by sea.[3] Shortly before the war Japan had 2337 merchant ships listed in Lloyd's Register. At the end of the war there were 231.[4] Most had been sunk by American submarines, which were also responsible for sinking over 200 Japanese warships.[5]

Unlike England, Japan failed to recognise the vulnerability of the sea lanes to submarines. Few resources were allocated to preventative measures. Britain and her Allies won the Battle of the Atlantic, but Japan lost the Battle of the Pacific. At the time of its surrender, Japan could still muster 5 million men under arms and 11 000 aircraft, but they were immobilised.[6] Literally and metaphorically, Japan had run out of gas. Many historians believe that the fire bombing of Japanese cities and the use of atomic weapons were unnecessary and that the submarine blockade would ultimately have won the war.

By the end of the Pacific conflict, the US submarine service represented only 2 per cent of the American forces in the Pacific, yet that tiny percentage was more effective than the rest put together.[7] However small, it was a glamour service, consisting exclusively of volunteers. It was also the service that suffered most in the American armed forces. Of the 228 American submarines in action during the war, 52 — almost a quarter — were lost. One in five submariners was killed.[8]

During the war, little was known of the exploits of the submarine service. And even postwar, despite successful books, films and a television series, the 'silent service' has still not been accorded credit appropriate to its decisive contributions.

By the end of the nineteenth century, motor, as opposed to manually powered submarines had become a crude reality. After many impractical designs, craft with internal combustion and electric battery power were perfected and were soon adopted by the major navies. Early submarines were actually surface craft that could submerge only for short periods before the batteries wore down and had to be recharged by surfacing.

From the very start, submarines and the men who manned them had an image and vernacular all of their own. In the early stages of their development, submarines were so small that many observers called them 'boats'. Ever since, every submarine, large or small, diesel or nuclear, friend or foe — has been called not a ship but a boat. In the early history of the submarine, the cramped confines of the boats were often plagued by stench, with dirty, foul air and foul bodies; everybody called them 'pigboats' and that name stuck too. The name given to the self-propelled missile fired from the submarine was derived from a species of electric ray, *Torpedo nobiliana*. The boats and torpedoes became the stuff of folklore.[9]

The German U-boat menace in World War I demonstrated the full potential of the submarine by sinking 5000 ships and almost starving England into submission.

The American submarine service in that war did not have the opportunity or resources to wage an effective campaign. However, although Australia had only two submarines, they made a modest though memorable contribution to Australian naval history. These were 'E' class boats built in Portsmouth and commissioned into the Australian Navy in February 1914. They were 181 feet overall, 725 tons in weight, had a complement of 35 officers and men, and cost the government £105 000 each.[10]

To *AE1* fell the unfortunate distinction of being the first Australian warship to be lost. On 14 September 1914 she vanished without trace east of New Britain. However, *AE2* had a brief but exciting career. Operating in the Dardanelles shortly after the Gallipoli landing, she created considerable concern for the Turkish navy before being immobilised. Her crew spent the rest of the conflict as prisoners of war.

Australia had no submarines in service at the beginning of World War II. America had 55 boats in the Pacific, based at Pearl Harbor and the Philippines. Japanese expansion and the strategic importance of Australia to the Allied war effort resulted in a considerable proportion of America's submarine war being conducted from Australian ports.

At the start of the Pacific war, the submarine service, like other American forces, was unprepared and underequipped. Half the submarines in service were the small, obsolete O, R and S classes of World War I vintage. The S class submarines had been designed primarily for defence duties and were not equipped for long range Pacific cruises. The P and Salmon class boats launched in the '30s were much improved, bigger and had better engines. They had four bow and four stern torpedo tubes, a 4-inch deck gun and could dive within 60 seconds. The crews also had the luxury of the boats being air-conditioned.

The Tambor class boats launched just before the war were better still, with the best of the new engines — the General Motors Winton. Six tubes were forward and four aft. They were armed with a 5-inch deck gun, had air-conditioning and could cruise for 12 000 miles.

The old S class subs were called 'sugar boats' by their crews, but serving in them was far from sweet adventure. They were 220 feet long, weighed less than 1000 tons and had a crew of 42. Designed only for coastal duties, they were not air-conditioned, although operating in a controlled temperature was not just important for crew comfort. Condensation and moisture due to excessive heat were continuing problems and at least one of the engines was usually malfunctioning. Crew members also called them 'whores'.[11]

George Holley, skipper of S-41, described some of the problems:

The failure of the sound gear happened at the start of the first patrol. There was also the failure of the radio transmitter, the gyro compass and the number one attack periscope. The failure of the refrigeration plant resulted in meat being quickly consumed until it was rotten and thrown overboard.

Lieutenant Commander Holley could not recall all the faults, merely concluding: 'and so it went'. Leaks were legion and crews cannibalised spare parts to survive.

The American Navy did not at first recognise the potential of the submarine in the Pacific war. Only a few boats were built and delivered in 1940–41 and it was believed they would be used mainly for defensive and reconnaissance duties. With the prospect of war, 65 new submarines were quickly ordered. They were the superb Gato class boats, all of them welded and with excellent seagoing qualities. They had a maximum diving depth of 400 feet, first-rate crew quarters, superior surface speed and, most essentially, they could stay submerged for up to 72 hours. One hundred and ninety-five Gato class boats were built during the war, although the majority did not enter service until 1942–44.[12]

The boats of the Pacific Fleet at Pearl Harbor escaped destruction, but those of the Asiatic fleet stationed in the Philippines were not so fortunate. At the Cavite navy yard in Manila Bay, the *Sealion* was damaged beyond repair while lying in dry dock. It was the first American submarine to be lost in the war. Japanese aircraft also damaged other submarines and much of the support facilities.[13]

The early challenge for the submarine service was the defence of the Philippines. In fact, submarines were the only offensive weapon of any value available. There was much excitement when *Swordfish* sank the 8500 ton freighter *Atsutusan Maru* off Hainan Island in the South China Sea. It was the first ship to be sunk by an American submarine in any war. Unfortunately, this early success was also isolated. The American submarine service had abysmal results early in the war. The problems were many, including timid captains, poor training and poor equipment. But without doubt, the main problem confronting submariners in the first year of the war was the quality of the torpedoes.[14]

Poor design and lack of practical testing resulted in the standard American torpedo having problems with depth control and in the firing mechanism. Many skippers were driven to rage and despair by torpedos exploding either prematurely or not at all. It was not until September 1943, almost two years into the war that the service had at its disposal an effective and reliable torpedo.

By March 1942, the Asiatic submarine force had failed even to inconvenience the Japanese advance. After four months of war and hundreds of sorties, only ten enemy ships had been sunk. Over the same period, German U-boats operating off the American east coast sank 244 ships. For the American submarine service, it was an ignominious result. By December 1942, one in three captains had been replaced, most often by younger, more aggressive junior officers with more enthusiasm than experience.

As the Japanese moved south, so did the American submarines, withdrawing to Australia to regroup and rethink. Senior officers were being replaced as well. Charles Andrews Lockwood became the new commander of United States submarines in the Pacific, replacing John Wilkes. At the age of 52, Lockwood was an experienced submariner. He had served on seven submarines over 30 years, from the early gasoline boats to the latest fleet boats. Nicknamed 'Uncle Charley', Lockwood took up residence in Fremantle in April 1942. Promoted to rear admiral in May, he could not have started his role under more adverse circumstances.

After addressing the poor performance of boats and captains, Lockwood focused his attention on the torpedo problem. When the Bureau of Ordnance suggested the problem was due to improper maintenance procedures by the submariners under his command, a less than convinced Lockwood took matters into his own hands. With practical field testing it was found that the main problems with the Mark 14 torpedo were failing magnetic exploders and the firing pins not striking the primer on impact. Once these problems had been identified they were quickly resolved.[15] The success of the new improved torpedoes owed more to the efforts of the men who used them than of those who had designed them.

Lockwood became an inspirational leader. He understood the

pressures of the silent service, and with morale a priority, he leased the Ocean Beach Hotel in Fremantle and the King Edward Hotel in Perth for submariner rest camps.[16] Other Western Australian locations, such as Albany and Exmouth Gulf, were briefly used by the Americans, but Fremantle was the main base for most of the war.

There was no announcement of the American arrival in Fremantle. One morning they were simply there — ships, men and equipment. One young Perth resident saw a convoy of peculiar looking vehicles that he was later told were jeeps. He was a little uneasy when they stopped:

'Hey, buddy,' one of the soldiers called out, 'Come here. Say buddy, can you point the way to the CML building?'[17]

The Colonial Mutual Life building was to be the headquarters for the battered Asiatic submarine force, and they immediately began to construct base facilities. The tenders *Holland* and *Otus*, together with several battered and weary boats, arrived in March 1942.[18]

If the submarines were craft like no other, then the men who manned them were likewise. The submarine force has always been an exclusive unit within the United States Navy and, particularly as the war progressed, the appeal of greater responsibilities, autonomy and the prospect of quick promotion attracted many of America's finest young officers. They all came from the Navy Submarine School in New London, Connecticut, and most were graduates of the Naval Academy at Annapolis, Maryland.

The normal course ran for six months and the annual number of graduates was about 50, but war escalated everything. Courses were cut back to three months and in 1944 there were 995 graduates. Enlisted men were chosen for emotional, psychological and physical qualities. The number of enlisted men selected was 336 in 1940 and peaked at 4734 in 1944. Courses were cut in half, with extended tuitional times, sometimes until midnight. New boats were being delivered from the builders' yards at the rate of one per week.[19]

Although American submarines enjoyed little early success, the standards set in training were very high. Ignatius J. Galantin, class of 1936, future skipper of the *Halibut* and later an admiral, has written of the criteria:

Graduation from sub school was just the first step in a submarine career. To earn the 'Qualified in submarines', which gave the right to wear the gold dolphins insignia, would require a year of satisfactory service in an operating sub, completion of a notebook in which all ship's systems were sketched and described, demonstration of proficiency in diving the ship and in operating its machinery, as well as the ability to make a successful torpedo attack. To earn their silver dolphins, enlisted men went through a similar, but less rigorous procedure. A year or two after qualification, subject to the CO's recommendation, would come the designation 'Qualified to command submarines'. It took me four years of duty to receive both designations.[20]

Circumstances might have made it necessary to short-cut this procedure, but as the war progressed the great majority of American submariners, both officers and other ranks, were skilled and resourceful.

The all-volunteer service enjoyed a special camaraderie and *esprit de corps*. Every man in the boats had a special responsibility; everyone depended on each other. Camaraderie was a result of service ethos but also of congestion. The stinking interior of old S class sub or even more modern ones were no place for those who lacked communication and social skills. After a cruise of 60 days, men finally had a chance to change their underwear. Clothes and most bed linen were not laundered at base — they were destroyed. Some ratings never breathed any air outside of the boat for up to two months.

Eighty men in an area the size of a railway carriage enjoyed an effective yet relaxed and informal discipline. Submerged, the officers removed their neckties and caps; open collars and baseball caps were more practical. Officers wore khaki shirt and trousers, ratings wore denim dungarees. Even facial hair was allowed. When it was hot they wore shorts and sandals, and when it became even hotter the men worked bare-chested.

The submariners felt good about their status. They enjoyed the life and the liberty. While nobody ever conducted a survey, it always seemed that the men from the 'pigboats' got more of the girls, and with the extra 50 per cent in pay a submariner received many a young lady would be spoilt.

In the early months of the war, the service slowly improved its effectiveness. However, this was not simply thanks to the Navy Submarine School in New London. No-one there could really teach you what to do about a dud torpedo, or a depth-charge attack from a group of destroyers, or engine failure, or running aground. The Pacific ocean was one big finishing school.

The first boats out of Fremantle achieved no results. The Pearl Harbor boats were doing well in the Marshall Islands, the Carolines and the East China Sea, but the areas of the Java Sea, Philippines and the South China Sea patrolled by Fremantle boats seemed to offer slim pickings. Maybe they were just unlucky.

The turning point for Australian-based boats seems to have come when *Skipjack* conducted a patrol to Camranh Bay which resulted in the sinking of four Japanese ships of 28 000 tons.[21]

Patrols from Fremantle usually averaged a dozen a month. The submariners loved the time between patrols, but there were soon complaints about the distance of rest houses from the city. What the sailors really wanted was booze and broads. Boats returning from patrols met the pilot boat that guided them to the berth; the navy band played on the wharf and fresh milk, fruit and mail were delivered. Then it was liberty. Staff officers knew the value of morale, and quality liberty was deemed as important as reliable machinery.

A tabloid service newspaper, *The Mirror*, kept everybody informed, entertained and up to date. The liberty haunts were many — the ANA Club, the Ocean Beach Hotel and the Embassy Ballroom. One 18-year-old submariner looked forward to his liberty in Fremantle with a passion: 'Freeo, with the sun, surf, broads and booze was like going to heaven'.[22]

In April 1942, Brisbane also become a major American submarine base. The former commander of the Atlantic-based submarines, Ralph Christie, was the new commander of the fledging Brisbane operation. With the tender *Griffin*, Christie and six boats sailed from Panama on 5 March, arriving in Brisbane on 15 April. The welcome was a typical Queensland tropical storm of 60-knot winds and hailstones the size of golfballs.

Five other boats arrived from Manila via Java and Fremantle. With eleven boats — all of them S class — and a tender, Christie began to construct the facility at New Farm wharf. Facing the immediate threat of Japanese invasion, Christie's orders were to conduct defensive operations from the east coast.[23] It was early days, but it wasn't long before the boats were being used offensively and the Brisbane base, with the exception of Pearl Harbor, became the largest American submarine facility in the war.

The patrols from Brisbane for officers and crew of the S class boats were often a nightmare. The heat generated by a tropical climate was overwhelming. These quintessential pigboats were also sweatboats. Nobody bothered to chase the cockroaches after a while. William Ruhe, a junior officer, described the conditions aboard *S-37*:

The bunks beyond the wardroom are filled with torpid, skivvy-clad bodies. Metal fans are whirring everywhere ... The deck in the control room is littered with towels, used to sponge up the water dripping off men and the submarine itself ... The food is routine — something canned. The dehydrated potato, powdered onions and reconstituted carrots have the same general taste — like sawdust.[24]

Mechanical failures were routine, but to turn the machinery off for maintenance was a risky business. It was feared that it would not start again. The diving planes were noisy and the sonar gear inadequate. Another young officer also recalled the repellent living conditions on an antiquated submarine:

'Hot bunking it', was aptly applied to this way of sleeping on an S-boat in tropical waters. If the previous sleeper had sweated profusely, the officer taking over the just vacated bunk would unlash the canvas from its iron frame, turn it over to dump out the puddle of sweat and then re-lash the canvas to the iron frame with the dry side up. Blankets were rarely used and sheets never. Pillows were formed from folded dungarees.[25]

S-37 was the worst of them all; it was a wreck. In June 1942 it returned to Brisbane shortly after starting a patrol. Somebody inadvertently put a hole in the hull.[26] Regardless of their condition, the old boats put in noble service. The most successful was *S-44*, commanded by John Raymond 'Dinty' Moore, class of '29. The old sub had the distinction of sinking a ship on each of its first two patrols.

Moore was a no-nonsense, competent officer. As far as the old boats went, *S-44* was in reasonable condition. The men had gathered their own funds and bought a makeshift air-conditioning unit which they installed before arriving in Brisbane. Moore was on patrol in the Solomons when the 1st Marine Division landed on Guadalcanal in 1942. He would not have been aware that Japanese Admiral Mikawa, with a large force of cruisers, had launched a surprise surface attack on the invasion fleet off Savo Island early in the morning of 9 August. The Australian cruiser, *Canberra*, and the American heavy cruisers *Vincennes, Quincy* and *Astoria* had been surprised and sunk with the loss of over 1000 sailors.[27]

Japanese casualties and damage were minimal. As the Japanese ships were returning to Rabaul, Moore saw them in his periscope. The four Japanese cruisers which had just inflicted the worst ever defeat on the American navy at sea were now confronted by the old *S-44*.

Moore decided to attack the last in line. It was the modern, 9000-ton heavy cruiser *Kako*. The old boat crept to within 700 yards of the *Kako* and fired a spread of four torpedos. Thirty seconds later there was a terrifying noise as the ship blew up, sinking in minutes. Moore successfully evaded a depth-charge attack and returned to Brisbane a hero. His was the first American submarine to sink a major Japanese warship.[28]

Not all patrols were assigned the destruction of Japanese shipping, and special-mission status was assigned to many patrols. *Spearfish* (Lieutenant Commander James C. Dempsey) was on the last leg of a successful patrol, having sunk two freighters of 11 000 tons, when Dempsey received an urgent message to enter the harbour of Corregidor and pick up some special American personnel and deliver them to Fremantle. Corregidor was under siege by the Japanese.

On 3 May 1942 *Spearfish* eased into Manila bay, cleverly evading Japanese surface craft. Later that night small boats arrived carrying passengers. Some officers bought with them a roster of all who remained on the Rock. There were also cabinets of documents. Dempsey thought he had seen it all, until he also saw an officer's wife. What really got the ranks talking was the last group of passengers — twelve army nurses. *Spearfish* was a new S class boat, built in 1938, which had a very tight complement of 70. Now there were nearly 100 on board plus their possessions. For over 20 hours the *Spearfish* remained submerged, delicately avoiding Japanese warships.

Forty-eight hours after the last nurse was helped aboard *Spearfish* and offered a piece of candy, the American forces at Corregidor surrendered to the Japanese.[29]

Unlike most American services, what the submarine force was not the subject of great publicity. No war correspondents were allowed on the boats. Anonymity in life and death was the pattern. The great deeds of the service during the war were censored to prevent the Japanese learning the tactics that were being employed. Moreover, the navy wanted the Japanese to believe that the submarines were ineffective and to underestimate them. Admiral Lockwood was a keen exponent of confidentiality.

Great pressure was being put on the Navy Department to publish play by play accounts of the war. We of the submarines wanted no part of this. To keep the enemy guessing, we wanted him to go about his routines and methods and to think that every time he dropped a depth-charge, another American submarine went to Davy Jones' locker.[30]

The American media, accustomed to many a scoop and lead story, were denied information by the submariners and many believe that the term silent service was as much a result of this policy as the subs' cruising and operating procedures.

'Loose Lips Sink Ships' said the posters in almost every bar and public facility. But in one of the great gaffes of the war, American newspapers published a story about submariners escaping escort attacks because Japanese depth-charges were set too shallow. This story caused outrage within the service. Most hoped that it had gone unnoticed. It had not. A Brisbane S-boat on patrol in the Solomons actually heard an American news broadcast discussing the fact that only three American submarines had been lost and that they could evade depth-charges simply by diving deeper. Only a few hours later the daily Tokyo Rose radio program issued a warning: 'To United States submarine sailors, our Japanese warships are going to start using far bigger depth-charges with settings so deep that there'll be no way to avoid being sunk'.

Many sailors died because of this one indiscretion. In future for the silent service, the press was treated with deep suspicion and with caution. One radio man developed the slogan: 'Shoot off your mouth and pull a rickshaw'.[31]

While the American submarine force struggled for success, Japanese submarines conducted a successful offensive campaign in or near Australian waters. Many of their attacks were in sight of the mainland. It is a little known fact that seventeen ships, nearly 10 per cent of those sunk by Japanese submarines during the war, met their fate off the east coast of Australia.[32]

The most famous Japanese naval attack on Australia was the

midget submarine raid on Sydney Harbour on the night of 31 May 1942.

A Japanese float plane had flown over the harbour the day before, passing over North Head at an altitude as low as 90 feet. The observer was frantically sketching the harbour and the distribution of ships, and in an attempt to get his bearings the pilot used Macquarie Lighthouse as a marker. Three large Japanese submarines then released three midget submarines for the attack.

Two of the midget submarines successfully evaded the boom nets at the harbour entrance while the third became entangled. In an evening of wild excitement and confusion, one of the submarines was destroyed by a depth-charge attack while a third managed to fire two torpedos at the USS *Chicago*, which was the main target for the operation. The torpedoes missed the cruiser but one hit the *Kuttabul*, a ferry which was being used as floating dormitory. Twenty-one young ratings were killed. The raid, although not a success for the Japanese, caused considerable alarm for the Australian public. It created enormous publicity and photographs of the captured Japanese craft were widely published.[33]

A few days later, Sydney received a further reminder of how close the war had come when the Japanese submarine *I-24* fired her deck gun at South Head, Rose Bay and Bellevue Hill. Ten rounds were fired and the action caused much alarm, but little damage. Two hours later, the *I-21* fired 34 rounds in the direction of Newcastle. One landed near the Parnell Place air raid shelter, but once again, the damage was insignificant; most of the shells did not explode.[34]

The most notorious episode in the Japanese submarine campaign against Australian shipping was the sinking of the hospital ship RHS *Centaur*, 58 kilometres north-east of Brisbane. The ship was on its way to Port Moresby to pick up wounded personnel when Commander Nakagawa, of the *I-177*, sighted her in his periscope. Despite displaying lights and hospital markings the ship was torpedoed shortly after 4 am on 14 May 1943. The *Centaur* went down in minutes, 268 of the 332 on board were lost and the survivors spent over 30 hours in the water. The death toll might have been higher still had it not been for the arrival of the American destroyer, *Mugford*, under Lieutenant Commander Howard S. Corey.

The sinking of the *Centaur* drew intense condemnation from both MacArthur and Curtin, and from the crew of the *Mugford* who donated nearly $500 for the survivors.[35]

All the while, a number of American submarines and their commanders were distinguishing themselves.

Lieutenant Commander Howard W. Gilmore was a unique officer, who had risen through the ranks to command a submarine. He knew both good and bad fortune. While on a peacetime cruise with the USS *Shark*, he and a junior officer were attacked by thugs in Panama and their throats were slashed. The scars had not yet healed when Gilmore's wife died of polio. While he was commanding the *Growler* in the Pacific, his second wife was seriously injured after falling down a flight of stairs. The other officer who was assaulted in Panama, Charles Triebel, said of Gilmore: 'Howard was one of the finest men I knew, but he was born under an unlucky star'.

Gilmore might have been unlucky, but he was also fearless. On an early patrol in *Growler* he attacked three Japanese destroyers, sinking one and damaging the others. In early 1943, *Growler* was a Brisbane-based boat on patrol in the Solomons. On 16 January she sank a 6000 ton Japanese ship; another was fired at but the torpedo failed to explode. On 7 February, *Growler* had surfaced and was recharging its batteries when Gilmore sighted what he believed to be a small gunboat. Calling the crew to action stations, Gilmore decided to sink the craft with his deck gun. The ship was not a gunboat but the 900 ton provision ship *Hayasaki* which prepared to ram. The ships collided and became locked together. The *Hayasaki* opened fire with machine-guns, killing an officer and a rating and wounding Gilmore. Refusing any aid, Gilmore ordered the bridge to be cleared and for the boat to submerge. The executive officer, Arnold Schade, stood at the bottom of the ladder waiting in vain for his captain. Howard Gilmore lost his life but gained immortality when he yelled the order, 'Take her down!' Schade crash-dived the boat with his captain and two dead crewmen still topside. The *Growler* was severely damaged but managed to crawl back to Brisbane with a sombre crew. For his unselfish devotion to duty Howard Gilmore was awarded the Medal of Honor. He was the first submariner to receive the award.[36]

William Leslie Wright was one of the most senior officers in the silent service, having graduated from submarine school in 1925. He told tall tales and drank tall whiskies; he was fearless and everyone called him 'Bull'. Wright and his boat, *Sturgeon*, could not have been in action any earlier in the war. The submarine had been berthed alongside the tender *Holland* in Manila when the Japanese attacked on 8 December. Wright had had a big night before. His executive officer, Reuben Whitaker, attempted to wake him with the news that the Japanese had attacked Pearl Harbor. 'Captain,' said Whitaker, 'I'm going to get the boat under way and move out into Manila Bay so we can dive if we have to.'

'Hey Reuben, take care of that for me,' said Wright. 'I'm going back to sleep.'

Whitaker took the boat out to sea and awaited orders. At 3.45 pm, *Sturgeon* and 50 other boats received explicit instructions: 'Submarines and aircraft will wage unrestricted warfare'.

The *Sturgeon* was a relatively modern boat, one of the new S class, delivered in 1938. It had a crew of 70 which included third officer Chester William Nimitz Jr. son of the famous Admiral. When Bull Wright believed he had sunk his first ship he sent a message to base: '*Sturgeon*, is no longer a virgin'.[37]

Like the rest of the submarine service, the *Sturgeon* had withdrawn to Australia. It left on its first war cruise from Fremantle in late June 1942, bound for the waters off Manila. At about the same time that *Sturgeon* was cruising up the Western Australian coast, a 7000-ton Japanese freighter was leaving Rabaul for Hainan Island off the coast of Japan. It was the freighter *Montevideo Maru*, serving as a naval auxiliary. The ship was sailing without escort, but with a top speed of 17 knots the crew were confident of being able to outrun American submarines. On the night of 30 June, Wright saw her in his periscope and noted in his log:

At 2216 sighted a darkened ship to southward. This fellow was really going, making at least 17 knots, and probably a bit more, as he appeared to be zig-zagging. At this time it looked a bit hopeless, but determined to hang on in the hope he would slow or change course toward us. Sure enough, about midnight he slowed to about 12 knots. After that it was easy. At 0225 — fired four torpedo spread, range 4000 yards, from after tubes. At 0229 heard and observed an explosion about 75–100 feet abaft stack. At 0240 observed ship sink stern first. Dove at dawn. No further contacts.

A few of the Japanese crew escaped in two boats which reached Luzon the following day. However the cargo was lost. The cargo included 19-year-old private D.R. Ainsbury, from Maryborough, Queensland; 23-year-old, Private P.J. Byrne from Fairfield; New South Wales; 24-year-old Corporal Kevin Geyer from Tenterfield, New South Wales and 41-year-old Corporal C.F. Hicks from Ballarat, Victoria — all of them prisoners of war. There were 845 other POWs on board, destined for slave labour camps in Japan. None survived. Most of them were from the ill-fated 2/22nd Battalion, captured in Rabaul in January 1942. There were also 205 civilians, mostly Europeans, on board — the youngest aged seventeen, the eldest sixty-three.

This little-known tragedy remains the worst Australian loss of life at sea, much worse than the loss of HMAS *Sydney*, which went down with the ship's company of 645 men. More Australian lives were lost in the *Montevideo Maru* than were lost in the Korean and Vietnam wars combined. It was not until after the war that the Australian government discovered the fate of the men from 2/22nd.

Unfortunately, this was not an isolated incident. Hundreds of Australian prisoners of war were also lost in 1944 when the US submarines *Tang* and *Growler* sank the *Tamahoko Maru* and the *Rakuyo Maru*. The loss of the *Tamahoko Maru* with 562 Australian prisoners of war was tragic, but for the captain and the submarine that sank her, fate would prove fickle.[38]

Tang was the most successful American boat of the war and Richard O'Kane was the most successful captain; the tally was 24 ships in five patrols, for a total of 93 824 tons. But on 24 October 1944, in the Formosa Strait, *Tang* suffered the ignominy of sinking herself with a faulty torpedo. Seventy-eight men died. O'Kane and eight others survived and became prisoners of war.[39]

The worst tragedy of friendly fire killing Allied prisoners of war was yet to occur. On the day that *Tang* was lost, *Shark 2*, a Pearl Harbor boat, sank a freighter in the Luzon Strait. There were five survivors from a total of 1800 American prisoners of war in transit from Manila to Japan. These were the men captured by the Japanese at Bataan and Corregidor.[40]

This was the worst tragedy at sea for the American armed forces. The death toll was more than twice that of the sinking of the USS *Indianapolis* in July the following year. No American unit of comparative size suffered as much as these men who had been abandoned in the Philippines. After enduring privation and cruelty in Japanese captivity, to be sunk by an American submarine was a tragic irony. Fate intervened once again when Captain Ed Blakely and the crew of *Shark 2* were killed the same day that the Battling Bastards of Bataan, as they were known, endured their last ordeal.

As many as 5000 Allied prisoners of war were drowned in ships torpedoed by American submarines. Of course, there was no way any submarine could have known of these ships' human cargoes. The blame rests with the Japanese military, who could have arranged for safe passage of these vessels by informing the Allies. Instead, they were prepared to run the gauntlet with tragic results.

The sinking of the *Rakuyo Maru* in September 1944 left many men adrift at sea. The rescue of 92 of them by the submarines *Barb, Pampanito, Sealion* and *Queenfish* demonstrated the extent of camaraderie among the Allies. The injured, oil-soaked and dehydrated survivors had been in the water for up to six days, but their courage and spirit is epitomised by the action of Arthur Bancroft. He had survived the sinking of the HMAS *Perth* and suffered two and a half years as a prisoner of war. Now he had spent six days in the open sea without food or water. As the *Queenfish* started rescue procedures, Bancroft, resisting any help, climbed from his makeshift raft on to the foredeck and stood before Lieutenant Commander Elliott Loughlin. In his oil-soaked rags, Bancroft jumped to attention, saluted and shouted: 'Permission to come aboard, Sir!' On the *Barb, Sealion* and *Pampanito*, the POWs were welcomed aboard.

'How long since you've eaten, Digger?'

'Hey, Aussie! where's your turned-up hat?'

'Do you want a cigarette, buddy?'

One Aussie yelled from his life raft, 'Are you the bastard that sank us?'

Phil Beilby said that the submariners were the kindest people he had ever met. Don Miller was from Pittsburgh and a crew member of *Barb*:

I remember the condition of the men as they came aboard. Some of our crew jumped overboard to assist. All were very weak and so thin — skin and bones. We spent as much time as possible on the surface for five days at the fastest speed to get them to Saipan for better medical treatment. Seeing how men could be so cruel to other men is something I will never forget. Of all the things the *Barb* did for the victory over Japan, this is the one I always have foremost in my mind.

When the boats arrived at Saipan, many of the sick and injured said they wanted to stay with those who had saved their lives. The men of the United States Navy were deeply moved.

Both the submariners and the interrogation officers in Saipan were keen to learn more about the loss of the *Perth* and the USS *Houston* in the Sunda Strait in March 1942. The Americans knew the *Houston* had been sunk but had few details. However, what really upset everyone were the Australians' descriptions of the fate of the Allied prisoners of war. This was the first explicit account of the cruelty of the Japanese captors.[41]

By late 1942, the base in Brisbane boasted the greatest concentration of submarine power in the Pacific to that time. Squadrons Two, Eight and Ten and the tenders *Holland* and *Sperry* were augmented by the *Fulton,* which replaced the *Griffin* in November 1942. Les Cottman had been with the *Fulton* since Pearl Harbor. He had wanted to became a submariner but was a talented code operator, which proved to be a more useful option for the navy:

The efforts of breaking the Japanese codes was a little known achievement that was a major factor in defeating Japan. We knew just about everything that they were doing. We would listen and then advise headquarters. The Japanese never knew what was going on until after the war.[42]

Jimmy Fife, who replaced Ralph Christie in December 1942, inherited a formidable command. A staff visitor from the Fremantle base noted in his diary: 'The base they're building in Brisbane is going to make Sub Base Pearl look like a farmer's garage'.[43]

The barracks at New Farm could accommodate 550 men. There were workshops for torpedoes, batteries and periscopes. Submariners returning from patrol could enjoy rest camps out of town in Coolangatta, Toowoomba and Redcliffe. In Brisbane, houses were rented for senior officers and staff members; many of these were shared with local women. While the men enjoyed social activity in rest houses or in the city, the boats were cleaned, serviced, rearmed and replenished. Soon there would be more patrols. Les Cottman knew many of the crews:

They were a unique bunch of men, all volunteers. They knew how to party and to have a good time. They acted like it was their last night, for many of them it was. They were all mentally tough and brave, they had to be, it was the most dangerous work in the navy.[44]

Most of the patrols from Brisbane were to the waters off New Guinea or the Solomons. The boats going on patrol were a familiar sight to the locals. As they made their way down the Brisbane River they passed the historic Newstead House, an example of Victorian splendour and the oldest home in the city. The crews could also see the Breakfast Creek Hotel, which was almost as old as the Newstead property and a favourite haunt for American servicemen; framed photographs of many of them hung on the walls of the pub. Kingsford Smith Drive was also visible for most of the trip. It was a main road for commercial and domestic traffic. On both sides of the river there were always people, young and old, watching the spectacle of the subs and waving to the crews. It was then mud banks, mangroves and swamps until the entrance to Moreton Bay, and then the open sea.

January 1943 is remembered as being the most productive month for the Brisbane base. Nine boats started their patrols, sinking twelve ships for a combined total of 44500 tons. The following month was the worst. Five boats left Brisbane that February and only two returned.

Amberjack was only four months old, one of the excellent new Gato boats that were now entering service. The boat, commanded by Lieutenant Commander John A. Bole Jr. was depth-charged off New Britain and lost with its crew of 74. Lieutenant Commander John R. Craig, with 70 of his crew and his boat *Grampus*, were lost somewhere in or near the Blackett Strait. Lieutenant Commander George K. Mackenzie Jr. and *Triton* had left Brisbane on 16 February. On 6 March, she sank the *Kiriha Maru*. Five days later, Mackenzie reported that he was chasing a convoy, but nothing more was heard of *Triton*, Mackenzie or his crew of 73. In one month the Brisbane base had listed three boats 'Overdue —

presumed lost'. It was a quiet base when it was realised that 219 men would not return.[45] Many men lost friends and buddies. Les Cottman was one of them. 'It was the loneliest of deaths,' he said. 'The submarines went out and just did not come back. In many instances no-one knows what happened to them. They lie together somewhere in the bottom of the ocean.'[46]

Depth-charging was the submariner's ultimate bad dream come true. One of them said the experience was like being in a 44-gallon drum and having someone hit it with a sledgehammer. *Ray*, a Fremantle-based Gato class boat, was attacked and depth-charged for seventeen hours, finally falling to a depth of 700 feet to the ocean floor before rising and returning to base.[47]

The classic depth-charge encounter of the war involved another Fremantle boat, the Gato class *Puffer* (Lieutenant Commander Marvin J. Jensen, class of '31). In October 1943, on her first patrol to the Macassar Strait, *Puffer* was attacked by two Japanese Chidori class submarine chasers. Submerged 200 feet below the recommended maximum depth, Jensen ordered the air-conditioner be turned off to minimise noise. What followed in 50-degree heat was a depth-charge attack that continued for an incredible 37 hours and 45 minutes. When the *Puffer* finally had to surface, Jensen discovered that the Japanese had left the area, presumably believing his submarine had been destroyed. Ralph Christie later wrote in his diary: 'strength of character ... skill and experience and knowledge, the excellent state of training, saved the ship ... A brilliant job carried through by guts, determination and the inspired example of the Commanding Officer.'[48]

Officer standards improved as the war progressed. Unproductive patrols were rare. Skippers considered unadventurous were replaced, usually with younger officers, some from the class of '39. In hotels and rest houses, submariners exchanged news, good or bad. They would talk about crazy brave skippers who took on a Japanese tin can with a 'down the throat' shot, about the exploits of the new wolf packs like Blair's Blasters and Hydeman's

Hellcats, or about colleagues and friends they would never see again.

Perhaps the most famous submarine to operate from the Fremantle base was the *Harder*. The commander was Sam D. Dealey, class of '30, a pugnacious skipper who earned the title 'Destroyer Killer' for sinking five Japanese warships during his boat's fifth war patrol. *Harder* is credited with sinking 16 enemy ships totalling 54 824 tons.

The tragedy of the loss of the *Harder* was tinged with irony. On the morning of 24 August 1944, *Harder*, *Hake* and *Haddo* were attacked by the Japanese escort vessels *CD-22* and patrol boat *102*. Lieutenant Commander Frank Haylor in *Hake* saw *Harder*'s periscope and later heard a string of depth-charge explosions in the same area. The *102* was an ex-American Flush-Deck class destroyer, originally the USS *Stewart* (DD-224). The old four-stacker' had been captured by the Japanese in a Surabaya dry dock in March 1942 and converted for anti-submarine duty. The *Harder* was lost with all hands six kilometres from Hermana Major Island, off the west coast of Luzon. Commander Dealey received a posthumous Congressional Medal of Honor, while the *Harder* received a Presidential Unit Citation. The Americans retrieved the *Stewart* from the Japanese in August 1945 and it ended its career being sunk as a target ship on 24 May 1946.[49]

By 1945, the submarine service had almost performed themselves out of a job. There was not too much left to sink, only small craft not worth the cost of a $10 000 torpedo. Reconnaissance duties became routine and continued until the end of the war. However, with the B-29 raids on the Japanese mainland, American submarines took part in many daring rescues of ditched aviators, 497 of whom were saved. In September 1944, off Chichi Jima, *Finback* rescued from his rubber dinghy an appreciative young flier and future US President called George Bush.[50]

Activity in the Fremantle and Brisbane bases diminished as the war was waged increasingly closer to the Japanese mainland. The big patrols now came out of Pearl Harbor, Midway Island and the Philippines. Although the Brisbane base conducted patrols until the end of the war, many of the boats and the equipment were transferred to the Philippines in March 1945.

On 30 July 1945, USS *Bullhead*, a new Gato class boat, under the command of Lieutenant Commander Edward R. Holt Jr. (class of '39) left Fremantle for a patrol in the South China Sea. Seven days later she was sunk by a solitary Japanese aircraft off Bali. Holt and his crew of 83 were lost. This was the last American submarine to be sunk just days before the end of war.[51]

As the war progressed, the courage and daring of the American submariners in the Pacific was complemented by an increased understanding of the strategic potential of submarine warfare. Had the torpedo fault been detected and corrected earlier, the war might have ended sooner.

Rear Admiral Jimmy Fife indoctrinated his crews with a simple, direct strategy that was conveyed through a standing order:

Press home all attacks. Pursue relentlessly, remembering that the mission is to destroy every possible enemy ship.

Do not let cripples escape or leave them to sink — make sure that they do sink.[52]

Approximately 35 per cent of all Japanese ships sunk were the victims of submarine patrols from Australian bases. The efforts of the American submarine force during the war have not been duly acknowledged. Nor has their sacrifice.

Fifty-two submarines were lost during the war — 37 going to the bottom with all hands. And 3506 officers and men were killed — a mortality rate of 22 per cent, the highest of any American service.[53] The character and courage of these men was unique. A former submariner, now a white-haired senior citizen, paused to reflect at a recent plaque commemoration:

I don't think of them as being old men. They were young and brave and good shipmates. I really don't think of them as being gone. I like to think that they are still out there somewhere on patrol — still serving their country. I miss them.[54]

CHAPTER THIRTEEN

WHEN A BLACK MAN'S BLUE

One of the most sensitive issues regarding the American forces during their occupation and their infiltration into Australian society was the arrival of black servicemen into the country.

Since Federation, Australia had advocated a strict White Australia policy which in practice created not just a colour barrier but also excluded most people who did not have an Anglo-Saxon heritage.

Unlike Australia, the United States had few ethnic or religious restrictions on immigration. In the decades before World War I people had come from every quarter of the globe to the land of opportunity and freedom — Irish, Italians, Greeks, Germans, Spaniards and Poles; Christians, Jews, Buddhists, Hindus, Muslims and others. It is estimated that 35 million people made their new home in the United States, with about 25 per cent coming from eastern and southern Europe.[1] By the first decades of the twentieth century these millions had become integrated into American society and culture. In 1941 there were also an estimated 13 million Afro-Americans in the United States.

★   ★   ★

However, the United States has had a sorry history regarding the battle for racial equality. The American Civil War may have freed the black man from the chains of slavery, but he was still socially manacled. As early as April 1866 Congress passed a seminal Civil Rights Act declaring that all persons born in the United States were US citizens and were entitled to full and equal benefits of its laws. It proved to be overly optimistic and the Act became impotent;

a century later attempts were still being made to achieve civil rights equality.

The term 'Jim Crow' became a term for any form of professional or domestic discrimination. This comes from a minstrel dance tune of that name dating back to the 1830s. In the South, Jim Crow laws ostracised blacks from white society.[2] The coming of the new century did little to ease the struggle for racial minorities. Every American president since Lincoln has had to negotiate the difficult, volatile and sensitive issue of the plight of Afro-Americans.

During World War I 380 000 black troops were enlisted for full service in the United States armed forces. Two hundred thousand served in France, but only 42 000 were in combat units, mostly with the 92nd and 93rd Infantry Divisions (Provisional). The majority were used in service and support units; unloading ships, building and repairing roads, digging trenches and burying the dead. Training was poor, as were the billeting, sanitation facilities and leadership. Despite some black troops serving with distinction, confidence in the fighting abilities of black soldiers was low; many were court-martialled for cowardice. Black troops accused their white officers of being 'poisoned by prejudice'.[3] The World War I experience for the Afro-Americans was disastrous and gave some credence to the myth of the inferiority of black soldiers in combat.

At the start of World War II the involvement of the black American in the United States armed services was, at the very least, modest and undervalued. The US Army had a total of twelve black officers and 5000 black soldiers. No blacks were permitted in the Army Air Force or the Marine Corps and 90 per cent of the black Americans in the navy were mess stewards.[4]

Although the road that led the Afro-American to wartime Australia began with the liberation of slaves during the Civil War, the main catalyst was the Selective Service Act of 1940. On 22 September 1940, two distinguished black leaders, Walter White and A. Philip Randolph, met with Roosevelt to discuss the ramifications of the Act and to define the terms of conscription of black Americans into the armed forces.

Asa Randolph was the son of a clergyman. He had studied economics, philosophy and science at the City College of New York and before the war, he had served as President of the National Negroes Congress.[5] A pacifist, Randolph nonetheless knew that the road to racial equality would start with the integration of the labour movement and a new role for blacks in the American military. Walter White was a journalist and novelist who had also served as the executive secretary of the National Association for the Advancement of Coloured People. For his investigation into lynchings and race riots he was honoured with the 1937 Spingarn Medal for the 'highest and noblest achievement by an American Negro'.[6]

Roosevelt knew he had an audience which could not be intimidated, placated or patronised. Here were black leaders whose qualities and stature were the equal of any member of his administration. Shortly after the meeting, Assistant Secretary of War James Patterson released a statement to the press which listed seven conditions applying to the deployment of Afro-Americans in the armed forces, the first being that the number of Afro-Americans in the Army would be in proportion to the population. This seemed a fair deal and was also practical. It meant that over a million black Americans could serve their country.

Conditions two through six related to equal opportunities and non-discrimination. However, the final condition was the policy of the War Department not to intermingle coloured and white personnel in the same regimental organisation.[7]

In training camps, blacks were segregated into separate eating and recreational facilities. Jackie Robinson, who later became a famous black sportsman, was a morale officer for a black company at Fort Riley. He wrote: 'They want to send me 10 000 miles away to fight for democracy when a hundred feet away they've got stools I can't put my black butt on to drink a bottle of beer'.[8]

For those blacks who ultimately found themselves in the American armed services, there would always be two wars to fight. Few black soldiers attained a rank higher than master sergeant and of those few who went further hardly any commanded white troops. However, it was standard procedure for white officers to command coloured troops. Red Cross blood banks initially refused to accept blood donations from blacks, and although they subsequently relented they kept the blood segregated.[9]

It was soon obvious that the US Army would offer no relief from racial suppression and bigoted ignorance. General Marshall in his capacity as Chief of Staff confessed in a letter to the Rev. Arthur Devan: 'The notion that blacks might serve on an equal footing with whites seems a perilous project in social engineering not to be attempted by an Army at war'. Marshall also believed it was difficult to fit black selectees into highly technical branches because of their 'relatively low intelligence average'.[10]

The black American had never been a prized acquisition for Uncle Sam and there were few demands for his services from the American military. Although the destroyer escort USS *Mason* had an all-black crew, it was commanded by a white officer; no black man wore a Marine Corps uniform until late in the war; and the army formed just one fighter squadron of blacks, which was seen as good for the image of equality.[11] In the light of this, it is particularly ironic that black Americans were distinguishing themselves in combat before most Americans even knew that the war had started.

One of the first inspiring stories of the war was that, during the attack on Pearl Harbor, an unidentified man was seen defiantly shooting at the Japanese from a gun mount on the battleship *West Virginia*. The press wanted the reluctant hero found. It was revealed that he was a naval rating called Doris Miller, who had the humble rank of messman third class. And it was further revealed that America's first war hero was black.

Miller had been below decks when the Japanese attacked. When the ship's captain, Mervyn Bennion, was almost cut in half by a piece of shrapnel, his subordinates called for a mess attendant to carry the wounded commander below. The one chosen was the huge Doris (Dorie) Miller, the heavyweight boxing champion of the ship. The captain soon died and Miller was ordered back below. But before returning to his station, Miller strapped himself to an automatic weapon and began firing at the Japanese and cursing them in his Arkansas drawl. On 27 May 1942, six months after the Pearl Harbor attack, Admiral Nimitz pinned the Navy Cross on the ample chest of the modest Miller. The black press loved the fact that a black man with the lowest naval rank became the first American to perform an act of valour in the war. Miller became a hero.[12]

There were others who, when given the opportunity, followed in Miller's footsteps and soon black Americans were in the enlisting queues. The Selective Service Act forbade any discrimination against any persons of race or colour in the service of their country. However, like most previous attempts from Capitol Hill to negate discrimination, it was impotent legislation, and as white married men were drafted perfectly healthy blacks were overlooked for selection.

Soon after Pearl Harbor, the Roosevelt Administration began tentatively sending black units overseas and was eager to gather the responses to this initiative from area commanders.

★   ★   ★

On 9 January 1942, Australia's minister to the United States, R.G. Casey, cabled the Department of External Affairs about the impending arrival of black Americans. 'United States are considering the dispatch of ground troops, principally anti-aircraft units to Australia, and in this connection are anxious to know what would be your reaction to proposals that a proportion of these troops would be coloured'.[13]

The next day, Casey cabled his government that as many as 2000 black troops might be bound for Australia. Casey's cables rattled through Canberra's teleprinters and found their way to

Curtin's desk. The Australian response was swift and explicit. On 13 January 1942, the Minister for External Affairs, Dr H.V. Evatt, relayed to Casey minute number 673, from the Advisory War Council meeting of January 12th: 'We are not prepared to agree to proposal that proportion of United States troops to be despatched to Australia should be coloured'.[14]

That same day, the government received assurances from the American Legation in Canberra of the disposition regarding the servicemen:

The Negro units all belong to the U.S. Army. They are all enlisted personnel and are trained and disciplined men. The intention is to use them at Darwin for the heavy labor in connection with installation of aircraft defences and aerodromes, for which they are peculiarly fitted.[15]

With the nation in a precarious position, and aware of the need to appease and placate the United States in their role as potential saviour, the Australian government began to suggest concessions. On 20 January there was another cablegram from Dr Evatt:

Whilst the Advisory War Council decided that the Australian reaction to the despatch of Negro troops to Australia would not be favourable, the composition of the forces that the USA government might decide to dispatch to Australia is a matter for that Government to determine.

Nevertheless it is assumed that the USA authorities being aware of our views, will have regard to Australian susceptibilities in the numbers they decide to despatch.[16]

The Advisory War Council may well have sat for another session had they been aware that two black Engineer Aviation Battalions, the 810th and 811th, were already on the water and due to arrive in Melbourne on 26 February.

The unwanted invasion had begun. By May 1942, 6364 out of 15 679 black Americans sent overseas were stationed in Australia. Only the Japanese were less welcome.[17]

As early as 25 March, Lieutenant General Brett had cabled

Washington: 'it is now strongly recommended that no other colored troops of any category be sent to Australia. It is further recommended that the colored troops now here be either returned to the US, be sent to New Caledonia or to India.' Brett mentioned that there were numerous clashes between blacks and other American soldiers. His cable continued:

Every effort is being made to prevent spread to civil community. The situation will inevitably lead to bloodshed. The problem being created by the presence of Negro soldiers will adversely affect relationships between Australians and Americans and nullify any military value derived from their use.[18]

When MacArthur was appointed Commander in Chief of the South-West Pacific Area, he cabled the US War Department:

I will do everything possible to prevent friction or resentment on the part of the Australian Government and people at the presence of American colored troops ... Their policy of exclusion against everyone except the white race known locally as the 'White Australia' plan is universally supported here. The labor situation is also more acute — perhaps than any place in the world.

The Australian Government was obviously still uneasy about the influx, but MacArthur's reaction was that if it asked for America's help then it should take what it was given. 'I visualise completely,' he wrote, 'that there are basic policies which while contrary to the immediate circumstances of a local area, are absolutely necessary from the higher perspective and viewpoint.'[19] Nevertheless, he believed that he could minimise racial friction by deploying black troops some distance from the great centres of population.

When they arrived, Australians were amazed to see negroes on the streets. Most of the populace had never seen a black person, certainly not one wearing a uniform, and nobody could deny that many of them were fine physical specimens. Less well informed citizens believed warnings not to go near them as myths about lunacy, disease and the rumour that they had tails circulated.

It soon became apparent that the latest influx of servicemen also included 'Jim Crow'. One night in 1942 a young woman was knocked down and robbed in the Brisbane suburb of Annerley. An American soldier was quickly on the scene and while assisting the woman to her feet he asked, 'Was it a nigger?'[20]

★   ★   ★

Australia's success at cohabitation with its indigenous population was even less impressive than that of the United States with its Afro-Americans. The Aborigines were a nomadic and isolated race that had settled in Australia at least 40 000 years before the first white Europeans. Within years of European settlement the independent, culturally coherent Aboriginal population was transformed into a dependent, poverty-stricken, brutally oppressed minority.

Decades of warfare and genocide followed, and Aborigines were all but exterminated in the island state of Tasmania. Elsewhere 'protection boards' were established and Aborigines were segregated on reserves and in harsh outback areas. Cohabitation, when attempted, was generally a failure. A lack of empathy, appropriate social setting and education coupled with the assumptions underpinning the White Australia policy, resulted in the race being neglected in the extreme.

Aborigines were not considered as being equal. In fact they were not considered at all. Generations of Australians had been raised to totally ignore them. If mentioned, they were 'Abos', 'Blackfellas' or 'Boongs'. They were not counted in the census and had limited voting and very few civil rights. The White Australia policy was so ingrained in the society that the findings of an opinion poll conducted during the war about the value of the policy surprised no-one. When asked the question, 'After the war, would you alter the White Australia Policy to admit a limited number of coloured people?' nine out of ten people voted for the continuation of the policy. Most were opposed even to a limited number of coloured people being admitted to the tropical north, where labour was in short supply.[21]

In 1939 the Australian armed forces mirrored the government's policies by rejecting applications from Aborigines and Islanders and anyone 'not substantially of European origan or descent'. However, many Aborigines joined the services early in the war at a time when many recruiting officers were confused about enlistment policies.[22] On 6 May 1940 the matter was clarified. A memo from the Military Board stated that the enlistment of persons of non-European origin or descent was 'neither necessary nor desirable'. Indigenous Australians were turned away from recruiting centres, but the matter would not rest. Protests from Aboriginal welfare organisations, state government departments and the Returned Sailors' and Soldiers' Imperial League of Australia championed the cause of black Australians. In August 1940, the Military Board made a modest amendment to the original policy:

This precludes the enlistment of full blooded aborigines, but, in deciding whether or not a person with some aboriginal blood is or is not substantially of European origin or descent, medical officers will be guided by the general suitability of the applicant and by the laws and practices of the State or Territory in which the enlistment takes place.[23]

As a result of this ambiguous statement, some Aborigines were now eligible to enlist. With the advent of the war with Japan and the desperate manpower shortages, a few more Aborigines began to be accepted in the armed services.

Despite the absence of welcome mats and invitations, approximately 3000 Aborigines served their country during the war. Reginald Saunders from Portland, Victoria, enlisted in April 1940. He served with distinction in North Africa, Crete and New Guinea, and in November 1944 was promoted to lieutenant; the only Aborigine to be commissioned during the war. Another Aborigine, Leonard Waters, became a fighter pilot with 78 Squadron in New Guinea. This was a major achievement for a young indigenous Australian. He had joined the service in August

1942, flying American P-40 Kittyhawks in the New Guinea campaign and later in Borneo.[24]

★   ★   ★

Nobody saw a black American flying a Kittyhawk in Australia. In fact, they were seldom seen anywhere. In the main, they were sighted only fleetingly on the streets in Sydney and Melbourne before most of them were posted north. By June 1942, over half the black Americans in Australia were in the north, many of them in isolated areas.

Amongst the earliest to arrive in Queensland were the 91st and 96th Battalions of the Engineers General Service, who landed in Townsville on 10 April 1942. There was little contact with civilians as the 96th were soon allocated to clearing ground for an airstrip eighteen kilometres south of the town. In June they were posted with another black unit, the 92nd Quartermaster Company, to the remote area of Reid River.

The 1218 officers and men of the 91st Battalion were to be even more isolated, being posted to a railway siding called Woodstock about 50 kilometres south. In May they moved to the remote town of Giru. Social interaction with locals was intermittent and with the exception of a few minor alcohol-induced offences the apartheid was effective; even more so when many of these units were transferred to Port Moresby in August and September 1942.[25]

Almost without exception, black units were commanded by white officers. Most white officers knew little about black Americans; they belonged to a society where blacks worked as porters, servants, labourers, waiters and jazz musicians.

The arrival of the black Americans was an obvious attraction to Australian jazz musicians and fans. There was little if any racism amongst this group. Most musicians, especially the jazz inclined, hailed the blacks as 'musical gods'. After all, most of the seminal figures in jazz were black. In fact, in jazz there was a sort of reverse racism. White musicians generally imitated the musical progressions of black innovators and often struggled for artistic credibility. In the world of music, this was known as 'Crow Jim'.

When Sid Bromley heard that black Americans were coming to Australia, he was ecstatic. He was determined to buy the first black man he met a beer and then ask him to play something. Bromley lived at Ipswich, which was the place to be if you wanted to meet black soldiers; there were 2000 of them in camps in nearby Wacol and Goodna. Then came the shock. Where were Fats Waller, Red Allen, Coleman Hawkins, Benny Carter and the rest? The guys Bromley met were okay, but they liked the Ink Spots and gospel or had little interest in music at all. Bromley and other disappointed jazz devotees thought that maybe all the black 'jazz cats' had gone to the European theatre. Here again was a classic example of stereotyping. Most Australians had little exposure to any form of black culture. The musicians had exposure only to records, some musical shorts at the pictures and a few articles in music magazines. The great black musical artists were as rare as the great white musical artists. It was a search in vain for uniformed Benny Goodmans' or Count Basies'. Australia had a very limited perception of any American culture other than what was depicted by the mass-entertainment industry.[26]

Integrating the black Americans into the wartime social structure proved to be a difficult task. Bigotry and ignorance abounded. Young women were warned to stay away from them or risk serious peril. But those inquisitive young girls who met them found the majority even more courteous than their white compatriots. However, many girls were castigated for associating with black Americans and any indiscretion or trouble relating to blacks was invariably exaggerated.[27]

In Brisbane there was an area set aside for black social activity in the city's south. Despite protests by local and state officials, black Americans soon had their own segregated entertainment complex. Dr Carver's Club for Colored Allied Servicemen opened on 5 May 1943. The facilities included dormitories for 250 men, a barber shop, pool room, dance hall, cafeteria and bar. By 1944 it had become the largest and most popular black club in the country.

South Brisbane was soon the black area, and such were the myths and superstitions surrounding it that few white women would visit. Some of the more timid ones who inadvertently strayed into the area saw it as a forbidden zone or a place to fear. The Red Cross attempted to match black soldiers with dark-skinned women, either Aborigines or Islanders, but this did not always prove to be harmonious. In fact, segregation was so efficiently handled that many Australians did not even know of the black American presence until after the war.

'Something must be done about the coloured soldiers in this area,' wrote a concerned resident from the Brisbane suburb of Goodna. 'We have women alone while we are at work and the coloured walk in packs and there's always a bit of trouble with the soldiers at Redbank.' This letter, addressed to the local police, was by no means an isolated one. There were two black battalions at the Goodna and Redbank camps while Amberley, a few miles south, was an all-white affair. There were altercations between black and white soldiers and several areas were classified as out of bounds.[28]

There was no doubt that the mere presence of black troops intimidated many locals. Mr T.W. Reid, the chairman of the Chinchilla Shire Council, was also concerned about the 'coloured problem'. In a letter to the American Legation Section in Brisbane, Reid mentioned that as a former member of the First AIF he knew well the value of morale and 'having fun', but 'something in the nature of picketing or leave limitation or perhaps an "out of bounds" section may be the answer'.

Reid was particularly concerned about the black troops from Columboola, an ordnance depot near Chinchilla.

What sort of place was Columboola? Opinions vary, but it seemed an absolutely ideal place to hide 36 blacks and one white officer. It was like a desert Devil's Island. For the black servicemen it was barren and completely unfamiliar but it was also all too typical of where most of them were posted. After the isolation and solitude of Columboola, Chinchilla must have seemed to be the entertainment capital of the world.

'Without being directly offensive,' continued Mr Reid in his letter,

they pass remarks and engage in a conduct that cannot go unnoticed. I cannot be too specific, but we fear the negroes will be given an opportunity of getting too familiar with local girls and women. Just the other day I was told that they were offering lollies to women in the local picture theatre.

The letter was not ignored and Toowoomba police sent an inspector to Chinchilla and then to Columboola, where Lieutenant Landis was in charge of the 636 Ordnance Ammunition Corps and of the 36 soldiers stationed there. 'Frankly, I cannot find anything wrong with the troops,' said the inspector in his report. 'In fact, they seem as well behaved — if not more so — than more local units.'[29]

It would be fanciful to believe that no black troops ever engaged in any mischief or irresponsible activities. Their behaviour was as varied as that of any other group of soldiers, but certainly no group of men was as carefully monitored or prejudged as were the coloured men in uniform. At best, their behaviour was exemplary; at worst, it was best confined to contemporary archival report and arrest sheets.

However, even in Columboola tempers could wilt under the hot sun. On 10 April 1943, there was a fist fight between Arthur Nathaniel Jones and Edward Garfield. The cause is unclear, but evidently the battle was monumental. It appears that Jones was bested. However, he was not to be denied. Walking into Lieutenant Landis' office, Jones pushed the officer aside, broke into the armoury, took a weapon, returned to the compound and shot Edward Garfield dead.[30]

Camooweal was another town with another story. Not to be confused with the 'metropolis' of Columboola, Camooweal was about 160 kilometres west of the Queensland mining town of Mount Isa. Troops stationed there had their sense of duty tempered by those of frustration and hardship. Black troops and civil construction crews were there to build the Mount Isa to Tennant Creek road, providing an alternative route to the Northern Territory and Darwin. Constructed in hostile terrain, the road stretched over 900 kilometres through rock, bush, dust, creeks and gullies.[31]

There were more black Americans in this area than in any other during the war. Over 3000 worked on the road-building project, mostly from the 1st Battalion, 48th QM Regiment. This group became the heart of the No. 1 Motor Transport Command which comprised 5000 men and nearly 2000 vehicles. It would be an understatement to say that the work was tough. As a major test of physical strength and character, it was the type of work which would have been delegated to the most incorrigible chain gang back in the States. The dust in which they worked was at times over a foot deep. Men rose at dawn when it was cool, as later in the day the heat was of a kind that no-one had previously experienced. The terrain was so rough that no trucks could get through with ease and digging vehicles out of bogs and repairing carburettors and tyres was commonplace. The water trucks did not just offer refreshment, they also saved lives.

Between May 1942 and April 1943, American forces logged over 15 million miles over the new route. Before the road was paved, men were required to wear respirators to prevent them from choking on the dust. After a few trips, the cabs of trucks would 'crack off' and have to be welded back together. Men who drove the road likened it to driving on a giant washboard. But there was one aspect of this operation involving black soldiers that drew admiration from all who witnessed it. This was the skill that they demonstrated as drivers.

One Australian soldier, Rex Erwin, commented:

The negro drivers had only one speed — flat out. The drivers were very good but took terrific punishment. Around their waists they used to wear belly-guards, like body belts, because the vibrations were that severe. Quite often they would bleed from the navel after a day's continual jolting. The dust just poured in. It was so difficult to see ahead that the negro drivers would stand out on the running board, with the door closed, and reach in to steer the truck through the open window.[32]

Private Clarence McDeaman was like most of his buddies who enjoyed liberty in Mount Isa after the slave-like labour on the Camooweal road project, but Clarence spent the night of 26 August 1942 in the Mount Isa watchhouse for drunk and disorderly behaviour. He was not the first, nor would he be the last soldier to enjoy the hospitality of the local 'drunk tank'.

However what followed for Private McDeaman is a classic example of what could be called over-zealous call of duty or racism.

As McDeamon was about to be released he was charged with another offence; specifically, the destruction of a cell bucket. He had no knowledge of damaging the item but was quickly shown the object, which appeared to have had the bottom kicked out of it. The aggressive level of prosecution for this trivial offence was nothing short of bewildering. Sergeant Lake of the Mount Isa police produced an arrest sheet full of witness statements and other details. There was also a report to the Commissioner of Police about the destruction. 'Sir, you will notice,' wrote Sergeant Lake, 'that I do not request a replacement bucket with this report. I can use one from the station office until I apply for a new one with my annual requisition.'

The next development occurred when Lieutenant Ray Peters from the 1st Battalion 48th QM Regiment arrived with an apologetic Private McDeaman to talk to Sergeant Lake. Peters asked for the cost of a replacement bucket. This was put at 10s 6d, a ridiculous amount, but McDeaman paid Lake the money believing that would be the end of the matter. However the charge was not dropped and the police requested that the American authorities prosecute the matter with vigour.

The Queensland Police repeatedly asked the American military for details of the outcome of the matter. In late September a letter was sent to the Queensland Commissioner of Police stating that McDeaman had been found guilty of wilful destruction and had been sentenced to seven days detention. He would also be given extra hard work to do.[33]

One can only imagine the type of extra hard work that could possibly be delegated on the Camooweal road project, and why the matter was allowed to proceed to the level of a court martial. One wonders too whether a Caucasian GI would have been prosecuted so energetically. The matter was not productive; the only result was an unnecessary stain on Clarence McDeaman's service record.

Provosts at the best of times possessed limited communication skills and questionable empathy for the difficulties of soldiers in a strange land, and they had even less empathy with black soldiers.

In late 1942 there was a disturbance outside the Argent Hotel in Mount Isa. After a brief scuffle, a black soldier was shot dead in front of local civilians, who then witnessed the body being lifted into the back of a vehicle. That same year another black soldier was shot dead in Cairns after attempting to flee from provosts. In 1943 a black soldier in the Royal Brisbane Hospital lost his composure and ran amok in Ward 16. When an American provost arrived on the scene he immediately reached for his holstered hand gun and would have shot the man dead in the public ward had it not been for the intervention of nurses and orderlies.[34]

The treatment of black soldiers became, on occasion, so vicious that members of the Australian public complained. Some even began to recognise in the treatment of black Americans, aspects of their own racism.

Most Australians saw little, or had anything to do with, Aborigines and were seldom confronted with the unsavoury aspects of their racial persecution.

As early as May 1942, the Australian government issued a

formal protest after an incident which occurred in Sydney. A group of newly arrived white soldiers stopped an army truck carrying black troops and told them to exit the vehicle, which they did amid jeers and much profanity. Fighting resulted, and when the provosts arrived, it seemed that the blacks were the main targets of the swinging batons. This incident happened in full view of Australian civilians who complained to the government and a protest letter was soon on MacArthur's desk. This forced the General to compile a response to Mr H.B. Chandler, a public official:

There is absolutely no discrimination against colored troops ... Without knowing anything of the circumstances, I will venture the opinion that any friction that may have arisen was based not upon racial lines but upon individual deportment and incidents of conduct. You may rest completely assured that so far as I am concerned, there is no differentiation whatsoever in the treatment of soldiers.[35]

Despite this letter, everyone in the US armed forces knew the extent of the discrimination, including the Commander in Chief, whose directives sent the black soldiers to remote areas. It would not have taken long to count the number of black soldiers of any authority in MacArthur's headquarters.

The potential sensitivity of the Afro-American presence was not helped by the often vociferous comments by elements of the militant press. On 21 February 1944 *The Worker* told its readers:

Crimes by negroes, particularly sex offences against white women, are causing considerable concern in those Australian areas where negroes are located. Respectable white women are afraid to go out of doors unattended. In Queensland negroes have figured in a number of crimes, including rape. Some are inclined to regard all white women as of the same type as the morally-low class who batten on to them for money. In Sydney the complaint is made that negroes prowl about the city at night, many of them carrying knives. Women who frequent the Domain draw them in their hundreds — an ugly sight in a white man's country.[36]

The American army was always monitoring the situation and in a counter intelligence bulletin released to the various base sections there were the following recommendations:

The results of undercover investigation and analysis of newspaper stories reveal that considerable bitterness has developed among Australian civilians towards negro soldiers. Needless to say, much of this ill will has been engendered by sensational press reports of alleged sex offences. Whether or not these stories are fact, it can be correctly pointed out that the overwhelming percentage of negro soldiers are conducting themselves in a soldierly manner. The unfortunate condition which causes sex stories to be magnified beyond their importance should make it clear to commanding officers that increased vigilance is necessary not only to prevent sex offences but also to prevent even the appearance of them.[37]

How ignominious it must have been for so many of these proud black Americans. Sent to Australia in the service of their country, they were subjected to offensive innuendo, posted to a remote area and, often regardless of their qualifications, given a pick and shovel.

Back in the land of the free, the plight of black Americans was no better. In the largest internal migration in the country's history, southern blacks moved north where there were more employment opportunities. Under increasing pressure, Roosevelt issued Executive Order 8802 which forbade any racial discrimination in defence industries.[38] This had not been altogether a Roosevelt initiative. Asa Randolph had told him that unless something was done for black labour, he would have 50 000 black protesters demonstrate outside the front lawn of the White House. In addition to Order 8802, there was a Fair Employment Practices Commission to enforce the Act, but it was a lame duck with no prosecution powers.

Detroit was a classic example of the problems accompanying northern migration. 60 000 blacks had arrived in the city to find work in the plants. Tension with whites — many of whom had also come from the South and had brought their prejudices with them — was commonplace. In June 1943, some fist fights escalated into the worst race riot in 25 years and culminated in the deaths of 9 whites and 25 blacks, 17 of whom had been shot by police. There was also $2 million worth of damage. Roosevelt had to declare a state of emergency and send in federal troops to restore order.[39]

This tragic affair received massive media coverage and made it clear that the Afro-Americans would not submit easily and would defend their civil rights. It also demonstrated that America's global concerns for the rights of free men should start with their own.

Mainstream American white society knew very little of its fellow black Americans. In a survey poll conducted in New York soon after the war started, 62 per cent of those polled said that they thought that black Americans were pretty well satisfied with things in their country. But in another, less highly publicised poll, nearly 20 per cent of all blacks thought that they would be better off under Japanese rule.[40]

The trepidation expressed by the Australian government about the arrival of the black soldiers during World War II was ill-founded. The few Australian citizens who came to know the Afro-Americans during the war soon realised that the stereotypical image of them as rogues with the propensity for violence, drunkenness and sexual debauchery was fallacious in the extreme. The typical black serviceman was no different from his Caucasian counterpart. In many instances he was more polite, courteous and affable. What many Australians remember decades after the departure of the black Americans is their smiles.

Conversely, although they endured many ordeals, black Americans left Australia with a generally favourable impression of the culture and the people. Many expressed a forlorn hope of staying in the country after the war.

As for the Australian Aborigines who served in the armed forces during the war, most enjoyed a rare period of equality. Unlike the Americans they were integrated into units rather than segregated.

Their conditions, discipline and pay were the same as those of other servicemen and army records became one of the few government documents that did not state their race.[41]

The fortunes of American segregated black units in overseas service embarrassed the great arsenal of democracy. It became obvious to American people at home and to democratic societies overseas that hypocrisy was being perpetuated. The cause of freedom concerned the defeat of powers who advocated racial superiority, yet America had practised segregation and discrimination within many areas of its own country. Roosevelt conceded: 'Americanism is not, and never was, a matter of race or ancestry'.[42]

Talk had been cheap before, but in World War II it heralded the beginning of a new era of social advancement. In a reflection of public awareness, more than 200 cities and towns within the United States set up interracial committees. Many public opinion polls indicated that whites were becoming more aware of the blacks' discontent.[43] There was also a major breakthrough in the armed services. During the war a study revealed that two-thirds of the men in an average white company disliked the idea of mixed-race companies. After the test of combat, only 7 per cent retained their original view.[44]

Towards the end of the war, black divisions — the 92nd and 93rd — served in Europe and the Pacific. During the crises with the German offensive through the Ardennes, Eisenhower deployed black troops and by March 1945 there were 57 platoons of black troops in Europe, comprising men who volunteered for front-line duty. There were also blacks serving with the Marines during the Iwo Jima campaign.[45]

The role of the black American in the service of his country was constantly under scrutiny. There were dramatic changes. Shortly after the war, various labour unions were pressured to accept blacks on the same level as whites. Blacks even began serving in senior capacities in the Truman administration. The National Association for the Advancement of Colored People became a more militant and influential organisation with over half a million members.

The most significant breakthrough for the military came on 26 July 1948 when President Harry Truman issued an executive order desegregating the armed forces. Two years later, black and white Americans were joining, training, travelling, fighting and dying together in the Korean War.[46]

CHAPTER FOURTEEN

I'LL BE SEEING YOU

(LONG AGO AND FAR AWAY)

The departure of American forces from Australian cities, towns and outback areas was not as dramatic as their arrival. If 1943 was the peak year of the occupation, it was also the beginning of the end of the American presence in Australia.

In July 1943, the United States Sixth Army Headquarters was established at Camp Columbia, Wacol, a few kilometres south of Brisbane, under the command of Lieutenant General Walter Kruger. A month later, a prepared area at Strathpine — a few kilometres north of Brisbane — became the new billet for the 1st Calvary Division under the command of Major General Dumas P. Swift. The majority of the 41st Division was still based in Rockhampton under the command of Lieutenant General Robert L. Eichelberger and the 32nd Division had temporarily returned to the bush billet at Camp Cable. The weary 1st Marine Division, fresh from triumphs at Guadalcanal, stayed at the camp for a few weeks before relocating at the malaria-free Mount Martha, near Melbourne.[1]

A major reason for the dwindling numbers of Americans in Australia was the success of the offensive operations in New Guinea. The beachheads at Buna and Gona had been captured, at great cost, in January 1943. By the end of the month resistance around Sanananda was eliminated.

The Japanese continued to defend the north-eastern coast of New Guinea against the Allies. It was decided to bypass the large Japanese base at Rabaul and MacArthur's South-West Pacific Forces began to clear the New Guinea coast, supported by Admiral Halsey's South Pacific Area forces. They would then join for an assault on the Philippines. In addition, forces under Admiral Nimitz were to conduct a series of island-hopping campaigns in the central Pacific before also joining in operations in the Philippines.[2]

With the war moving ever northwards, MacArthur also needed to move north. In early April 1944, a fleet of transports left Brisbane loaded with Base Section 3 personnel and equipment. The destination was Hollandia, on the coast of Dutch New Guinea. It was here that MacArthur would relocate his headquarters.[3]

The Australians might have earned the right to contest the liberation of the Philippines, but MacArthur did not ask for their assistance. Instead Australian forces conducted campaigns against reluctant and isolated Japanese in Bougainville and Borneo. There was no apparent strategic or political motive, other than looking for a 'good scrap', and the Australian Army fought and died in battles that made little difference to the outcome of the war.[4]

The lack of MacArthur newspaper stories, empty streets, empty bars, smaller lines at picture theatres, coupled with better service in service related industries, made it clear that the Yank was moving on. On 21 October 1944, the *Herald* carried a dispatch from Frank Kluckhorn, a credited and favoured correspondent from the MacArthur camp in the Philippines:

It may now be revealed that the American Army and Navy have evacuated Australia completely, except for a few skeleton supply units, after a 'friendly invasion' which lasted two and a half years. A few weeks ago the streets of Australian cities, like Brisbane, were filled with American uniforms of all types. Australian girls walked arm-in-arm with Yanks.

Today there is none of that bustle and excitement which a busy Army creates.[5]

Where was MacArthur? The Australian people would never see him again; all they could do was read about his exploits. Later, like the rest of the world, they saw newsreel footage and photographs of MacArthur — flanked by his staff — wading in knee-high surf towards Red Beach at Leyte in the Philippines. He had returned.

By December 1944, Brisbane was designated United States Army Headquarters, Australia Base Section. Its jurisdiction covered all United States Army troops remaining on the Australian mainland. Brigadier General William H. Donaldson was the officer in charge. Brisbane became a supply and administration centre. Base Section 3 was no more.[6]

During the period from December 1941 to the end of the Pacific war the base processed 2 290 757 military personnel. (Many servicemen had regularly travelled to and from the Base.) A phenomenal 45 208 782 tons of supplies had also been processed.[7] But in the last days of the war there were no more than 5000 Americans on the continent. This was about the same number who arrived on the *Pensacola* convoy nearly four years before.[8]

On Thursday 16 August 1945, Prime Minister Ben Chifley told a national radio audience: 'Fellow citizens, the war is over'. A crowd estimated at a million people gathered in the streets of Sydney to celebrate. John Curtin was not alive to witness the jubilation; he had died on 5 July 1945 — three months after the death of Roosevelt. Chifley continued his address: 'Let us remember those whose lives were given that we may enjoy this glorious moment and may look forward to a peace which they have won for us'.[9]

Those few American servicemen in Australia to join in the celebrations were basically concerned with the release of surplus supplies and the settlement of a multitude of claims resulting from the occupation. With the end of the war, the United States military presence in Australia was terminated as quickly as possible and by January 1946 the Americans were only a memory.

It was, however more than a memory that inspired almost 15 000 war brides to join their husbands in the land of the Stars and Stripes. The exact number of women who left their homes and their country 'for the love of a soldier', is not known, but in 1946 many of the ships that had brought the Americans to Australia in the early days of the war were transporting fiancées and wives to their new homeland. The *Lurline, Holbrook, Mariposa, Marine*

Phoenix, Monterey and others became 'brideships'. The women came from all over Australia to ports of embarkation.

The Australian women were, in some ways, as brave as any soldier. Most had never been out of the country before and many had never left their towns or cities.[10] Many of them had not seen their men for up to two years. A new organisation called The American Wives' and Fiancées' Club was formed to discuss and advise on issues relating to the departure, the voyage and their impending arrival in the United States. The club boasted nearly 1000 members. The fortnightly meetings included the reading of letters from girls already in their new country. The mood was solemn when letters describing unions that failed, or husbands who had vanished, were read. However the club was quick to diffuse concerns: 'Only twenty of the 1500 Australian brides in the United States have been deserted by their husbands,' a newspaper reported. 'We want to hear more about the happy marriages.'[11]

For 1200 war brides and their 400 children, the *Mariposa* became a floating social centre and nursery. The converted quarters included play pens, basinets, 500 toys, 18 000 safety pins and 20 000 paper nappies. Conditions on the long voyage varied. Several women and children often shared the same cabin. Many women frolicked and socialised at improvised functions with the crew and the occasional troop units which were also returning to the States. Some women became withdrawn and reserved, full of sadness for leaving their homeland and full of trepidation for what lay ahead. The American military looked after the formal arrangements for the voyage and the processing through Customs. Special trains were organised for women whose spouses were not available to meet them at the dock. Telegrams were sent to the American husbands and fathers to notify them of time, date and place of arrival. Like a goods consignment, the American signed on the line for his wife, who was then duly delivered.

It was not just Australian women who were arriving in American ports. In February 1946 thirteen bride ships arrived in

America. They came from England, New Zealand, Canada and other countries that had been 'occupied' by the Americans. It is estimated that around 50 000 wives and 20 000 children were the legacy of the American war machine. It was a fantastic effort; 70 000 new acquisitions were enough to start a whole new nation.[12]

War brides were not just leaving Australia, they were arriving as well. By June 1944, 132 women and 21 children had arrived in Sydney Harbour.[13] These were new family members for Australians who had served overseas. Although most were wives of RAAF airmen who had served in England with the Empire Air Scheme, some came from Canada and America, while those few from the Middle East must have tested the White Australia policy.

Newspaper reports about the Yanks going north, or going home, were usually concerned with the loss of girls to matrimonial unions or with cultural acquisitions including donuts, Coca-Cola, coffee and Sunday movies. However, as early as October 1944, a perceptive editorial in the *Telegraph* put the invasion in perspective:

> Their presence here did more than countless ambassadorial visits could have done to create a clearer understanding of the community of interest between America and Australia, and laid a sound foundation upon which closer relations, essential in the post-war world, can be built.
>
> We have learned much from the Americans, particularly about the value of mechanisation, and we have benefited not only from what we have learned from them, but from the opportunity of emerging from our self-contained insularity and measuring our own achievements against those of our highly-developed neighbour.
>
> For Australia, with her small population and her correspondingly small services, to have to meet the demands of a big influx of population was no easy task, particularly when it had to be performed under all the disabilities of war and emergency. Not only have we found out some of our strong points, but we have also discovered some of our weak spots, and that is equally important.[14]

There were also many Americans who did not desire to return

home. In November 1945, United States officials stated that hundreds of servicemen had submitted applications to remain in Australia. Others journeyed from elsewhere in the Pacific to formally apply for Australian citizenship. Many had married Australian girls. No Australian was more pleased than the Queensland Premier, Mr Frank Cooper.

Americans who have married Australian girls have purchased properties and interests in businesses here.

I expect 2500 Americans to settle in Australia with a combined capital of at least £300 000. We are proud of the Americans as Allies, and will welcome them as citizens.

Some might have believed that the immigration criteria had at long last become more open but government officials quickly announced certain requirements: 'Only the US Forces of European race or descent are eligible to remain in Australia'.[15]

Despite this, the war affected many Australian postwar policies and challenged some traditions. America had clearly demonstrated that a multicultural population could not only exist, but could prosper. Australians at all levels of society had witnessed the largely successful blending of American military personnel, and realised that was also a reflection of their cosmopolitan society. There were US servicemen of Italian, Greek, Polish and of course Anglo-Saxon descent. Americans were still struggling with equal rights for the Afro-Americans, but at least they were integrated into mainstream society.

Australia had much to contend with in 1945 and 1946. The immediate problems were the demobilisation of nearly a million members of the Armed Forces and facing the challenges of a future which promised to be dramatically different from the past. The end of the war was also the beginning of the end of the White Australia policy. It would soon be modified and, much later, discarded. 'Populate or perish,' said the Minister for Immigration, Arthur Calwell, who added:

The call to all Australians is to realise that without adequate numbers this wide brown land may not be held in another clash of arms.

A policy of planned immigration is essential in protecting Australia's welfare and defence.

Calwell was no visionary. He also said that he hoped that for every foreign migrant there would be ten people from the United Kingdom.[16]

In December 1947 the last Yanks went home — 1409 of them. All had lost their lives while serving their country and helping Australians serve theirs. Most had died in the numerous accidents that are an unfortunate legacy of any substantial build-up of armed forces; some had died of wounds after being repatriated from battle zones to mainland military hospitals. The War Graves Unit of the American Armed Forces was prepared to do whatever a grateful country could for servicemen who had paid the ultimate price. If so desired by relatives, the boys would go home — or they would rest in sacred military ground in Hawaii.

A funeral cortege with an unknown American soldier was the focus of attention for a procession that commenced at the American cemetery in Ipswich and ended at King George Square, Brisbane. In a fitting gesture of Allied admiration and loyalty, the casket was handled by American officers and given to their Australian counterparts, who escorted it to Newstead Wharf where the *Goucher Victory* was waiting to take the boys home. Many government and military officials were included in the procession and 30 000 people lined the streets in a display of solemnity never before experienced with any public event that involved the American armed forces.

At the wharf, a 70-year-old Brisbane woman walked from the crowd and placed a hibiscus flower on the casket of the unknown soldier. 'I am an Australian,' she said, 'but the Americans came here to fight for us and I wanted to thank them.'

By coincidence, the entourage carrying the last Americans to go home passed through the same gate to the same wharf at which six years earlier, almost to the hour, the first Americans had disembarked.[17]

Shortly after the war, Mr F.S. Parkes, a Main Roads Department engineer, suggested a Cairn of Remembrance for the Americans who served at Camp Cable. The area had been levelled and there were few reminders of the once thriving camp, but the monument was placed near the location of the main entrance. The wording on the plaque was in doubt until Mrs Parkes provided a suggestion that was deemed appropriate:

U.S.A.
CAMP CABLE
THEY PASSED THIS WAY
1942–1944 [18]

The full impact of the Americans in Australia during the war could never be adequately recorded on any plaque. The Americans arrived in a vulnerable country that was in a perilous situation; they were not motivated by Australia's needs but by their own. Australia simply offered the logistical and geographical requirements necessary for the prosecution of the war against Japan. It was both unintentional and inadvertent that, in the process, they influenced Australia domestically, culturally and industrially.

Australia always had the potential to prosper, the resources and the skills, but before the war the pace was pedestrian and the motivation variable. The impetus and example of the Yanks down-under were major contributions to Australia successfully meeting the challenges of the future, while still retaining the better qualities of the past.

An ideal plaque commemorating the Americans and the alliance with Australia during the war could read:

They Passed This Way And They Helped Show The Way.

CHAPTER FIFTEEN

THE SONG IS ENDED, BUT THE MELODY LINGERS ON

There are few reminders in Australia today that nearly six decades ago a million Americans passed this way during the country's darkest hours.

Six years after the end of World War II the Australian-American Association unveiled a stark monument to commemorate the wartime alliance. It stands in the middle of Newstead Park in Brisbane. The area in which it is displayed is called Lyndon B. Johnson Place; a reminder of another alliance in the 1960s, when both countries where committed to the tragedy of Vietnam. Curious onlookers can make out some by now faded and tarnished text on the base of the monument.

> They Passed This Way
>
> This monument was erected by the people of Queensland in grateful memory of the contribution made by the people of the United States of America to the defence of Australia during the 1939–1945 war. Long may it stand as a symbol of unity of English-speaking people in the cause of freedom.

An eagle is perched above the memorial, gazing in the direction taken by the American submarines as they cruised the Brisbane River on their way to operations in the waters off New Guinea and the Solomons.

A few metres from the eagle's perch, one can see a new plaque mounted in 1992: 'Dedicated to the memory of the allied submarines and their crews who operated from Brisbane 1942–1945'. Over 50 submarines are listed, including several English boats which used the facility in the later stages of the war.

On 2 November 1999, bulldozers levelled what remained of the United States submarine base at New Farm in Brisbane. A property developer paid the Brisbane City Council $7.25 million for the site. Fifty-five years since the last boats left on the last patrols, the area will become the city's first multi-million dollar, inner city, riverside housing precinct. As a matter of historical conscience, it was agreed to preserve the old machine shed, which will be heritage-listed. Apart from the shed, all that now remains of the base and the silent service is the legacy of its exploits.

At the beginning of the new millennium the city of Brisbane is virtually unrecognisable when compared with the gloomy garrison city it was during the war. The Brisbane City Hall remains but it has been dwarfed by the high rise development of the past three decades. In the 58 years since the notorious Battle of Brisbane, the battleground has changed. Most of the buildings of that era were destroyed or renovated during the city's redevelopment during the '60s. The tram bells stopped ringing in 1969.

The two buildings that housed the Australian canteen and the American PX still stand in Adelaide Street. It seems that, like the events they witnessed, they refuse to fade easily into the anonymity of history. But unlike in their heyday, they are now semi-occupied and quiet. You can still stand at the spot where O'Sullivan and company came to blows. The footpath where Webster fell is still the same, but the American post office is now an Australian government building. The Gresham Hotel has long gone. The battleground for round two of that battle has changed less over the years. The AMP building that housed MacArthur's headquarters still stands, although MacArthur Chambers are empty and decrepit. Next door is the GPO building; it has been there for a hundred years. The provost's baton may still be on the roof.

MacArthur has not been a part of the city's history for over 50 years. But if his reputation is under siege, his profile is not. In recent years a plaque has been mounted on the outside of the AMP building which says in part: 'In this building General Douglas MacArthur, Supreme Commander Allied Forces South-West Pacific, established his headquarters on 21st July 1942 and here he formulated the initial plans which led to final victory'.

The first thing one sees when entering the foyer of Lennons Hotel is Macarthur's Bar — spelt thus. Although a temperate man, the General would undoubtedly have been impressed.

In June 1999 it was announced that the State government and the Brisbane City Council had agreed to restore and permanently preserve MacArthur Chambers in the AMP building. The Premier, Mr Peter Beattie, immediately pledged $70 000 toward the project and explained: 'What we need to do is not only have some respect and appreciation for the contribution MacArthur made to protect Australia, but clearly there is an American tourism component.'

The restoration is expected to be completed by the time Queensland hosts the Goodwill Games in October 2001. It will be promoted in tourism material that will be distributed throughout the United States.

Douglas MacArthur is still good 'box office'. The publicity from the initiative was so positive it was as if MacArthur and Pick Diller had written the press releases the night before. American Legion Brisbane adjutant, Chris Boen, told the press: 'We have hundreds of people come here every year and they want to see MacArthur Chambers, but we've had to turn them back'.[1]

In October 1999, amidst much fanfare, a new restaurant complex opened in Adelaide Street. Situated a few blocks from the AMP building, it offers the ultimate homage. A caricature of the General, complete with braid cap, sunglasses and corncob pipe, adorns the façade and the menus. Plaques, posters and photos are strategically located and restaurant staff tell inquisitive diners of MacArthur's exploits. 'I shall return' is still a familiar catchcry at MacArthur's H.Q., but this time it has a different connotation.

Camp Cable, near Logan Village in Queensland, was a busy, well appointed but isolated camp. The home of the Red Arrow had some distinguished visitors, including Eleanor Roosevelt and Douglas MacArthur. Today, it is a most tranquil place. Since 1945 scrub and a commercial timber plantation have overgrown the area. However where the front gate to the self-contained camp that housed up to 20 000 men stood there are three quaint memorials. One is dedicated to the memory of Robert Dannenberg who, like nearly a thousand of his buddies, trained at Camp Cable before losing his life in New Guinea in December 1942. Another small stone commemorates a mascot called Vicksburg, a dog who was born in Mississippi City that somehow ended up at Camp Cable before becoming another American road fatality at Southport in 1942. The third, and more formal, memorial is the cairn discussed in the previous chapter.

Darwin is now a modern city and bears few scars of that momentous day in February 1942. There is a memorial to Second Lieutenant Robert J. Buel USAAF, 33rd Pursuit Squadron, whose valour was belatedly recognised.

In 1986, when Marekumi Takahara revealed that his aircraft was engaged by a lone Kittyhawk near Darwin and that both aircraft were shot down, Northern Territory historians, Bob Piper and Bob Alford began a long campaign to honour the American pilot. Buel's sister, Mrs Katharine Brothers, was contacted in California and travelled to Darwin to honour her late brother and unveil the memorial in May 1993. Buel was posthumously awarded the Distinguished Flying Cross. It was presented to Mrs Brothers on the day the memorial was unveiled.[2]

In Port Pirie, South Australia, there is an Airmen's Memorial Park. The man responsible for the dedication is a local alderman Ken Madigan. As a young boy during the war, he witnessed an American Kittyhawk crash nearby; he and his mates rode their bikes to the scene and inspected the wreckage. The memory of the incident had a profound effect on the youngster. He later learnt that the pilot was Second Lieutenant Richard E. Pingree of the 33 AAF Pursuit Squadron. Many years later Madigan received community assistance in realising his dream of a memorial to Pingree and other airmen who lost their lives in the area.[3]

Shortly after the war an American War Graves Unit arrived in Darwin to locate the USS *Peary*. Despite their efforts and those of many locals, the wreck was not located until 1956. In 1989 the 'Knox' class destroyer USS *Robert E. Peary* visited Darwin as part of the Kangaroo 89 defence exercises. Local scuba divers presented the ship's captain with a brass shell casing and the wardroom keys of the original *Peary*.[4]

Other heroes and casualties of the Darwin raid are also commemorated. A Walk of Remembrance in Coolangatta on Queensland's Gold Coast contains plaques dedicated to ships sunk around Australia's coastline during the war. The *Peary* and other ships lost at Darwin have pride of place. Sister Margaret de Mestre is honoured on a plaque in Central Queensland. St Christopher's Chapel in Rockhampton is a sacred reminder to the memory of the 41st Division, which had such a positive influence on the town during the war.[5]

Every day, weather permitting, Bob and Vivien Deakin raise the American and Australian flags on the Bakers Creek Memorial near Mackay ; it is not far from where the B-17C crashed in 1943, killing 40 men. They are a retired couple who have been conducting the ceremony since 1992, when the memorial was unveiled. They ask nothing for their trouble. Like many others, they were moved by the extent of the disaster and saddened by the subsequent anonymity of the victims. If it were not for the efforts of Col Benson and the Mackay RSL, together with Teddy Hanks in Wichita Falls and a few others, there would be no memorial. For interests other than their own, this small group of men have persevered for years in collating information on the crash and the men who died in such futile and tragic circumstances.

Every anniversary of the crash, Mrs Faye Cole places a wreath on the memorial. Mrs Cole is the sister of Joan Harris, who first reported the crash to Mackay police. The funds are from a small group of contributors in America, including the only survivor of the disaster, Foye Roberts, who all these years later still carries emotional and physical wounds from the tragedy. On 14 June 1997, a new American flag was unfurled and raised at the memorial. It was purchased by Foye Roberts, in memory of his buddies.[6]

For most Australians, however, the Americans have left only memories. Few of the old city pubs and saloons survive. The delis, milk bars, cafes and fish and chip shops, so popular with the invaders, have long gone, destroyed by the next generation of invaders — a commercial army with franchises the strategy and fast food the weapon. The great dance halls have long since relinquished their sites to developers. They had become empty and idle, with no orchestras left to play on the stand and no-one to fill the dance floors.

The participants who passed this way and those who greeted them are also fading into history. The most eminent, General Douglas MacArthur, lived to enjoy more triumphs, the last being his invasion of Inchon during the Korean war. MacArthur was commander of the United Nations forces but his intention to extend the war to China led to a confrontation with President Truman and MacArthur was relieved of his command. He never did run for public office, but continued to enjoy the adulation of the American people. However, without a war and without an army, MacArthur grew old.

'The shadows are lengthening for me,' he told cadets at his beloved West Point. 'The twilight is here. My days of old have vanished, tone and tint; they have gone glimmering through the dreams of things that were. Their memory is one of wondrous beauty, watered by tears, and coaxed and caressed by the smiles of yesterday.'

The methodical MacArthur had always planned his life, and he also planned his own modest funeral. When President John Kennedy told him that a more 'suitable national tribute', would be required, with the involvement of West Point cadets, MacArthur responded,

'By George, I'd like to see that'. Neither he nor Kennedy would do so. On Kennedy's death MacArthur was amongst those who pleaded with President Johnson not to become involved in a land war in Vietnam.

'I've looked that old scoundrel death in the face many times,' said the General in old age. 'This time I think he has me on the ropes. But I'm going to do the very best I can.' Douglas MacArthur died on 5 April 1964, at the age of 84.[7]

Jean MacArthur remained devoted to the memory and grandeur of her late husband until she died on 16 January 2000. She was 101. Arthur MacArthur is now a man in his sixties. He has a music degree and it is music and not military matters that have always interested him. Arthur MacArthur has never married and the MacArthur military dynasty has thus ended with its most illustrious figure.[8]

The General's coterie has followed him in death. Perhaps appropriately the Bataan Gang's press officer, LeGrand Diller was the last to go.

In 1986, he wrote to a former staff member in MacArthur's old headquarters:

Those early days were very busy and trying days. With the General champing at the bit to get a relief force going toward the Philippines and no troops in Australia and none promised. We all wondered why we were there. My job was particularly difficult for the press wanted to know much more than I was permitted to tell them.[9]

Joy Foord never forgot Diller. For some years, she received courteous correspondence from Pick and Hat Diller. In 1987, she received a short letter. It was the first from Diller's new wife and the last she would receive relating to the debonair senior officer she had met for the first time 45 years earlier:

Dear Miss Foord,

It is with a sad heart that I must tell you that Pick died on 2 September here in Reynolds, Georgia where we were building our home since we were married. His home in Florida has been sold.

Sincerely,

Mary Lou Diller

Joy Foord is now in her eighties and lives a quiet life near Brisbane. She still radiates that charm and dignity that must have impressed Diller, Sutherland, Lynn and the rest.

The honeymoon for Les and Yvonne Cottman is now in its 58th year. Seldom have a couple been so devoted to each other. Living in Brisbane, Les still has his Arkansas accent, but claims an ocker disposition. Yvonne retains her teenage crush on Americans, especially the one she married. They still hold hands and compose sonnets to each other.

Joan and Bill Bentson also live in Brisbane. Joan is still an army wife, simply because Bill has never left it. The phone book lists him as 'Bentson Major USA (retired) William A.' He has devoted his life to compiling information about the American and Australian alliance.

It was Bill Bentson and a few others who were responsible for the plaque outside of MacArthur's office in Brisbane. The General always inspired loyalty and respect and, although Bentson remains objective, he has enormous admiration for the late, great soldier.

Grady Gaston never returned to his base at Iron Range, nor did he ever return to Australia. He was always reluctant to discuss his ordeal following the crash of the *Little Eva* Liberator in the outback. The emotional and physical scars he endured during his five-month ordeal may never have healed. He seldom attended any reunions or functions organised by the veterans of the 90th Bomb Group.[10] Gaston was invited to return to Australia for Australia Remembers, the 50 year commemoration of the end of the Pacific war, but he declined. He lived out the rest of his life in his beloved Frisco City, Alabama, where he died on 8 January 1998.

His fellow survivors of the crash are also gone — Norman Grosson in May 1989 and Roy Wilson in July 1991. All that remains of the *Little Eva* saga is the aircraft itself. It lies, rusty and overgrown, near Moonlight Creek — 110 kilometres north of Burketown.[11]

There are many other American expatriates who have remained in Australia since the end of the war, or have migrated since. Like the thousands of Allied soldiers who defended the country during the war, they now see a totally different culture.

Australia has a population of nearly 20 million and a liberal immigration policy. Many of Australia's economic allies are former enemies. The conflict that now exists in the Asia-Pacific region is one of trade and commerce. Australia is waging a war for market share and influence in the area. America is still a valued ally, and although Australia is still a member of the British Commonwealth it is impossible to imagine Australians rushing to aid the Mother Country.

In the last 50 years Australia has come of age, but this has not pleased everyone, in particular some of those who fought the old battles and the old enemies when the country was young and in peril. They accept the transitions of the last half century only reluctantly, and providing Australians of all ages and backgrounds do not forget the 100 000 of its people who died in the twentieth century defending their ideals.

'Don't get me wrong,' said a white-haired American expatriate. 'Things change, it's the way of the world, but I want to tell you something. When we came here during the war we thought that Australia was a little innocent and about 20 years behind the United States, but that was okay by us. That's what we loved about it then — and that's what we miss about it now.'

CHAPTER NOTES

CHAPTER ONE

1. Paul Hasluck, *The Government and the People, 1939–1941*, p. 152.
2. Margaret Olds (ed.), *Australia Though Time*, p. 216. See also Ian Grant, *A Dictionary of Australian Military History*.
3. Robin Brown, *Collins Milestones in Australian History*, p. 562.
4. Olds (ed.), *Australia Through Time*, p. 300.
5. Michael Page, *Bradman: The Illustrated Biography*, p. 232.
6. Olds (ed.), *Australia Through Time*, p. 300.
7. Olds (ed.) *Australia Through Time*, p. 300.
8. *Sun News-Pictorial*, 16 September 1939.
9. Olds (ed.), *Australia Through Time*, p. 301.
10. Conversation with Bill Bentson, June 1997.
11. Michael McKernan, *All In! Australia During the Second World War*, p. 65.
12. Hasluck, *The Government and the People, 1939–1941*, p. 403.
13. G. H. Gill, *Royal Australian Navy, 1939–1942*, pp. 184 –94.
14. Grant, *Dictionary of Australian Military History*, pp. 97, 147.
15. Vic Cassells, *For Those in Peril*, p. 73.
16. Cassells, *For Those in Peril*, p. 46.
17. *Northern Lines* (BHP newspaper), June 1998, p. 4.
18. Olds (ed.), *Australia Through Time*, p. 307.
19. Brown, *Collins Milestones in Australian History*, p. 569.
20. Brown, *Milestones*, p. 569.
21. Brown, *Milestones*, p. 569.
22. *Courier-Mail*, 8 December 1941.
23. Hasluck, *The Government and the People, 1939–1941*, p. 558.

CHAPTER TWO

1. Neil Wenborn, *A Pictorial History of the U.S.A.*, p. 260.
2. Wenborn, *Pictorial History*, pp. 259, 260, 261, 263.
3. Wenborn, *Pictorial History*, pp. 262, 263. See also Tad Tuleja, *The New York Public Library Book of Popular Americana*, pp. 373.
4. Wenborn, *Pictorial History*, p. 265.
5. Wenborn, *Pictorial History*, p. 269.
6. Ronald H. Bailey, *The Home Front: U.S.A.*, p. 43.
7. Lee J. Ready, *World War II: Nation by Nation*, p. 304.
8. Frank Freidel, *Franklin D. Roosevelt: A Rendezvous With Destiny*, p. 360.

9. Wenborn, *Pictorial History*, p. 271.
10. Robert Goralski, *World War II Almanac*, pp. 186, 187.
11. Gordon Prange, *At Dawn We Slept*, p. 539.
12. Bailey, *The Home Front*, p. 43.
13. W. F. Kimbal (ed.), *Churchill and Roosevelt: The Complete Correspondence*, Volume 2, p. 283.
14. Brogan Hugh, *Longman History of the United States of America*, p. 589.
15. B. Charles MacDonald, *The Mighty Endeavour: The American War in Europe*, p. 21.
16. Lee Kennett, *For the Duration*, p. 24.
17. Captain Howard L. Steffy, diary, December 1941.

CHAPTER THREE

1. Tom Frame, *Pacific Partners: A History of Australian –American Naval Relations*, p. 10.
2. Frame, *Pacific Partners*, p. 10.
3. Frame, *Pacific Partners*, p. 16.
4. *Daily Telegraph*, 10 August 1908.
5. *Daily Telegraph*, 23 July 1925.
6. Barbara Winter, *HMAS Sydney: Fact, Fantasy and Fraud*, p. 4.
7. Winter, *HMAS Sydney*, p. 251.
8. Frame, *Pacific Partners*, p. 33.
9. *Pages of History: The Best of the Daily Telegraph Mirror*, p. 80.
10. *Pages of History*, p. 81.
11. Margaret Olds (ed.), *Australia Through Time*, p. 295.
12. *Courier-Mail*, 15 February 1938.
13. *Courier-Mail*, 15 February 1938.
14. *Pages of History*, p. 83.
15. *Courier-Mail*, 15 February 1938.
16. John Hammond Moore, *Over-Sexed, Over-Paid and Over Here*, p. 2.
17. *Courier-Mail*, 19 March 1941.
18. *Courier-Mail*, 19 March 1941.
19. *Courier-Mail*, 19 March 1941.
20. *Sydney Morning Herald*, 21 March 1941.
21. *Courier-Mail*, 25 March 1941.
22. *Courier-Mail*, 25 March 1941.
23. *Courier-Mail*, 25 March 1941.
24. *Courier-Mail*, 26 March 1941.
25. *Courier-Mail*, 26 March 1941.
26. *Courier-Mail*, 26 March 1941.
27. *Courier-Mail*, 3 April 1941.
28. *Toowoomba Chronicle*, 15 April 1941.
29. *Courier-Mail*, 30 April 1941.
30. Gordon Prange, *At Dawn We Slept*, p. 537. See also Larry Sowinski, *The Pacific War*, p. 26.
31. Steven L. Carruthers, *Australia Under Siege: Japanese Submarine Raiders, 1942*, p. 24.
32. Denis and Peggy Warner, *Disaster in the Pacific*, p. 256.
33. Warner, *Disaster in the Pacific*, p. 222.
34. C. W. Kilpatrick, *Naval Night Battles in the Solomons*, p. 169.
35. Kilpatrick, *Naval Night Battles*, p. 101.
36. Nigel Hamilton, *JFK: Reckless Youth*, p. 548.
37. Hamilton, *JFK*, p. 548.
38. Ibid., p. 565.
39. Kilpatrick, *Naval Night Battles*, p. 149.

40. Robert Sinclair Parkin, *Blood on the Sea: American Destroyers in World War II*, pp. 260–1.

41. Paul H. Silverstone, *United States Warships of World War II*, p. 118.

CHAPTER FOUR

1. Captain Howard L. Steffy, diary, 7, 8 December 1941.

2. A. Willard Heath, *Letter to Justin*, p. 11.

3. Heath, *Letter to Justin*, p. 12.

4. Howard L. Steffy, diary, 10, 12, 14, 18 December 1941.

5. Howard L. Steffy, diary, 22 December 1941.

6. Douglas Gillison, *Royal Australian Air Force, 1939–1942*, p. 296. See also Daniel and Annette Potts, *Yanks Down Under*, p. 5.

7. Gillison, *Royal Australian Air Force, 1939–1942*, pp. 184–5.

8. John Hammond Moore, *Over-Sexed, Over-Paid and Over Here*, p. 41.

9. Interview with the author, 21 December 1991.

10. Interview with the author, 10 May 1992.

11. Moore, *Over-Sexed, Over-Paid and Over Here*, pp. 41–2.

12. Heath, *Letter to Justin*, p. 12

13. Interview with the author, 20 May 1992.

14. *Weekend Australian*, 21–22 December 1991

15. *The Brisbane Line*, television documentary, Channel 7 1987 (producer, Frank Warwick).

16. Interview with the author, 6 May 1992.

17. Moore, *Over-Sexed, Over-Paid and Over Here*, p. 42.

18. Paul Hasluck, *The Government and the People, 1942–1945*, p. 58.

19. Hasluck, *The Government and the People, 1939–1941*, Appendix 3.

20. M. Healy, *Wharfie*, Vol. 1, No. 10, 10 May 1943: 'for and on behalf of the Communist Party of Australia, Waterfront Branch'.

21. Hasluck, *The Government and the People, 1942–1945*, p. 33.

22. Elizabeth Anne Wheal, Stephen Pope and James Taylor, *Encyclopedia of the Second World War*, pp. 288, 289. See also David G. Chandler, *Battles and Battle Scenes of World War II*, p. 145.

23. *Herald*, 27 December 1941.

24. Victor W. Madej (ed.), *U.S. Army and Marines Corps Order of Battle: Pacific Theater of Operations, 1941–1945*, Volume 1, pp. 33–6.

25. Peter Stone, *The Lady and the President: The Life and Loss of the SS* President Coolidge, p. 94

26. Paul H. Silverstone, *United States Warships of World War II*, p. 85; David Brown, *The Royal Navy and the Falklands War*, p. 136.

27. Peter Elphick, *Singapore: The Pregnable Fortress*, pp. 1, 356. See also Chandler, *Battles and Battle Scenes of World War II*, p. 145.

28. John Robertson, *1939–1945: Australia Goes to War*, p. 219.

29. Hasluck, *The Government and the People, 1942–1945*, pp. 110, 112.

30. Potts, *Yanks Down Under*, p. xiv; also, Bill Bentson, interview with the author, 11 May 1997.

31. John Marriott, *Disaster at Sea*, pp. 129–35.

32. Interview with the author, 11 May 1997.

33. Hasluck, *The Government and the People, 1942–1945*, p. 225. See also Clay Blair Jr., *Silent Victory: The U.S. Submarine War Against Japan*, pp. 191, 218.

34. *Truth* (Brisbane), 14 June 1942.

35. Captain Howard L. Steffy, diary, 15 March, 20 May 1942; Bill Bentson, interview with the author, 18 May 1997.

36. United States Army, Special Services Division, *The Pocket Guide to... booklets, 1941–43.

37. *Truth* (Brisbane), 22 March 1942.

38. *Herald*, 10 April 1942.

39. *Sun News-Pictorial*, 24 March 1942. See also John Costello, *Love, Sex and War: Changing Values, 1939–45*, p. 327.

40. Hasluck, *The Government and the People, 1942–1945*, p. 225.

41. Queensland State Archives, A/2878 M 78, 21 November 1942.

42. Bill and Joan Bentson, interview with the author, 11 May 1997.

43. Camp Cable—32nd Division Red Arrow staging area. Original map drawn by E. D. Hawkins, August 1942. See also R. A. Judd, *The Camp Cable Incident*, plaque dedication ceremony program, published by 32nd Division Veterans Association and American Families Association of Queensland, 1968.

44. Potts, *Yanks Down Under*, p. 83.

45. Robertson, *1939–1945: Australia Goes to War*, p. 140.

46. Ian Grant, *A Dictionary of Australian Military History*, p. 190.

47. Robert Dalleck, *Lone Star Rising: Lyndon Johnson and his Times*, p. 237.

48. Charles Messenger, *World War II Chronological Atlas*, p. 114.

49. Grant, *Dictionary of Australian Military History*, p. 242.

50. Messenger, *World War II Chronological Atlas*, p. 114.

CHAPTER FIVE

1. Frank Alcorta, *Australia's Frontline: The Northern Territory's War*, p. 5.

2. Alcorta, *Australia's Frontline*, p. 6; Robert N. Alford, *Darwin's Air War*, p. 6.

3. Alcorta, *Australia's Frontline*, p. 6.

4. Amelia Earhart, *Last Flight*, p. 127.

5. Alford, *Darwin's Air War*, p. 7.

6. Earhart, *Last Flight*, pp. 127, 128.

7. G. H. Gill, *Royal Australian Navy, 1939–1942*, p. 586.

8. Alan Powell, *The Shadow's Edge: Australia's Northern War*, p. 56.

9. Douglas Lockwood, *Australia's Pearl Harbour: Darwin, 1942*, p. 17.

10. Lockwood, *Australia's Pearl Harbour*, p. 17.

11. Peter Dennis, Jeffrey Grey, Ewan Morris and Robin Prior, *The Oxford Companion to Australian Military History*, p. 3.

12. Douglas Gillison, *Royal Australian Air Force, 1939–1942*, p. 294.

13. Powell, *The Shadow's Edge*, p. 65.

14. Powell, *The Shadow's Edge*, p. 66; also W. Victor Madej (ed.), *U.S. Army and Marine Corps Order of Battle: Pacific Theater of Operations, 1941–1945*, Volume 1, p. 33.

15. Mark T. Muller, interview with Lieutenant Robert F. McMahon, USAF (ret.), 13 April 1986, Austin, Texas. Transcript, p. 2.

16. Major Floyd Joaqhin Pell, Service Record and Distinguished Service Cross Award details, February 1942.

17. McMahon interview transcript, 1986, p. 2.

18. Powell, *The Shadow's Edge*, pp. 65, 66.

19. McMahon interview transcript, 1986, p. 3.

20. Powell, *The Shadow's Edge*, p. 69.

21. Powell, *The Shadow's Edge*, pp. 68, 69.

22. Alford, *Darwin's Air War*, p. 13.

23. Alford, *Darwin's Air War*, p. 13.

24. Lockwood, *Australia's Pearl Harbour*, pp. 2, 3–4.

25. Alford, *Darwin's Air War*, p. 13.

26. Ian Grant, *A Dictionary of Australian Military History*, p. 369.

27. Gill, *Royal Australian Navy, 1939–1942*, p. 581; Robert J.

Rayner, *The Army and the Defence of Darwin Fortress*, p. 177.

28. Rayner, *The Army and the Defence of Darwin Fortress*, p. 179.

29. Rayner, *The Army and the Defence of Darwin Fortress*, p. 179; *RAAF News*, May 1993, p. 16.

30. McMahon interview transcript, 1986, p. 1.

31. Robert Sinclair Parkin, *Blood on the Sea: American Destroyers in World War II*, pp. 16, 21.

32. Paul H. Silverstone, *United States Warships of World War II*, p. 103.

33. Samuel Eliot Morrison, *The Two-Ocean War: A Short History of the United States Navy in the Second World War*, p. 79

34. Morrison, *The Two-Ocean War*, p. 81.

35. S. E. Smith (ed.), *The United States Navy in World War II*, Chapter 5; W. L. White, *The Philippine Expendables*, p. 49.

36. White, *The Philippine Expendables*, p. 50

37. White, *The Philippine Expendables*, p. 53.

38. Parkin, *Blood on the Sea*, p. 18; also Lockwood, *Australia's Pearl Harbour*, p. 49.

39. Harry Holmes, *The Last Patrol*, p. 12.

40. Parkin, *Blood on the Sea*, p. 18.

41. Clay Blair, Jr, *Silent Victory: The U.S. Submarine War Against Japan*, p. 134.

42. Smith (ed.), *The United States Navy in World War II*, p. 48.

43. White, *The Philippine Expendables*, p. 50.

44. Parkin, *Blood on the Sea*, pp. 17, 18.

45. Parkin, *Blood on the Sea*, p. 19.

46. McMahon interview transcript, 1986, p. 5.

47. McMahon Interview transcript, 1992, p. 2.

48. Rayner, *The Army and the Defence of Darwin Fortress*, p. 180; also Lockwood, *Australia's Pearl Harbour*, p. 26.

49. Alford, *Darwin's Air War*, p. 13; also McMahon interview transcript, 1986, p. 6; 1992, p. 3.

50. Lockwood, *Australia's Pearl Harbour*, p. 47.

51. Gill, *Royal Australian Navy, 1939–1942*, p. 589; also Lockwood, *Australia's Pearl Harbour*, pp. 44–6.

52. McMahon interview transcript, 1986, p. 7; also Lockwood, *Australia's Pearl Harbour*, p. 31

53. Alford, *Darwin's Air War*, p. 14.

54. McMahon interview transcript, 1986, p. 7.

55. Lockwood, *Australia's Pearl Harbour*, pp. 23, 24.

56. Gillison, *Royal Australian Air Force, 1939–1942*, p. 426.

57. Lockwood, *Australia's Pearl Harbour*, p. 25.

58. Robert Oestreicher report, 1942; Lockwood, *Australia's Pearl Harbour*, p. 32.

59. McMahon interview transcripts, 1986 and 1992; also Lockwood, *Australia's Pearl Harbour*, pp. 32–8.

60. John Keegan (ed.), *Encyclopedia of World War II*, pp. 175, 192–3.

61. Lockwood, *Australia's Pearl Harbour*, p. 32–8; McMahon interview transcript, 1986, pp. 7–10; 1992, p. 4; Powell, *The Shadow's Edge*, pp. 83, 86; Robert F. McMahon, letter to Group Captain Ross H. Glassop, 25 October 1973.

62. Powell, *The Shadow's Edge*, p. 80.

63. Parkin, *Blood on the Sea*, pp. 20–1; Lockwood, *Australia's Pearl Harbour*, p. 49.

64. Gill, *Royal Australian Navy, 1939–1942*, p. 593.

65. Rupert Goodman, *Hospital Ships*, p. 68. Also Goodman, *Our War Nurses*.

66. Lionel Wigmore, *The Japanese Thrust*, p. 386.

67. David Jenkins, *Battle Surface: Japan's Submarine War Against Australia, 1942–44*, pp. 102–5.

68. Powell, *The Shadow's Edge*, p. 82

69. Powell, *The Shadow's Edge*, p. 89; also Lockwood, *Australia's Pearl Harbour*, p. 101.

70. Alford, *Darwin's Air War*, p. 14; also Powell, *The Shadow's Edge*, pp. 93, 94.

71. Alford, *Darwin's Air War*, p. 21; also Powell, *The Shadow's Edge*, p. 93; Lockwood, *Australia's Pearl Harbour*, p. 183.

72. Grant, *Dictionary of Australian Military History*, p. 95.

73. Rayner, *The Army and the Defence of Darwin Fortress*, p. 224.

74. Lockwood, *Australia's Pearl Harbour*, p. 46.

75. Alford, *Darwin's Air War*, p. 20.

76. J. Rohwer and G. Hummelchen, *Chronology of the War at Sea, 1939–1945*, p. 127

77. Rohwer and Hummelchen, *Chronology of the War at Sea*, p. 126.

78. *Sabretache*, April/June 1995, p. 7; Tom Lewis, *Wrecks in Darwin Waters*.

CHAPTER SIX

1. Robert Leckie, *Delivered From Evil: The Saga of World War II*, p. 322.

2. For details on MacArthur's early life and career, see: Leckie, *Delivered From Evil*, pp. 316–24; Eric Larrabee, *Commander in Chief*, pp. 305–11; William Manchester, *American Caesar*; Perret Geoffrey, *Old Soldiers Never Die*. I also benefited from conversations with John Lillback, May 1997, and Bill Bentson, June 1997.

3. Larrabee, *Commander in Chief*, p. 311; Lee J. Ready, *World War II: Nation by Nation*, pp. 231–2.

4. Larrabee, *Commander in Chief*, p. 311; Manchester, *American Caesar*, pp. 162–4.

5. Manchester, *American Caesar*, p. 164.

6. Leckie, *Delivered From Evil*, p. 324; Manchester, *American Caesar*, p. 161.

7. Manchester, *American Caesar*, p. 165, Perret, *Old Soldiers Never Die*, pp. 219, 227–9; D. Clayton James, *The Years of MacArthur*, Volume, 2 p. 100.

8. Leckie, *Delivered From Evil*, p. 350; Larrabee, *Commander in Chief*, p. 318

9. Manchester, *American Caesar*, pp. 205–6.

10. John Costello, *Days of Infamy*, p. 28.

11. James, *The Years of MacArthur*, Volume 2, pp. 6 –14, Costello, *Days of Infamy*, p. 15–43.

12. Larrabee, *Commander in Chief*, p. 316.

13. Larrabee, *Commander in Chief*, p. 317.

14. Charles Messenger, *World War II: Chronological Atlas*, pp. 82–3; Robert Goralski, *World War II Almanac*, p. 192; James, *The Years of MacArthur*, p. 24.

15. Messenger, *World War II Chronological Atlas*, p. 82.

16. Messenger, *World War II Chronological Atlas*, p. 82.

17. James, *The Years of MacArthur*, Volume 2, p. 33–4.

18. Manchester, *American Caesar*, p. 223.

19. James, *The Years of MacArthur*, Volume 2, p. 47.

20. Manchester, *American Caesar*, pp. 242–3; Perret, *Old Soldiers Never Die*, p. 268; Larrabee, *Commander in Chief*, p. 320.

21. Manchester, *American Caesar*, pp. 235.

22. Costello, *Days of Infamy*, pp. 269–71, 407; Larrabee, *Commander in Chief*, p. 315

23. Manchester, *American Caesar*, p. 250.

24. Manchester, *American Caesar*, p. 256; Perret, *Old Soldiers Never Die*, p. 274.

25. Manchester, *American Caesar*, pp. 255–8; James, *The Years of MacArthur*, Volume 2, pp. 100–5; Perret, *Old Soldiers Never Die*, p. 275.

26. Edward Vernorff and Rima Shore, *The International Dictionary of Twentieth Century Biography*, pp. 146, 421.

27. Manchester, *American Caesar*, p. 275.

28. James, *The Years of MacArthur*, Volume 2, p. 127.

29. Manchester, *American Caesar*, pp. 258–67; Perret, *Old Soldiers Never Die*, pp. 276–83; James, *The Years of MacArthur*, Volume 2, pp. 100–8.

30. Peter Donovan, *Alice Springs: Its History and the People Who Made It*, p. 213.

31. Paul Hasluck, *The Government and the People, 1942–1945*, p. 110; Manchester, *American Caesar*, pp. 267–8.

32. Hasluck, *The Government and the People, 1942–1945*, p. 110; *Daily Mirror* (Sydney), 18 March 1942.

33. Manchester, *American Caesar*, p. 270.

34. Manchester, *American Caesar*, p. 270

35. *Herald*, 21 March 1942; Manchester, *American Caesar*, pp. 272–3; James, *The Years of MacArthur*, Volume 2, pp. 109–10.

36. *Herald*, 21 March 1942.

37. James, *The Years of MacArthur*, Volume 2, p. 127–8.

38. Messenger, *World War II: Chronological Atlas*, pp. 82–3.

39. Conversation with Bill Bentson, June 1997.

40. James, *The Years of MacArthur*, Volume 2, pp. 111–12.

41. Hasluck, *The Government and the People, 1942–1945*, p. 112–

13. See also, James, *The Years of MacArthur*, Volume 2, p. 120.

42. Hasluck, *The Government and the People, 1942–1945*, p. 113, 114.

43. James, *The Years of MacArthur*, Volume 2, p. 122.

44. Warren F. Kimball (ed.), *Churchill and Roosevelt: The Complete Correspondence*, Volume 1, pp. 477–80.

45. Manchester, *American Caesar*, p. 280.

46. Conversation with Bill Bentson, June 1997.

47. Messenger, *World War II: Chronological Atlas*, pp. 82–3.

48. James, *The Years of MacArthur*, pp. 147–52.

49. Leckie, *Delivered From Evil*, p. 459.

CHAPTER SEVEN

1. Leonski material from: Queensland State Archives, 1263M; *Sun News-Pictorial*, 4, 13, 23 May, 17 July 1942; *Herald*, 17 May 1942; *Courier-Mail*, 11 May 1942; Ivan Chapman, *Leonski: The Brownout Strangler*; Daniel E. and Annette Potts, *Yanks Down Under*, pp. 233–5; Alan Sharpe, *The Giant Book of Crimes That Shocked Australia*, pp. 265–70.

2. Alan Sharpe, *Murder: 25 True Australian Crimes*, pp. 49–55.

3. Queensland State Archives, A/12034.

4. John Hammond Moore, *Over-Sexed, Over-Paid and Over Here*, p. 213; Potts, *Yanks Down Under*, p. 236.

5. *Telegraph* (Brisbane), 8 June 1963.

6. Queensland State Archives, A/6504 (60).

7. Queensland State Archives, A/12034: Inkerman Shooting [complete police report, 141 pages]; Coroner autopsy report on Frederick Theodore Simons, 408th Bomb Squadron, 7 November 1942.

8. Queensland State Archives, A/12037 1268.

9. Queensland State Archives, A/12029, A/12035 A/12040, A/12044.

10. *Courier-Mail*, October 1943; Queensland State Archives, A/12036, A/12037 231/25.

11. Queensland State Archives, A/12036.

12. Brigadier General L. S. Ostrander to Police Commissioner Carroll, September 1943. Queensland State Archives.

13. Australian National Archives, File Q 18451, Letter to American Consul Brisbane from Captain W.D. Chandler, USS *Northampton*, 10 August 1941; American Consulate, Joseph P. Ragland, to CIB Brisbane, 14 August 1941; American Consulate to CIB Brisbane, 19 August 1941; Inspector Foote, CIB Brisbane, to CIB Canberra, 19 August 1941; American Consulate to CIB Brisbane, 26 August 1941; American Consulate to CIB Brisbane, 4 September 1941; Inspector Foote to Intelligence Section, Victoria Barracks, 5 September 1941; Inspector Foote, CIB Brisbane, to American Consul Brisbane, to CIB Brisbane; Inspector Foote, CIB Brisbane, to Northern Command, Victoria Barracks, copy to CIB Canberra; Major H. A. Cummins, Australian Military Forces, Northern Command, 17 September 1941; Meal vouchers and miscellaneous expenses, authorised Tom Adams, 22 September 1941; G. C. Streng, officer Matson Navigation Company, confirmation of receipt of five American absentees for boarding SS *Monterey*, 18 September 1941; Postal telegram from Tom Adams to R. Retallack, 18 September 1941.

CHAPTER EIGHT

1. Paul, Hasluck, *The Government and the People, 1942–1945*, p. 225.

2. John Costello, *Love Sex and War — Changing Values, 1939–45.* p. 324

3. Daniel E. and Annette, Potts, *Yanks Down Under*, p. 133.

4. Potts, *Yanks Down Under,* p. 135.

5. *Truth* (Melbourne), 18 April 1942.

6. Potts, *Yanks Down Under,* p. 136.

7. *Sun News-Pictorial,* 17 April 1942; John Hammon Moore, *Over-Sexed Over-Paid and Over Here*, p. 106; Potts, *Yanks Down Under*, pp. 134, 135.

8. *Sun News-Pictorial,* 20 April 1942.

9. Diane Collins, *Hollywood Down Under*, p. 3

10. Simon Brand, *Picture Palaces and Flea-Pits*, pp. 80, 81.

11. Brand, *Picture Palaces and Flea-Pits*, p. 111–27.

12. Brand, *Picture Palaces and Flea-Pits*, p. 144.

13. Brand, *Picture Palaces and Flea-Pits*, p. 146.

14. Interview with Bill Bentson, May 1997.

15. Brand, *Picture Palaces and Flea-Pits*, pp. 216–19; Personal recollection, Cec Parsons; John Walker (ed.), *Halliwells Film and Video Guide*, 1998 edn. p. 848; Eric Reade, *History and Heartburn: The Saga of Australian Film*, 1896–1978, pp. 89, 123, 124.

16. Brian McKinlay, *Australian, 1942: End of Innocence*, p. 139

17. Moore, *Over-sexed, Over-paid and Over Here*, p. 107.

18. Andrew Bisset, *Black Roots White Flowers: A History of Jazz In Australia*, pp. 61, 64, 76; Bruce Johnson, *The Oxford Companion to Australian Jazz*, pp. 133–5; conversations with Sid Bromley, April 1997, Paddy Fitzallen, 1985 and Allan Campbell, March 1999.

19. Potts, *Yanks Down Under*, p. 128; Bisset, *Black Roots White Flowers*, p. 84.

20. Joseph Csida, *American Entertainment: A Unique History of Popular Show Business*, p. 231.

21. Roger Kinkle, *The Complete Encyclopedia of Popular Music and Jazz 1900–1950*, entries 1939–44; Colin Larkin (ed.), *The Guinness Encyclopedia Of Popular Music.*

22. George Simon, *The Big Bands* (1972 ed.); Donald Clarke, *The Rise and Fall of Popular Music.*

23. Recollections of Sid Bromley and examination of original 78s, April 1997.

24. Herbert G. Goldman, *Jolson: The Legend Comes to Life*, p. 253.

25. *Courier-Mail*, 9 November 1943; *Truth* (Brisbane), 14 November 1943.

26. *Cairns Post*, 17 January 1979; Randy Roberts and James S. Olson, *John Wayne: American*, p. 253.

27. Larry Adler, *It Ain't Necessarily So*; conversation with Larry Adler, April 1997.

28. *Courier-Mail*, 7 September 1943; Eleanor Roosevelt, *My Day*, pp. 306–7.

29. Michael Pate, *An Entertaining War*, p. 189.

30. Pate, *An Entertaining War*, p. 71; Bisset *Black Roots White Flowers*, p. 75.

31. Pate, *An Entertaining War* p. 106; conversation with Sid Bromley, February 1997.

32. Bisset, *Black Roots White Flowers*, p. 48; Jack Mitchell, *Australian Jazz On Record, 1925–80.*

33. Bisset, *Black Roots White Flowers*, pp. 76, 77; conversation with John Best, December 1994.

34. David Wallechinsky and Irving Wallace, *The People's Almanac #2, 'Time Capsules In America'*, p. 161.

35. Mike Sutcliffe, 'Artie Shaw in Australia', *Jazz Journal* April 1981; Bisset, *Black Roots White Flowers*, p. 76; conversations with Don Burrows, May 1985, Artie Shaw August 1997, and John Best, December 1994.

36. Conversation with Artie Shaw, May 1995.

37. Edward Vernoff and Rima Shore, *The International Dictionary of Twentieth Century Biography*, p. 533.

38. *Sun News-Pictorial*, 14 July 1944.

39. *Sun News-Pictorial*, 24 July 1944.

40. Robin Brown, *Milestones in Australian History*, p. 564.

41. John Crampton and Evie Hayes, *And I Loves Ya Back*, pp. 87, 98–121.

42. *Courier-Mail*, 26 July 1942; National Archives (original scripts).

43. Potts, *Yanks Down Under*, p. 145.

44. *Herald*, 18 July 1942.

45. *Herald*, 27 July 1942.

46. *Herald*, 15 June 1942.

47. *Herald*, 18 July 1942.

48. *Herald*, 8 September 1942.

49. *Herald*, 30 July 1942.

50. *Herald*, 30 December 1943; Potts, *Yanks Down Under*, p. 144; conversation with Beryl Lynagh, former nursing sister, Royal Brisbane Hospital, April 1997.

51. *Herald*, 5 March 1942.

52. Conversations with Bill Bentson, Sid Bromley, February–May 1997; Daniel E. and Annette Potts p. 146, 147, 151.

53. *Herald*, 12 May 1943.

54. Norman Polmar and Thomas B. Allen; *World War II: America at War*, p. 545.

55. *Herald*, 12 May 1943.

56. *Herald*, 11 June 1943.

57. Moore, *Over-Sexed, Over-Paid and Over Here*, p. 211.

58. Survey, 14–26 September 1942; David Reynolds, *Rich Relations: The American Occupation of Britain, 1942–1945*. p. 248.

59. *Herald*, 28 April 1942.

60. *Queensland Times*, 18 May 1992.

CHAPTER TEN

1. John Hammond Moore, *Over-Sexed, Over-Paid and Over Here*, p. 208.

2. State Archives, A/12035, A/12040; Moore, *Over-Sexed, Over-Paid and Over Here*, p. 219; Daniel E. and Annete Potts, *Yanks Down Under*, p. 302; Rosemary Campbell, *Heroes and Lovers*; Sunday Mail (Brisbane), 16 April 1989.

3. *Courier-Mail*, 12 September 1942.

4. *Courier-Mail*, 4 June 1942.

5. *Courier-Mail*, 24 October 1942.

6. Potts, *Yanks Down Under*, p. 303.

7. Tony Maiden and Adele Horin, 'The Battle of Brisbane', *National Times*, 10–11 February 1975.

8. Maiden and Horin 'The Battle of Brisbane'.

9. Campbell, *Heroes and Lovers*, p. 77.

10. Potts, *Yanks Down Under*, p. 299.

11. Moore, *Over-Sexed, Over-Paid and Over Here*, p. 222.

12. Queensland State Archives, A/12034, Shooting and use of firearms by American Forces, 1944–44.

13. Queensland State Archives, A/12034, Letter from Eunice Hargrave to Townsville Police, 12 October 1942.

14. Queensland State Archives, A/12034; Vic Cassells, *For Those in Peril*, p. 257.

15. Conversation with Cec Parsons, former post office delivery boy.

16. *Courier-Mail*, 26 November 1942.

17. Moore, *Over-Sexed, Over-Paid and Over Here*, p. 222.

18. Battle of Brisbane account: Personal recollections of Cec Parsons, Bill Bentson, Les Cottman (April–May 1997), Allan Campbell (February 1999) *The Brisbane Line*, television documentary, Channel 7, 1987 (producer, Frank Warwick); Queensland State Archives, A/12035, A/12040; *Courier-Mail*, 27, 28 November 1942; Maiden and Horin, 'The Battle of Brisbane'; *The National Enquirer*, 10–15 February 1999; *Telegraph* (Brisbane), 18 August, 10 October 1978; *Sunday Mail* (Brisbane), 16 April 1989; *Sun*, 3 May 1989, 19 November 1990; *Courier-Mail*, November 1992; *Sun*, 4 October 1991; Moore, *Over-Sexed, Over-Paid and Over Here*, pp. 217–24; Potts, *Yanks Down Under*, pp. 302–9. Libby Connors, Lynette Finch, Kay Saunders and Helen Taylor, *Australia's Frontline:*
Remembering the 1939–45 War, pp. 177, 179; Peter Thompson, 'Invasion, 1942' (unpublished MS).

19. State Archives, B260A, letter from Police Commissioner Carroll to Minister for Health and Home Affairs (copy to State Premier), 27 November 1942.

20. State Archives, B260A, letter from Prime Minister to Premier of Queensland, 29 December 1942.

CHAPTER ELEVEN

1. Elizabeth Anne Wheal, Stephen Pope and James Taylor, *Encyclopedia of the Second World War*, pp. 494–5.

2. John Lillback, 'One Man's Journey' (unpublished MS), p. 10.

3. John Lillback, conversations with author, 4–5 May 1997.

4. Victor W. Madej (ed.), *U.S. Army and Marine Corps Order of Battle: Pacific Theater of Operations, 1941–1945*, Volume 1, pp. 33–4.

5. John Lillback, conversations with author, 4–5 May 1997.

6. Lillback, 'One Man's Journey', p. 17. See also Wallace Fields, *Issue In Doubt*, p. 96.

7. John Lillback, conversations with author, 4–5 May 1997.

8. Ian Grant, *A Dictionary of Australian Military History*, p. 93. See also Wheal, Pope and Taylor, *Encyclopedia of the Second World War*, pp. 112–13.

9. Dan van der Vat, *The Pacific Campaign — The US–Japanese Naval War 1941-1945*, p. 182–95.

10. P. D. Wilson, *North Queensland, WWII: 1942–1945*, pp. 26, 61.

11. Wilson, *North Queensland*, pp. 26, 27.

12. John Hammond Moore, *Over-Sexed, Over-Paid and Over Here*, p. 199. Also Sharnee Lillback, conversation with author, 5 May 1997.

13. Daniel E. and Annette Potts, *Yanks Down Under, 1941–1945*, p. 259.

14. Wilson, *North Queensland*, p. 35.

15. Roger R. Marks, *Queensland Airfields*, Appendix 1, pp. 187–206. See also Wilson, *North Queensland*, p. 34.

16. *Northern Miner*, 9 May 1942.

17. *Northern Miner*, 18 May 1942.

18. Wilson, *North Queensland*, p. 24.

19. Marks, *Queensland Airfields*, p. 19.

20. Marks, *Queensland Airfields*, p. 27.

21. Marks, *Queensland Airfields*, p. 27.

22. John S. Alcorn, *The Jolly Rogers: A History of the 90th Bomb Group During World War II*, Chapter 9.

23. Queensland State Archives, A/64580 M 78, Report from Cloncurry Police to Commissioner of Police, January 12 1943, March 21 1943.

24. Queensland State Archives, A/64580 M 78, Cloncurry Police Report to Commissioner of Police, 21 March 1943. See also Report from C. J. Carroll (Queensland Commissioner of Police) to Captain M. J. Beyers, Graves Registration Officer, U.S.A.S.O.S. Base Section 2, 21 May 1943.

25. Queensland State Archives, A/64580 M 78.

26. Queensland State Archives, A/64580 M 78.

27. Alcorn, *The Jolly Rogers*, Chapter 9.

28. Staff Sergeant Grady Gaston, Report, May 1943.

29. SBS television documentary, 1993.

30. Marks, *Queensland Airfields*, p. 9.

31. Marks, *Queensland Airfields*, p. 9.

32. Douglas Gillison, *Royal Australian Air Force, 1939–1942*, p. 457. See also Marks, *Queensland Airfields*, p. 258.

33. Gillison, *Royal Australian Air Force, 1939–1942*, p. 552.

34. Wilson, *North Queensland*, p. 23.

35. Wilson, *North Queensland*, p. 21.

36. *Mackay Daily Mercury*, 7 July 1944.

37. *Mackay Daily Mercury*, 18 August 1944.

38. Marks, *Queensland Airfields*, pp. 112–13.

39. Conversations with the author, August 1997. Queensland State Archives, A/64580 M 78, Mackay Police report to Commissioner of Police, 16 June 1943; Letter from Police Commissioner to American Headquarters Base Section Three, June 18 1943.

40. RSL, Mackay Sub Branch newsletter, 28 April 1996; conversation with RSL historian, C. E. Benson; list of casualties B-17c s/no 40-20272, courtesy C.E. Benson / T. Hanks, Wichita Falls Texas.

41. *Truth* (Brisbane), 4 July 1943.

42. Queensland State Archives, E64581 7298, Police report to Commissioner of Police from Yaamba Station, 21 December 1943.

43. Queensland State Archives, E64581 7280, Police report to Commissioner of Police from Rockhampton station, 28 December 1943.

44. Neville Meyers, conversations with author, November 1997. See also John Hammond Moore, *Over-Paid, Over-Sexed and Over Here*, pp. 257–61.

45. Clayton D. James, *The Years of MacArthur*, Volume 2, p. 245; Geoffrey Perret, *Old Soldiers Never Die*, p. 308. Also Bill Bentson, conversations with the author, 14 November 1997.

46. James, *The Years of MacArthur*, Volume 2, p. 250.

47. Lex McAulay, *To The Bitter End: The Japanese Defeat at Buna and Gona*, pp. 11, 310.

48. Ronald H. Spector, *Eagle Against the Sun: The American War With Japan*, pp. 215–18.

49. Perret, *Old Soldiers Never Die*, p. 318.

50. William Manchester, *American Caesar*, p. 325.

51. Michael Schaller, *Douglas MacArthur: The Far East General*, p. 71.

52. John H. Bradley, *The West Point Military History of the Second World War*, Volume 2, pp. 281–2.

53. Perret, *Old Soldiers Never Die*, p. 326.

CHAPTER TWELVE

1. Keith Wheeler, *War Under the Pacific*, p. 8.

2. *Purnell's History of the Second World War*, Volume 6, Number 88; Robert E. Walters, *Naval War in the Pacific*, p. 2462; Samuel Eliot Morison, *The Two-Ocean War: A Short History of the United States Navy in the Second World War*, p. 493.

3. Anthony Preston, *Submarines*, p. 123.

4. Preston, *Submarines*, p. 127.

5. Wheeler, *War Under the Pacific*, p. 23.

6. Walters, *Naval War in the Pacific*, p. 2462.

7. Walters, *Naval War in the Pacific*, p. 2464; Mochitsura Hashimoto, *Sunk: The Story of the Japanese Submarine Fleet, 1942–1945*, pp. 178–9.

8. Clay Blair Jr., *Silent Victory: The U.S. Submarine War Against Japan*, p. 877; Harry Holmes, *The Last Patrol*, pp. 189, 190.

9. Blair, *Silent Victory*, p. 25.

10. Vic Cassells, *For Those in Peril*, pp. 15 16.

11. Blair, *Silent Victory*, pp. 65–9; Paul H. Silverstone, *United States Warships of World War II*, pp. 176–94; *Jane's Fighting Ships of World War II*, pp. 288–9.

12. *Jane's Fighting Ships*, pp. 290–1;

Silverstone, *United States Warships of World War II*, pp. 195–203.

13. Holmes, *The Last Patrol*, pp. 11–12.

14. Wheeler, *War Under the Pacific*, p. 34; Holmes, *The Last Patrol*, p. 7.

15. Wheeler, *War Under the Pacific*, pp. 40–7; Ronald H. Spector, *Eagle Against the Sun: The American War With Japan*, pp. 484–5.

16. Blair, *Silent Victory*, p. 274.

17. *Australia at War: The Home Front*, television documentary; Wheeler, *War Under the Pacific*, p. 43.

18. Blair, *Silent Victory*, p. 191.

19. Wheeler, *War Under the Pacific*, p. 50.

20. I. J. Galantin, *A Submarine Against Japan in World War II*, pp. 11–12.

21. Blair, *Silent Victory*, pp. 906, 910.

22. Conversation with the author.

23. Blair, *Silent Victory*, pp. 217–18

24. Blair, *Silent Victory*, p. 297.

25. William J. Ruhe, *War in the Boats: My World War II Submarine Battles*, p. 11.

26. Blair, *Silent Victory*, p. 297.

27. Morison, *The Two-Ocean War*, p. 177.

28. John Hamilton, *War at Sea, 1939–1945*, p. 147: Edwin P. Hoyt, *Guadalcanal*, p. 48; Blair, *Silent Victory*, p. 298.

29. Blair, *Silent Victory*, pp. 196–7.

30. Wheeler, *War Under the Pacific*, p. 62.

31. Ruhe, *War in the Boats*, p. 55.

32. Mochitsura, *Sunk*, p. xi; David Jenkins, *Battle Surface: Japan's Submarine War Against Australia, 1942–44*, p. 286.

33. Jenkins, *Battle Surface*, pp. 185–223; G. H. Gill, *Royal Australian Navy, 1942–1945*, pp. 61–74; Cassells, *For Those in Peril*, p. 36.

34. Jenkins, *Battle Surface*, pp. 247–51; Gill, *Royal Australian Navy, 1942–1945*, pp. 77–8.

35. Jenkins, *Battle Surface*, pp. 277–85; Christopher S. Milligan and John C. H. Foley, *Australian Hospital Ship* Centaur: *The Myth of Immunity*; Ian Grant, *A Dictionary of Australian Military History*, p. 78.

36. Blair, *Silent Victory*, pp. 270, 374; Wheeler, *War Under the Pacific*, pp. 63–4.

37. Blair, *Silent Victory*, pp. 127–8; conversation with Les Cottman, June 1997.

38. Wheeler, *War Under the Pacific*, p. 178.

39. Holmes, *The Last Patrol*, pp. 137–9; Blair, *Silent Victory*, pp. 768–9; Wheeler, *War Under the Pacific*, pp. 179, 182.

40. Blair, *Silent Victory*, p. 769; Holmes, *The Last Patrol*, pp. 134–5.

41. Clay and Joan Blair, *Return from the River Kwai*, p. 179.

42. Conversation with Les Cottman, June 1997.

43. Blair, *Silent Victory*, p. 371.

44. Conversation with Les Cottman, June 1997.

45. Holmes, *The Last Patrol*, pp. 30–7.

46. Conversation with Les Cottman, June 1997.

47. Conversation with author.

48. Wheeler, *War Under the Pacific*, pp. 73, 76.

49. Holmes, *The Last Patrol*, pp. 119–24; Blair, *Silent Victory*, pp. 719–20; Henry C. Keatts and George C. Farr, *Dive Into History*, Volume 2, p. 109.

50. Hamilton, *War at Sea, 1939–1945*, p. 214.

51. Holmes, *The Last Patrol*, p. 187.

52. Blair, *Silent Victory*, p. 878.

53. Holmes, *The Last Patrol*, p. 9; Blair, *Silent Victory*, p. 877.

54. Conversation with the author, 1997.

CHAPTER THIRTEEN

1. Hugh Brogan, *Longman History of the United States of America*, p. 404

2. *The New York Public Library Book of Popular Americana*, p. 195.

3. Alexander A. C. Gerry, 'A Tribute to Black Americans in the Military', *The Officer*, February 1996, pp. 103–5.

4. Norman Polmar and Thomas B. Allen, *World War II America at War, 1941–1945*.

5. Edward Vernoff and Rima Shore, *The International Dictionary of Twentieth Century Biography*, p. 584.

6. Vernoff and Shore, *Dictionary of Twentieth Century Biography*, p. 751; Claire Walter, *The Book of Winners*, p. 13.

7. Alan Pomerance, *Repeal of the Blues*, pp. 165–6.

8. Ronald H. Bailey, *The Home Front: U.S.A.*, p. 55.

9. Polmar and Allen, *World War II America at War 1941–1945*, p. 723.

10. Lee Kennett, *For the Duration: The United States Goes to War: Pearl Harbor, 1942*, p. 93.

11. Polmar and Allen, *World War II America at War 1941–1945*, p. 724.

12. Kennett, *For the Duration*, p. 210; Gordon W. Prange, *At Dawn We Slept: The Untold Story of Pearl Harbor*, pp. 514–15.

13. Bryan D. Barnett, *Race Relations in Queensland During the Second World War Pertaining to American Negro Regiments*, p. 23, 24; *Sunday Mail* (Brisbane), 6 October 1996.

14. Barnett, *Race Relations in Queensland*, p. 24; *Sunday Mail* (Brisbane) 6 October 1996.

15. Barnett, *Race Relations in Queensland*, p. 24.

16. Barnett, *Race Relations in Queensland*, p. 25.

17. Barnett, *Race Relations in Queensland*, p. 31; Moore, *Over-Sexed, Over-Paid and Over Here*, p. 210.

18. Barnett, *Race Relations in Queensland*, p. 30.

19. Barnett, *Race Relations in Queensland*, p. 31; D. Clayton James, *The Years of MacArthur*, Volume 2, p. 257

20. Libby Connors, Lynette Finch, Kay Saunders and Helen Taylor, *Australia's Frontline: Remembering the 1939–45 War*, p. 185; conversation with Agnes Black, June 1997.

21. *Herald*, 17 April 1943.

22. Robert Hall, in Desmond Ball (ed.), *Aborigines in the Defence of Australia*, p. 35.

23. Hall, p. 36; Alan Powell, *The Shadow's Edge: Australia's Northern War*, p. 249.

24. Hall, p. 36; Peter Dennis, Jeffrey Grey, Ewan Morris and Robin Prior, *The Oxford Companion to Australian Military History*, p. 528.

25. Barnett, *Race Relations in Queensland*, pp. 48, 49.

26. Conversation with Sid Bromley, August 1997.

27. Conversations with Yvonne Cottman, June 1997, and Agnes Black, July 1997.

28. Queensland State Archives, A/12035 1268.

29. Queensland State Archives, A/12035 1268M.

30. Queensland State Archives A/12034 1268M.

31. P. D. Wilson, *North Queensland, WWII: 1942–1945*, p. 23.

32. Powell, *The Shadow's Edge*, p. 103; Barnett, *Race Relations in Queensland*, p. 47.

33. Queensland State Archives, A/12035.

34. Connors, Finch, Saunders and Taylor, *Australia's Frontline*, pp. 185, 186; conversation with Beryl Lynagh, December 1997.

35. Ronald H. Spector, *Eagle Against the Sun: The American War With Japan*, p. 391.

36. *The Worker*, 21 February 1944.

37. Base Section Communique, US Army, 1943.

38. Bailey, *The Home Front: U.S.A.*, pp. 149–50

39. Bailey, *The Home Front: U.S.A.*, p. 153.

40. Bailey, *The Home Front: U.S.A.*, pp. 149, 153.

41. Dennis, Grey, Morris and Prior, *The Oxford Companion to Australian Military History*, p. 14.

42. Dinesh D'Souza, *The End of Racism*, p. 191.

43. Bailey, *The Home Front: U.S.A.*, p. 153.

44. Polmar and Allen, *World War II America at War: 1941–1945*, p. 724.

45. Gerry, 'A Tribute to Black Americans in the Military', p. 107.

46. Bailey, *The Home Front: U.S.A.*, pp. 149, 153.

CHAPTER FOURTEEN

1. Howard L. Steffy, diary; Daniel E. and Annette Potts, *Yanks Down Under*, p. xiv.

2. Charles Messenger, *World War II Chronological Atlas*, pp. 144–5.

3. Howard Steffy, diary; conversation with Bill Bentson, May 1999.

4. Peter Charlton, *The Unnecessary War*, p. 1.

5. *Herald*, 21 October 1944.

6. Victor W. Madej, *U.S. Army and Marine Corps Order of Battle: Pacific Theater of Operations, 1941–1945*, Volume 1, p. 33; Howard Steffy, diary.

7. Howard Steffy, diary.

8. Paul Hasluck, *The Government and the People, 1942–1945*, p. 225.

9. Hasluck, *The Government and the People, 1942–1945*, pp. 589, 595–6.

10. Annette Potts and Lucinda Strauss, *For The Love of a Soldier*, p. 5; conversation with Yvonne Cottman, June 1997.

11. *Sun News-Pictorial*, 9 February 1945; conversation with Yvonne Cottman, June 1997.

12. David Reynolds, *Rich Relations: The American Occupation of Britain, 1942–1945*, pp. 420–1; Potts, *Yanks Down Under*, p. 362.

13. *Herald*, 1 August 1944.

14. *Telegraph,* 23 October 1944.

15. *Courier-Mail*, 17 November 1945.

16. Margaret Olds (ed.), *Australia Through Time*, p. 329.

17. *Courier-Mail*, 23 December 1947.

18. R. A. Judd, *The Camp Cable Incident,* dedication program, 1968.

CHAPTER FIFTEEN

1. *Courier-Mail*, June 1999.

2. 'The Valley Bomber March', *Air International*, October 1986; Northern *Territory News*, 22 May 1993; *RAAF News*, May 1993; conversation with Bob Alford, October 1997.

3. Bob Alford, *Darwin's Air War*, pp. 25, 45; conversation with Bob Alford, October 1997.

4. Tom Lewis, *Wrecks in Darwin Waters*.

5. McIvor, Trevor and Shirley, *Salute the Brave: A Pictorial Record of Queensland War Memorials*, pp. 187, 208.

6. 'The Crash of B-17C Flying Fortress at Bakers Creek on 14 June 1943', Newsletter, RSL. Mackay Sub Branch, 1997; letter from Col Benson, 19 October 1997.

7. William Manchester, *American Caesar*, pp. 699, 704, 705.

8. Geoffrey Perret, *Old Soldiers Never Die*, pp. 589–90; conversation with Bill Bentson, August 1999.

9. Letter from LeGrande Diller to Bill Bentson, 2 June 1986.

10. Conversation with Loyde Adams, 90th Bomb Group Association, June 1999.

11. *Jolly Rogers, The 90th Bomb Group Association Roster*, 15 August 1998.

BIBLIOGRAPHY

Adler, Larry. *It Ain't Necessarily So*. London: Collins, 1984.

Alcorta, Frank. *Australia's Frontline: The Northern Territory's War*. Sydney: Allen & Unwin, 1991.

Andrews, Michael. *Australia and the Pacific War*. Sydney: Dreamweaver Books, 1985.

Avery, Derek (ed.) *A History of the US Fighting Forces*. London: Chevprime Press, 1989.

Bailey, Ronald H. *The Home Front: U.S.A.* Alexandria, Virginia: Time-Life Books, 1978.

Bauer, Eddy. *History of World War II*. London: Orbis, 1983.

Bisset, Andrew. *Black Roots White Flowers: A History of Jazz in Australia*. Sydney: Golden Press, 1979.

Blair, Clay, Jr. *Silent Victory: The U.S. Submarine War Against Japan*. New York: J.B. Lippincott, 1975.

Blair, Clay and Joan. *Return from the River Kwai*. London: Raven, 1979.

Boardman, Gerald. *The American Musical Theatre: A Chronicle*. New York: Oxford University Press, 1978.

Bolt, Andrew (ed.) *Our Home Front, 1939–45*. Melbourne: Wilkinson Books, 1995.

Brand, Simon. *Picture Palaces and Flea-Pits*. Sydney: Dreamweaver, 1983.

Brogran, Hugh. *Longman History of the United States of America*. London: Guild, 1985.

Brown, Bruce. *A Changing Destiny: Australia in the Twentieth Century*. Melbourne: Edward Arnold Australia, 1989.

Brown, Robin (comp.). *Collins Milestones in Australian History, 1788 to the Present*. Sydney: Collins, 1986

Brune, Peter. *Those Ragged Bloody Heroes*. Sydney: Allen & Unwin, 1991.

Burns, Ross. *War in the Pacific, 1937–1945*. London: Bison Books, 1991.

Campbell, Christy. *The World War II Fact Book, 1939–45*. London: Macdonald and Co., 1985.

Campbell, Rosemary. *Heroes and Lovers*. Sydney: Allen & Unwin, 1989.

Cassells, Vic. *For Those in Peril*. Kenthurst: Kangaroo Press, 1995.

Chapman, Ivan. *Leonski: The Brownout Strangler*. Sydney: Hale & Iremonger, 1982.

Charlton, Peter. *The Thirty-Niners*. Melbourne: Macmillan, 1981.

Charlton, Peter. *The Unnecessary War*. Melbourne: Macmillian, 1983.

Charlton, Peter. *War Against Japan, 1941–42*. Sydney: Time-Life Books, 1988.

Charlton, Peter. *War Against Japan, 1942–45*. Sydney: Time-Life Books, 1989.

Charlton, Peter. *South Queensland, WWII 1941–1945*. Brisbane: Boolarong Publications. 1991.

Collins, Dianne, *Hollywood Down Under*. Sydney: Agus & Robertson, 1987.

Connors, Libby, with Lynette Finch, Kay Saunders and Helen Taylor. *Australia's Frontline. Remembering the 1939–45 War*. St Lucia: University of Queensland Press, 1992.

Costello, John. *The Pacific War*. London: Collins, 1981.

Costello, John. *Days Of Infamy*. New York: Pocket Books, 1994.

Costello, John. *Love, Sex and War: Changing Values, 1939–45*, London: Collins, 1985.

Csida, Joseph and June. *American Entertainment: A Unique History of Popular Show Business*. New York: Watson-Guptill, 1978.

D'Souza, Dinesh. *The End of Racism*. New York: The Free Press, 1995.

Day, David. *The Great Betrayal: Britain, Australia and the Onset of the Pacific War, 1939–42*. Sydney: Angus & Robertson, 1988.

Dennis, Peter with Jeffrey Grey, Ewan Morris and Robin Prior. *The Oxford Companion to Australian Military History*. Melbourne: Oxford University Press, 1995.

Donavan, Mavis. *The Stars Shine On*. Brisbane: Boolarong Publications, 1984.

Elphick, Peter. *Singapore: The Pregnable Fortress*. London: Hodder and Stoughton, 1995.

Evans, Alun. *A Navy For Australia*. Sydney: ABC Enterprises, 1986.

Foley, John and Milligan, Christopher S. *Centaur*. Hendra: Nairana Publishers, 1993.

Frame, Tom. *Pacific Partners: A History of Asutralian-American Relations*. Sydney: Hodder & Stoughton, 1992.

Frank, Richard B. *Guadalcanal*. New York: Random House, 1990.

Freidel, Frank. *Franklin D. Roosevelt: A Rendezvous with Destiny*. Boston: Little Brown, 1987.

Gailey, Harry A. *The War in the Pacific, From Pearl Harbor to Tokyo Bay*. California: Presido, 1995.

Galantin, I.J. *Take Her Deep*. London: Unwin & Hyman, 1987.

Gill, G.H. *Royal Australian Navy, 1939–1945*, 2 vol. Canberra: Australian War Memorial, 1957 and 1968.

Gillett, Ross. *Australian Air Power*. Sydney: The Book Shop, 1996.

Gillison, Douglas. *Royal Australian Air Force, 1939–1942*. Canberra: Australian War Memorial, 1962.

Goldstein, Donald M., Dillion, Katherine V. and Wenger, J. Michael. *The Way It Was: Pearl Harbor, The Original Photographs*. New York: Brassey's, 1991.

Goodman, Rupert. *Our War Nurses*. Brisbane: Boolarong Publications, 1991.

Goodman, Rupert. *Hospital Ships*. Brisbane: Boolarong Publications, 1992.

Goralski, Robert. *World War II Almanac, 1931–1945: A Political and Military Record*. New York: Bonanza Books, 1981.

Grant, Ian. *A Dictionary of Australian Military History: From Colonial Times to the Gulf War*. Sydney: Random House, 1992.

Griess, Thomas E. (ed.) *The West Point Military Series: The Second World War*, vol. 3. Wayne, New Jersey: Avery, 1989.

Griffith, Tony. *From Kokoda to Keating*. Adelaide: Wakefield Press.

Hasluck, Paul. *The Government and the People 1939–1941*. Canberra: Australian War Memorial 1952.

Hasluck, Paul. *The Government and the People 1942–1945*. Canberra: Australian War Memorial, 1970.

Dalleck, Robert. *Lone Star Rising. Lyndon Johnson and His Times, 1908–1960*. New York: Oxford University Press, 1991.

Hall, Timothy. *Darwin, 1942: Australia's Darkest Hour.* Sydney: Methuen, 1983.

Halliwell, Leslie. *Halliwell's Film Guide*, 7th Edition. London: Harper Collins, 1989.

Holmes, Harry. *The Last Patrol.* Shrewsbury: Airlife, 1994.

Horner, D.M. *High Command, Australian and Allied Strategy 1939–45.* Allen & Unwin, 1982.

Hoyt, P. Edwin. *America's Wars.* New York: Da Capo Press, 1988

James, Clayton D. *The MacArthur Years, Volume 2, 1941–1945.* Boston: Houghton Mifflin, 1975.

Jane's Fighting Ships of World War II. London: Bracken Books, 1989.

Jane's Fighting Aircraft Of World War II. London: Bracken Books, 1989.

Jenkins, David. *Battle Surface: Japan's Submarine War Against Australia, 1942–44.* Sydney: Random House, 1992.

Jose, A.W. *The Royal Australian Navy, 1914–1918.* Canberra: Australian War Memorial, 1928.

Keatts, Henry C. and Farr, George C. *Dive Into History: Volume 2; U.S. Submarines.* Houston: Pisces Books, 1991.

Kennett, Lee. *For the Duration. The U.S. Goes to War.* New York: Charles Scribner's & Sons, 1985.

Kilpatrick, C.W. *Naval Night Battles in the Solomons.* Pompano Beach, Florida: Exposition Banner, 1987.

Kimball, W.F. *Churchill and Roosevelt: The Complete Correspondence.* Princeton, New Jersey: Princeton University Press, 1984.

Kinkle, Roger D. *The Complete Encyclopedia of Popular Music and Jazz, 1900–1950,* 4 vol. New Rochelle, New York: Arlington House, 1974.

Laffin, John. *Greece, Crete and Syria.* Sydney: Time-Life Books, 1989.

Larrabee, Eric. *Commander in Chief.* London: Andre Deutsch, 1987.

Leckie, Robert. *Delivered From Evil: The Saga of World War II.* New York: Harper & Row, 1987.

Lewis, Tom. *Wrecks In Darwin Waters.* Sydney: Turton & Armstrong, 1992.

Lockwood, D. *Australia's Pearl Harbour: Darwin 1942.* Melbourne: Cassell, 1966.

Luck, Peter. *A Time to Remember*. Richmond: William Heinemann Australia, 1988.

MacArthur, Douglas. *Reminiscences*. London: Heinemann, 1978.

MacDonald, Charles. *The Mighty Endeavour: The American War in Europe*. New York: Da Capo, 1991.

Magnusson, Magnus. *Chambers Biographical Dictionary*. Edinburgh: Chambers, 1995.

Manchester, William. *American Caesar*. Melbourne: Hutchinson Group, 1978.

Manchester, William. *Goodbye Darkness*. London: Michael Joseph, 1979.

Marks, Roger R. *Queensland Airfields, 50 Years On*. Brisbane: R & J Marks, 1994.

Marriott, John. *Disaster at Sea*. London: PRC, 1987.

Martinez, Mario. *Lady's Men*. London: Leo Cooper, 1995.

Mayer, S.L. *Great American Generals of World War II: MacArthur*. Greenwich: Bison Books, 1982.

Mayo, Lida. *Bloody Buna*. Canberra: Australia National University Press, 1975.

McIvor, Trevor and Shirley. *Salute the Brave: A Pictorial Record of Queensland War Memorials*. Toowoomba: USQ Press, 1994.

McKernan, Michael. *All In! Australia During the Second World War*. Melbourne: Thomas Nelson Australia, 1983.

McKinlay, Brian. *Australia, 1942: End of Innocence*. Sydney: Collins, 1985.

Messenger, Charles. *World War II Chronological Atlas*.

London: Bloomsbury, 1989.

Miller, Nathan. *War at Sea: A Naval History of World War Two*. New York: Schribner, 1995.

Millett, Allan R. and Maslowski, Peter. *For The Common Defense: A Military History of the United States of America*. New York: The Free Press, 1994.

Moore, John Hammond. *Over-Sexed, Over-Paid and Over Here*. St Lucia: University of Queensland Press, 1981.

Morris, Eric. *Corregidor*. London: Hutchinson, 1982.

Morris, James M. *History of the U.S. Army*. London: Bison Books, 1986.

Morton, H.V. *Atlantic Meeting*. Melbourne: Methuen, 1943.

Odgers, George. *Air War Against Japan, 1943–45*, Canberra: Australian War Memorial, 1968.

Olds, Margaret (ed.) *Australia Through Time*. Sydney: The Softback Preview, 1993.

Olson, James S. and Roberts, Randy. *John Wayne American*. New York: The Free Press, 1995.

Overy, Richard. *The Road to War*. London: Macmillian, 1989.

Parkin, Robert Sinclair. *Blood on the Sea: American Destroyers in World War II*. New York: Sarpedon, 1995.

Pate, Michael. *An Entertaining War*. Sydney: Dreamweaver Books, 1986.

Perret, Geoffrey. *Old Soldiers Never Die*. New York: Random House, 1996.

Pitt, Barrie (ed.) *History of the Second World War*, 8 vol. London: Purnell and Sons, 1966.

Pomerance, Allan. *Repeal of the Blues*. New York: Citadel Press, 1991.

Potts, Annette and Strauss, Lucinda. *For the Love of a Soldier*. Sydney: ABC Books, 1986.

Potts, Daniel E. and Annette. *Yanks Down Under 1941–1945*. Melbourne: Oxford University Press, 1985.

Powell, Alan. *The Shadow's Edge: Australia's Northern War*. Carlton: Melbourne University Press, 1988.

Prange, Gordon. *At Dawn We Slept: The Untold Story of Pearl Harbor*. New York: McGraw-Hill, 1981.

Prange, Gordon. *December 7, 1941*. London: Harrarp, 1981.

Rayner, Robert J. *The Army and the Defence of Darwin Fortress*. Sydney: Southwood Press, 1995.

Ready, Lee J. *World War Two: Nation by Nation*. London: Arms and Armour, 1995.

Reynolds, David. *Rich Relations: The American Occupation of Britain, 1942–1945*. London: Harper Collins, 1995.

Robertson, John. *1939 – 1945: Australia Goes to War*. Sydney: Doubleday, 1984.

Ross, Lloyd. *John Curtin: A Biography*. Melbourne: Sun Papermac, 1977.

Schaller, Michael. *Douglas MacArthur: The Far Eastern General*. Oxford University Press, 1989.

Shaw, Artie. *The Trouble with Cinderella*. London: Jarrolds, 1955.

Shaw, John (ed.). *The Concise Encyclopedia of Australia*. Sydney: William Collins, 1984.

Silverstone, Paul H. *United States Warships of World War II*. London: Ian Allan, 1965.

Sowinski, Larry. *The Pacific War*. London: Conway Maritime Press, 1981.

Spector, Ronald H. *Eagle Against The Sun: The American War With Japan*. Harmondsworth: Viking, 1984.

Steinberg, Rafael. *Island Fighting*. Alexandria, Virginia: Time-Life Books, 1977, van der Vat, Dan. *The Pacific Campaign*. New York: Simon and Schuster, 1991.

Van der Vat, Dan. *The Pacific Campaign — The US–Japanese Naval War 1941-1945*. New York: Simon & Schuster, 1991.

Walke, Claire. *The Book of Winners*. New York: Harcourt Brace Jovanovich, 1978.

Wall, Don. *Heroes at Sea*. Adelaide: Griffin Press, 1991.

Wheal, Elizabeth Anne, Pope, Stephen and Taylor, James, *Encyclopedia of the Second World War*. New Jersey: Castle Books, 1989.

Wheeler, Keith. *War Under the Pacific*. Alexandria Virginia: Time-Life Books, 1981.

Weinberg, Gerhard. *A World at Arms: A Global History of World War II*. Cambridge: Cambridge University Press, 1994.

Wenborn, Neil. *The Pictorial History of the U.S.A.* London: Hamlyn, 1991.

Wigmore, Lionel. *The Japanese Thrust*. Canberra: Australian War Memorial, 1957.

Willliams, David. *Wartime Disasters at Sea*. Somerset: Patrick Stephens, 1997.

Wilson, P.D. *North Queensland, WWII. 1942–1945*. Brisbane: Government Printing Office, 1988.

Winter, Barbara. *HMAS Sydney: Fact, Fantasy and Fraud*. Brisbane: Boolarong, 1984.

Wright, Christopher. *Over One Hundred and Fifteen Years of News From the Daily Telegraph Mirror*. Cremorne: Adrian Savvas, 1995.

INDEX

United States Army Airforce
194-5

3rd Light Bomb Group 199
3rd Pursuit Squadron 56
17th Pursuit Squadron 56
19th Bomb Group 195, 198
20th Pursuit Squadron 56
22nd Bomb Group 111
90th Bomb Group 210, 279
321st Bomber Squadron 201
408th Bomb Squadron 111
435th Squadron 195-6

United States Navy

PT 31 61
PT 34 61
PT 41 27
PT 109 27
S-37 228
S-41 221
S-44 228-9
USS Amberjack 238
USS Astoria 26, 228
USS Barb 236
USS Bullhead 241
USS Cassin 21, 26
USS Chicago 21, 23, 25, 26, 27, 231
USS Clark 21
USS Conyngham 21, 28
USS Downes 21, 26
USS Finback 240
USS Fulton 151, 152, 159, 237
USS Grampus 238
USS Griffin 160, 161, 227, 237
USS Growler 232
USS Haddo 240
USS Hake 240
USS Harder 240
USS Holland 233, 237
USS Houston 58, 59, 72, 77, 78, 237
USS Indianapolis 235
USS Langley 57, 77
USS Lexington 26, 197
USS Louisville 15-16, 27
USS Mason 246

USS McCawley 27
USS Memphis 15
USS Milwaukee 15
USS Missouri 79
USS Mugford 232
USS Niagara 29
USS Northampton 25, 27, 117-18 120, 155
USS Pampanito 236
USS Peary 59-62, 64-5, 72-3, 78, 276
USS Pensacola 27, 29
USS Phoenix 38
USS Portland 21, 22, 27
USS Puffer 239
USS Queenfish 236
USS Quincy 26, 228
USS Ray 239
USS Reid 21, 27
USS Robert E Peary 276
USS Salt Lake City 25, 27, 117, 118, 122, 153 154
USS Sealion 61, 222, 236
USS Shark 232
USS Shark 2 235
USS Skipjack 226
USS Spearfish 229
USS Sperry 237
USS Stewart 240
USS Sturgeon 233-4
USS Swordfish 222
USS Tang 235
USS Trenton 15
USS Triton 238
USS Vincennes 26, 228
USS West Virginia 246
USS Whippoorwill 61
USS Yorktown 151, 197, 198

United States Organisation (USO) 134-5

Vacchiano, Seaman F.J. 118, 120
Vargas, Jorge 87
Vaughan, Colonel Harry H. 173, 189
Vaught, Lieutenant Robert H. 65, 72

Veale Brigadier WCD 58
Venereal Disease 146-7
Verrall, Yvonne 152-61
Voce, Dudley 52

Wainwright, Lieutenant General Jonathan M. 85-95, 100
Walker, Lieutenant William 66, 68, 72
Wallace, George 137
War Brides 267-8
Waters, Warrant Officer Leonard 251
Waterside Workers' Federation of Australia 36
Wax, Harold 139
Wayne, John 90, 135
Webster, Private Edward S. 183, 273
White, Captain Robert M. 180
White, Walter 244
Whittaker, Reuben 233
Wiecks, Lieutenant Max B. 66, 68, 69, 72
Wilkes, Rear Admiral John 223
Wilkes, Lieutenant Charles 13
William B. Preston 65, 73, 75
Williams, Fountain B. 178
Willoughby, Colonel Charles A. 82
Wilson, Staff Sergeant Roy 202, 205, 280
Wilson, Woodrow T. 80
Women's Auxiliary Australian Air Force (WAAF) 4
Wren, Able Seaman David J. 177-8
Wright, Lieutenant Commander William Leslie 233
Wrobleski, Seaman E.J. 118-20

Yamashita, General Tomoyuki 38
Yokoyama, Colonel Yosuke 100

Zealandia 65
Zuikaku 197